Preface to Pastoral Theology

Preface to
Pastoral Theology

Seward Hiltner

Abingdon   Nashville

THE AYER LECTURES

The substance of this volume constitutes the Ayer Lectures for 1954. The Ayer Lectureship was founded in May, 1929, in the Rochester Theological Seminary by the gift of twenty-five thousand dollars from Mr. and Mrs. Wilfred W. Fry, of Camden, New Jersey, to perpetuate the memory of Mrs. Fry's father, the late Francis Wayland Ayer. At the time of his death Mr. Ayer was president of the corporation which maintained the Rochester Theological Seminary.

Shortly after the establishment of the lectureship the Rochester Theological Seminary and the Colgate Theological Seminary were united under the name of the Colgate Rochester Divinity School. It is under the auspices of this institution that the Ayer Lectures are given.

Under the terms of the foundation the lectures are to fall within the broad field of the history or interpretation of the Christian religion and message. It is the desire of those connected with the establishment and administration of the lectureship that the lectures shall be religiously constructive and shall help in the building of Christian faith.

Four lectures are given each year at the Colgate Rochester Divinity School at Rochester, New York, to be published in book form within one year after their delivery. They are known as the Ayer Lectures. The lecturer for the academic year 1953-54 was Seward Hiltner.

PREFACE TO PASTORAL THEOLOGY

Copyright © 1958 by Abingdon Press

All rights in this book are reserved.
No part of this book may be reproduced in any manner
whatsoever without written permission of the publisher
except brief quotations embodied in critical articles
or reviews. For information address Abingdon,
Nashville, Tennessee.

Library of Congress Cataloging in Publication Data

HILTNER, SEWARD, 1909-
  Preface to pastoral theology
  Biblio. p.
  1. Pastoral theology   2. Spencer, Ichabod Smith 1798-1854. A pastor's sketches.
  I. Title.
  BV4011.H5   250   58-5398

ISBN 0-687-33912-X

MANUFACTURED BY THE PARTHENON PRESS AT
NASHVILLE, TENNESSEE, UNITED STATES OF AMERICA

TO

Dorothy Stuart, William Bisseth,
and the late George Gray

Faithful, Efficient, and Creative Custodians
of MacMahan Island, Maine

Foreword

IN THE HISTORY OF MANY FIELDS OF INQUIRY THERE ARE OCCASIONS WHEN
the use of valuable data is hindered because basic theory is inadequate.
Pastoral theology has such a character in our time. Much valuable
knowledge has emerged from the various sciences that study human
personality. Some good practical use has been made of this knowledge
by ministers and churches, in pastoral counseling and pastoral care, in
group dynamics, in religious education, and elsewhere.

But when these data are viewed as a whole, it becomes clear that we
have not had up to this point a fundamental and unifying theory that
would enable us to do justice to these modern contributions while relating them critically and explicitly to the theological tradition. If these
potential riches are not to be regarded merely as external and peripheral,
they must be assimilated into a theological context. That task calls
for theory of a theological order.

As the content of this volume will make clear, I do not believe that
the entire work needing to be done can be carried out by pastoral theology as I shall define it. But I believe the potential contribution of pastoral theology to the total task can be large.

Beginning in Chapter 5, this volume has a hero in the person of
Ichabod S. Spencer, Presbyterian minister in Brooklyn at the middle of
the nineteenth century. Spencer wrote and published in dialogue or
direct discourse form accounts of his ministry to individuals and families.
There is nothing else like this in Christian history before the present
century. I am indebted to John T. McNeill for calling Spencer originally
to my attention, and to Joseph Havens for suggesting the idea of studying Spencer's cases intensively. Spencer's so-called "sketches" give us

an unparalleled opportunity to examine our modern ways of shepherding in the light of some of the ways of the past.

The original compilation of the material that has finally resulted in this book was made for the Ayer Lectures of 1954 at the Colgate Rochester Divinity School. Formal acknowledgment of this occasion is made elsewhere. In more personal vein I wish to express my warmest appreciation to President Wilbour G. Saunders, Dean Oren H. Baker, Professor Emeritus Justin Wroe Nixon, and to other members of the faculty and administration for their gracious invitation, delightful hospitality, and trust in giving me extra time to commit the material to paper as the lectureship requires.

The three groups of students who have been with me in year-long seminars about pastoral theology have made more contributions to my thinking than they know. My deepest thanks go to Joseph Fletcher, of the Episcopal Theological School, Cambridge, and to my colleague at Chicago, T. Mallary Fitzpatrick, Jr., for their thoughtful reading of and detailed comment on the entire manuscript. I want also to thank another Chicago colleague, Jaroslav Pelikan, for his penetrating and helpful counsel on the first draft of my historical chapter. Whatever its present deficiencies, they are less than they were at first. Marian Cronheim, of the Menninger Foundation, gave valuable help in preparing the index.

In addition to Dorothy Stuart, William Bisseth, and the late George Gray, to whom this book is dedicated, I want to thank all the other residents of MacMahan Island, Maine, for helping to write this book by letting me alone. Seated at the typewriter in a shack at the middle of the island, surrounded by spruce and fir and pine trees and with a distant view of the water, I was satisfactorily treated as a leper so long as my machine gave indication that I was really at work. Perhaps only the habitual city dweller can appreciate the combination of pine trees, sea air, and lack of interruption. Thanks to these friends, animate and inanimate, there was no excuse for failure to write. Since few of the animate friends are professional theologians, they may not understand the whole of this inquiry. But I trust they will not misunderstand the warmth of my appreciation to them.

SEWARD HILTNER

Contents

PART I. Definition

PART II. Transition

PART III. Content

PART IV. Cognates

Contents

PART I

Definition

CHAPTER 1

Task

WHAT IS PASTORAL THEOLOGY? HOW IMPORTANT IS IT? TO WHOM?

It is the thesis of this book that pastoral theology is a formal branch of theology resulting from study of Christian shepherding, that it is just as important as biblical or doctrinal or historical theology, and that it is no less the concern of the minister of the local church than of the specialist.

From the days of the Reformation the term "pastoral" has been used in two senses. Beginning with Zwingli's book *The Shepherd*, "pastoral" was used as the functional extension of the noun "pastor." [1] Whatever the pastor or shepherd did was pastoral or shepherding. Functions followed from title. By implication everything done by one called a "pastor" was shepherding. Followed to its logical end, this would have meant either an imperialism of shepherding over other possible ends or else a loss of the original biblical metaphor of shepherding as the exercise of tender and solicitous care.

"Pastoral" was also used in a second sense, which attempted to emphasize the thrust of the original metaphor. The eighteenth and nineteenth centuries spoke of "poimenics." [2] This meant the study of shepherding since it came from the Greek word for shepherd, *poimen*, which in turn came from a verb form that meant to feed or to tend the flock. "Poimenics" appeared along with a list of other important functions of minister and church, such as "catechetics," the study of religious instruction; "homiletics," the study of preaching and religious communication; and certain others. Had this view of shepherding been followed to its logical end, shepherding would have been seen as only one among a dozen functional goals of the church. Perhaps one out of every twelve events could then be regarded as "shepherding," while other events would fall under other headings.

We believe that neither of these ways in which Protestantism has understood shepherding can be fruitful in itself in establishing an adequate pastoral theology. But we believe it of great positive importance that neither of these views within the tradition has pushed out the other. Literally stated, each view is mistaken. Not everything done by one with the title of "pastor" is shepherding. But neither is shepherding a kind of faucet to be turned on only at occasional times and places. Each view testifies, we believe, to an important aspect of the truth. A normative definition of shepherding can learn from both views. But it will require more than a sum, since the two views appear mutually exclusive.

The truth of the first view, in which shepherding was seen as whatever one does who is known as shepherd, is attitudinal. If one is genuinely a pastor, then no act that he performs can avoid having behind it as motivation and as disposition or readiness an attitude of tender and solicitous concern for person or group with whom he is dealing. The attitude is always present as a readiness and comes into the open when called for by need. In some degree it is present in every actual event, and as readiness it is alert to becoming dominant in any event where the need exists.

The truth of the second view, in which shepherding was associated with one type of event as against other types, is structural or categorical. There are some events, or functions, or operations, in which shepherding is properly the dominant and overriding end. There are other events or types of events in which another immediate end may be dominant. Thus shepherding, while it may be involved in every event as an attitude or readiness, is not properly dominant in every actual event. In principle shepherding may be one category among others or one aspect in a structure defining the several legitimate ends.

We are grateful, then, that both ways of looking at Christian shepherding have been retained in the tradition, for each has truth to contribute to a normative conception. But until that conception has actually been stated, using whatever intellectual and spiritual tools are necessary and available, we cannot have a relevant pastoral theology. It is to that task that this entire volume is devoted.

It would be pleasant and gratifying to reader and writer alike if the task of defining first shepherding and then pastoral theology could be carried out on a relatively uncomplicated level, as if the intellectual dimensions of the job were simple and nothing were required except vivid illustrative material. Unfortunately, the facts are otherwise. We must include the truth from both views of shepherding as these have

16

been in our tradition, and that requires us to pay some attention to history. The study of shepherding demands some looking at actual events that involve shepherding, so there must be both an empirical and a contemporary dimension to our study. And since our concern goes beyond the activity of shepherding to a pastoral or shepherding theology, we must pay attention to the content and the method of any valid branch of Christian theology. In these several senses our inquiry must be theoretical, since we seek general and comprehensive principles worthy of the name "pastoral theology."

At the same time this inquiry is immensely practical. Every minister, whatever his specific location or branch of the ministry, must carry out shepherding when that is properly defined. And in carrying out this aspect of his ministry, either he has a grasp of fundamental principles or he must operate half blindly or by rule of thumb. In addition he needs to interpret to his people the meaning of shepherding. Perhaps we still confront the situation to which Richard Baxter addressed himself in 1656: "And because the people are grown unacquainted with the office of the ministry, it belongeth to us to acquaint them herewith, and to press them publicly to come to us for advice in such cases of great concernment to their souls." [3] Every minister, he added, is a "known counsellor for their souls." [4] He should, therefore, know what this function is and be able to interpret it to his people.

Shepherding occupies a quite unique place in Christianity. Bishop Gregory Bedell of Ohio, a great leader of the Protestant Episcopal Church, wrote in 1880, "No other religion than that of Christ absorbs all ideas of ministration within the idea of Pastorship, and concentrates the thoughts of its ministry upon Pastoral care. . . . The idea of Pastorship . . . is the whole of . . . Gospel ministry." [5] This is an overstatement of which the main thrust, however, is correct. Other high religions have spiritual directors, or guides, or teachers; but that which we hold to be focal and central about shepherding is distinctive of Christianity.

The unique place occupied by shepherding in Christianity comes from the way in which our relationship to God and our relationship to our fellow men are regarded as inseparable. The Great Commandment of Jesus, "You shall love the Lord your God with all your heart, and with all your soul, and with all your mind. . . . You shall love your neighbor as yourself," shows this relationship and of course emerges from our Jewish religious heritage. [6] It became clear to Paul and others that this commandment followed upon the fact that God had first loved us. This is

17

the basis for the high position held by shepherding in Christian practice, and we believe the understanding or theory of it, then, can occupy
no less significant a position in Christian thought and Christian theology.

The Meaning of Shepherding

We propose to consider shepherding as a perspective. The term "perspective" suggests that there is a certain point of view in the subject who
is performing the viewing or feeling or helping. But it implies also that
this subject is not completely described by this slant or point of view.
If he were not capable of other points of view as well, which need not
be competitive, we should be speaking of him in entirety and not of an
aspect of him. Thus the term "perspective" enables us to think of the
subject, or shepherd, as having and exercising an attitude or point of
view or type of feeling that is basic to him and not just something tacked
on. At the same time the subject is and has and feels more than this perspective.

"Perspective" implies also a relation to an object or other person. The
point of view is directed somewhere in particular, in act, in feeling, in
attitude. Thus the need or readiness of the object person will have something to do with what perspective becomes dominant in the subject person. Used in this way, the term "perspective" is relational. The shepherd
never looks at all without doing so in part, but not wholly, through the
shepherding perspective. But whether this is his dominant perspective depends upon the need and readiness of the other person or persons.

To view shepherding as a perspective solves in principle the problem
of the two kinds of meanings that shepherding has had in Protestantism.
From the one view we want to retain the truth that shepherding is in
some degree present in everything done by pastor or church. A group
meeting, a sermon, or a letter may contain as much shepherding intent
and effect as does a bit of personal counseling. The notion of tender and
solicitous concern that is behind the metaphor is in some measure to be
seen as present in everything done by pastor and church, if these are
rightly done. The view of shepherding as a perspective enables us to think
of shepherding as a readiness, an attitude, or a point of view that is never
absent from the shepherd and is therefore in some way involved in all his
feelings and actions.

From the other view of shepherding in Protestantism we wish to keep
the truth that shepherding, although much, is not everything, that it is
properly dominant when need and readiness so indicate, but that some-

thing else may properly be dominant under other conditions. Used in a relational sense, perspective makes this possible. When the one sheep is lost, attention is devoted to finding it. The shepherding perspective has for this sheep in this specific situation become dominant. Once this sheep is found and restored to the fold, other perspectives can and should take the foreground. But even though the ninety and nine for a time require no special shepherding, the idea of perspective suggests the readiness of the shepherd to be attentive to them at any time they need or wish tender and solicitous concern.

The idea or model of shepherding as a perspective enables us to answer the next question: Is shepherding the same as pastoral care? The answer is No if pastoral care is viewed as one of the so-called "offices" of the ministry, correlative with such other offices as preaching, church administration, religious education, evangelism, or the church's social outreach. The answer is Yes if pastoral care is seen to be involved in some degree in every act of church and minister, and to be dominantly important in some act but not in others.

Especially during the nineteenth century the acts and functions of the church were organized into types of offices.[7] There was, for instance, preaching as one of these offices or types; while the study of preaching was known as homiletics. There was religious education or instruction, the theory or study of which was called catechetics. The theory of pastoral care was called poimenics. Pastoral care was generally divided into a general branch and a special branch. The special branch dealt with types of individual cases. The general branch dealt with the whole group or with subgroups. There is something simple and natural about organizing the functions of the church about these offices, and they will continue to have positive value.

But the system of offices is, after all, only one possible way in which to examine what the minister and the church do. Let us look at a specific act or event. Here is a particular minister on a particular Sunday morning preaching a particular sermon to a particular group of people. If we are using the scheme of offices, we simply classify this event as preaching. But some members of the congregation may say the sermon was instructive and mean it literally. To others it brought a solicitous concern easing their burden. Calling this whole event "preaching," therefore, does not deal exhaustively with its meaning and significance. It is simply one useful way of classifying events or functions, but not the sole way and not necessarily the way best calculated to get at basic theory.[8]

When pastoral care is regarded as one of the offices of the church, the same things about its virtues and defects may be said as have been indicated above about preaching. And in that sense pastoral care would not be shepherding as we use it, as a perspective upon all operations and dominant in some. Pastoral care *could* be used as we are using the term shepherding, but in that case we should have to be careful not to revert to thinking by way of the offices.[9] For the purposes of our inquiry it has seemed better to return to the ancient metaphor of shepherding rather than attempting to wrest the idea of pastoral care from the typological context in which it is embedded.

The Meaning of Pastoral Theology

Pastoral theology is defined here as that branch or field of theological knowledge and inquiry that brings the shepherding perspective to bear upon all the operations and functions of the church and the minister, and then draws conclusions of a theological order from reflection on these observations.

This means, first, that pastoral theology comes out of inquiry from the shepherding perspective, when the latter is defined as in the previous section. I hold that there are two other perspectives cognate with shepherding, which I call "communicating" and "organizing," which should also lead to branches of theology; and these are discussed later in this volume.

Second, the definition asserts that pastoral theology is a branch of theology in the strict sense of the term.[10] It has the same kind of autonomy as any other branch of theology—biblical, doctrinal, historical, ethical, and so on—although all branches are of course interrelated. But pastoral theology is not derivative from the other branches except in the same sense in which all branches derive in part from one another.[11]

Third, the definition implies that pastoral theology is an operation-centered or function-centered branch of theology rather than what we shall call for lack of a better name a logic-centered branch of theology.[12] Within the whole body of divinity what is distinctive about the operation-centered inquiries such as pastoral theology is that their theological conclusions, or theory or basic principles, emerge from reflection primarily on acts or events or functions from a particular perspective. There are other branches of theology, such as biblical theology or doctrinal theology, whose organizing principle is of a different nature. The study of the Bible, or biblical theology, is centered logically around anything that contributes to understanding the meaning, devolopment, and significance of that book and the people and events and experiences lying behind the book. The study of doctrine is organized systematically and logically around the relation of doctrines to one another and their mutually reinforcing capacity to give testimony to the total faith. From these focal concerns each of the logic-centered fields of theology pursues its special investigations, which of course include the questions of practical significance and implication.

The logic-centered fields of theology are so obviously indispensable that they have led unwittingly to a misconception, namely, that any branch of theology must proceed as they do. They find their focuses in something that is overridingly logical and necessary, such as the Bible, the interrelation of doctrines, the development of history, or the meaning of morals. The contention here is that there is another kind of branches of theology, whose focuses are a particular perspective upon operations.[13] We distinguish three such branches, of which pastoral theology is one. A picture of the "body of divinity" is indicated schematically in the table on page 28.[14]

Fourth, our definition suggests that pastoral theology is systematic, as any branch of theology must be, but that the principles around which the system is organized are those given by the nature of the shepherding perspective.[15] For instance, doctrinal theology is organized systematically around doctrines and their interrelationship. It uses the common currencies of the faith—such as God, sin, salvation—primarily in terms of the relation of their meaning to one another. Pastoral theology, like any branch of theology, also uses these common currencies of the faith. But it organizes its material according to the data secured from inquiry according to the shepherding perspective. Thus pastoral theology is not a different kind of theology in terms of ultimate content. It is not a competitor of any other branch of theology, but its principle of self-organization is uniquely its own, just as theirs are.[16] As we shall see in this brief historical inquiry about pastoral theology, confusion about these apparently abstract points led sometimes to odd conclusions about pastoral and practical theology.

Fifth, our definition of pastoral theology enables us to use a method in relation to it that is consistent with the standards for any critical theological method.[17] How do we approach critical and discriminating inquiry in any branch of theology? We first acknowledge that we do not bring a blank mind, that our whole previous experience with the faith and with the world affects the questions and presuppositions we bring. In so acknowledging, we are in a better position to see what is in the material we are studying. So it is with pastoral theology. We do not come at this with minds wiped blank of experience with the faith. We acknowledge our views and convictions, and thus become more open to what study of this particular kind, namely, reflection on acts viewed from the perspective of shepherding, has to teach us.

Our method proceeds from and through revelation as in any branch of theology, in the sense in which William Temple defined revelation as the "coincidence of event and appreciation." [18] We seek to cultivate the appreciation, the reception, the assimilation, the understanding— recognizing that only so can we know the event. The event may indeed exist independently of our appreciation, but we never know it so. So revelation calls not for the stifling of inquiry but for the most discriminating inquiry that can be made.

All realms of theological inquiry involve relationship between faith and culture. Sometimes the questions raised in culture—for example, What kind of stability can man have in a world of instability?—can be answered by faith.[19] And at times questions asked within the faith—for example, How can a man avoid simple repetition of actions he deplores? —can have at least partial answers given by the world of culture—perhaps to this question the insights of psychology into our inner ambiguous motivations. Material of tremendous potential significance for the questions of theology is now available in the personality sciences. When pastoral theology studies this material, as it pertains to the perspective of shepherding, it is following not a nontheological or an extratheological method but something that is part of method in every branch of theology. Faith can remain faithful and relevant only when it is in constant and discriminating dialogue with culture.

In concluding this initial discussion of the meaning of pastoral theology, it will be well to note briefly the definitions that are excluded. First, pastoral theology is not merely the *practice* of anything.[20] The practice or functions or events are examined reflectively and thus lead to theory. Any merely practical study of practice, if it failed to lead to fundamental theory, could not be pastoral theology.

Second, pastoral theology is not merely applied theology. Such a notion implies that principles are acquired through, for example, study of the Bible or of Christian doctrine and that these are applied in one-way fashion to acts and functions. We acknowledge fully that study of

Bible and doctrine results in principles that may and must be applied. We assert further, however, that the process moves the other way also, that adequate critical study of events from some significant perspective makes creative contributions to theological understanding. Pastoral theology, like any branch of theology, applies some things learned elsewhere. But it is more than that as well.

Third, pastoral theology is not just pastoral psychology or pastoral sociology under a new name. The data considered may frequently be the same. What pastoral theology insists on is that the knowledge gained from observation and reflection be placed in a theological context. The principal criteria and methods employed are themselves theological. Pastoral psychology deals with insights emerging out of psychological inquiry for any and all aspects of the pastor's work and thought. Pastoral theology deals with the theological theory of the shepherding perspective upon the pastor's acts and functions. There is much overlap; but the two studies are not identical in scope, method, or aim.

Fourth, pastoral theology is not, as it has sometimes been held to be in the past, the theory of all the functions and operations of pastor and church. Such a view has seldom been held to completely, for the theory of preaching was usually excluded from the rubric of pastoral theology. We hold equally that pastoral theology cannot be the theory of all pastoral operations save preaching, for that gives it a kind of "Whatever is left over" definition. We believe attempts to define pastoral theology in this way will lead to either imperialism or amorphousness, as in the past, and we reject both.

Finally, we reject the possible conception of pastoral theology as the link betweeen the organized fields of theological study and the acts and functions of minister and church. We reject this for two reasons. On the one hand, it implies that study of operations and functions cannot lead through reflection and systematization to a branch of theology, and we believe it can and must do so. We reject it, on the other hand, because it implicitly defines any branch of theology in terms of what we have called a "logic-centered" point of reference. We must acknowledge the great importance of bringing together the findings from the logic-centered fields with those from the function-focused fields. But we believe this task is the job of all the branches and is not a function that can be performed by any alleged "master discipline."

As we shall see in the historical chapter, some astute theologians in the nineteenth century proposed a branch of theology known as "practical theology," which would in turn have subbranches, of which pastoral theology might be one. There are two senses in which our conception of pastoral theology agrees with the intention behind the formation of practical theology. The first is the implication that the study of operations can and must be theological in character, must somehow lead to theological understanding. The second is that pastoral theology is not the sole branch of theology that can emerge from proper study of the functions of pastor and church.

With other aspects of this nineteenth-century idea of practical theology, we must take issue. We do not believe there is or can be a discipline of "practical theology" or "operational theology" that can be regarded as co-ordinate with biblical theology, doctrinal theology, and historical theology, and seen in the same series. The branches of theology whose focus is operations are *collectively* co-ordinate to the branches of theology whose focus is some logical reference point, such as the Bible. Further, we do not believe there can be a master perspective on acts and operations that would swallow all the others, any more than there can be a master perspective in the logic-centered fields, such that Bible would swallow up doctrine or history or ethics or that doctrine would consume the others.

Pastoral theology, to present the definition in slightly different language, is an operation-focused branch of theology, which begins with theological questions and concludes with theological answers, in the interim examining all acts and operations of pastor and church to the degree that they involve the perspective of Christian shepherding.

Importance of Pastoral Theology

There are five reasons why the study of pastoral theology is important today. The first is the peculiar nature and extent of the need for shepherding in our time. In our country more people belong to churches, both absolutely and proportionately, than at any previous time. Joining the church and professing faith in Jesus Christ do not automatically eliminate personal needs and problems. The churches and ministers now have an opportunity to help many persons to whom previously they would have been denied access.

Whatever one's diagnosis of our present cultural climate—age of anxiety, trend toward comformity, confusion in moral standards, or cult of success—the deepest need is to come somehow to a valid sense of meaningfulness. At least the start toward this must often be made

24

through shepherding. But the details of the shepherding process must be up to date or they will not make contact. In the culture in which the shepherding metaphor was first developed, the single shepherd, with his crook to guide and redirect the strays, took his sheep into green pastures by day and at night brought them to the safety of home. Today a sheep grower has to help the pasture by fertilizer, by alternate plantings, or by irrigation. He adds vitamins and antibiotics to the sheep diet. He does these things, not because sheep are inherently more complicated now than they used to be, but because modern knowledge enables him to do more about helping more sheep in more dimensions of their life. The spiritual shepherd of today has as much obligation as the literal shepherd to bring his methods up to date, in order to meet the peculiar needs and dangers of our time.

A second reason why the study of pastoral theology is important lies in the development of new knowledge, new tools, and new professions that bear upon helping and healing. The new knowlege that is coming from psychology, from psychiatry, from anthropology, and from other sources is not easy to assimilate; but its riches are such that no thoughtful person can set them aside.[21] This knowledge is about more than methods and techniques. It may teach the spiritual shepherd the equivalent of how to prevent the grass from disappearing from a green pasture through knowledge of irrigation, crop rotation, and tree planting.

There are new problems and opportunities through the rise of new helping professions or through extension of functions among older helping professions such as the medical. Some modern shepherds, it is true, may be quacks, consciously or otherwise. In either event they need to be so recognized. But what is the shepherding function of the ordained minister in relation to the shepherding actually being carried out by the social worker, the psychiatrist, the student personnel worker, the clinical psychologist, the leader of group therapy, and all the others?[22] It is not the minister's Christian faith that distinguishes him from them. They too may well be Christians. How does he co-operate with them? Where do their skills extend beyond his and his beyond theirs? These questions and relationships demand continued study and discussion at a basic theoretical level as well as in terms of daily practice. Without a pastoral theology the minister has no theoretical structure to use in trying to answer them but must resort to a kind of practical opportunism. And we must speak not only to the question of the ordained minister as shepherd but also to that of the universal pastorhood of believers when some of those unordained Christian shepherds have skills and knowledge to which the ordained do not profess.

Third, pastoral theological study is important because without it the acts of shepherding, though they be many and mighty, will not illumine our understanding of the faith. In the United States it is clear that there is much shepherding activity within the churches. But it is not always clear that this is based on understood Christian presuppositions, and that reflection upon the activities is regarded as something more than the application of psychology or sociology in a purely practical sense.[23] Unless pastoral theology is studied, we lose many of the best opportunities with which God has provided us for deepening and correcting our understanding of the faith and that of those we try to help.

Fourth, the study of pastoral theology is important because of the peculiarly psychological intellectual climate of our time. Harry A. Overstreet has suggested that the language of our century is psychological in a way not true of any previous age.[24] Whether the psychology is good or bad, true or false, it is a mode of thinking in some respects unique to our time. Unless this modern man learns that this psychological language may also be a theological language, he is disposed to relegate theology as irrelevant to his thought and his concerns. There seems to be a growing amount of popular psychological thought that really deals with theological questions but that, by failing to acknowledge accurately the theological context, distorts theology and drives a deeper wedge between a misunderstood theology and an apparently more "comfortable" psychology. These trends should be arrested. Pastoral theology, studying shepherding in the light of theological questions and returning with theological answers, can take full account of psychology but can help prevent the false bifurcation that many now believe to represent the relation of theology and psychology. Of course there are difficult problems in this relationship. But the real problems are quite different from those posed in the popular mind.

Finally, the study of pastoral theology is important in the context of our general theological revival today. The renewed and widespread concern among laymen as well as clergy for a deepened understanding of biblical and doctrinal theology, and sometimes of historical and moral theology, is incomplete unless there is a new depth to pastoral theology. And at this point, as the historical chapter will suggest, there is no clear structural norm in our Protestant tradition. From this tradition we can learn much about attitude, about concern, about diligence,

He who would be of a shepherding character had better do some shepherding acting and some shepherding thinking.

The great Swiss pastor and teacher Alexander Vinet wrote in the middle of the nineteenth century, "It is at last only by the care of souls that he can realize and identify to himself his flock as a flock, and not only as an auditory. 'I know my sheep, and am known of mine' (John 10:14)— he only is the good Shepherd who can thus speak." [4] Baxter made a similar point, "This serious dealing with sinners for their salvation will help you to far deeper apprehensions of these saving principles, than will be got by any other means; and a little more of the knowledge of these is worth all the other knowledge in the world." [5] Becoming acquainted with "saving principles" through shepherding is itself a vital element in the formation of the shepherd's character.

Although our predecessors were far from ignorant of the darkness in the motives of even the best of men, it has remained for the personality studies of our day to present the mixture of human motivation in richness of detail. The qualities needed in the shepherd are always in fact mixed with others. For instance, we cannot love our parishioners any more than we can love our children without somewhere inside hating them a bit too. Our most sincere attempts to be reverent can never be wholly unmixed with some irreverence. We believe today that a certain ambiguity or ambivalence of motivation is not necessarily harmful unless we deny and distort this fact. We believe, for instance, that a conscious recognition of hostility within us helps to relieve it of its power.

On some details of this kind we know things of which our ancestors were ignorant. But they knew the crucial point quite well. If one had any genuine motivation at all for shepherding, this was due finally to God's gracious favor and not to any intellectual or spiritual virtues of one's own "unregenerate nature." To them as to us one did not fix his gaze upon a list of desirable qualities and then strive to realize these in his life. Instead, one acknowledged his imperfection or "corruption." Then, in response to Christ's own shepherding he went about among others in the faith that needed qualities would arise through response to what God had already given.

Today we tend to put such things more prosaically. We say no man can have all the qualities in the needed degree. No shepherd can be perfectly understanding, accepting, wise, tender, or loving. But a recognition of one's own biases, ambiguities, and inadequacies can go a long way toward making one available to others in need. The shepherd need not be perfect. But he does need a certain kind of attitude toward his imperfection and inadequacy. And while this attitude may begin with a gift, it requires diligent cultivation: through shepherding activity, through self-criticism in the course of that activity, and through intellectual and spiritual reflection on what the shepherding contributes to understanding of the faith. Modern as these statements may be, we share their meaning with Zwingli, Baxter, and Vinet.

Every Minister a Pastoral Theologian

Whatever his specific occupation within the larger calling and profession of the ministry, every minister must serve as shepherd; and therefore, among other things, he must be a pastoral theologian.

It requires no argument that the minister of the local church and the chaplain in hospital, prison, or armed forces performs many functions that are primarily shepherding in nature. We believe the fact is equally true of ministers who are teachers of religion or of those who administer the complexities of ecclesiastical life.

If a teacher should merely lecture to his classes and pay attention to nothing but the content of questions put by his students, disdaining any responsibility for either the religious or the emotional development of his pupils, he would have ceased in some measure to operate as a minister. And he would probably not be an effective teacher either, for teaching involves more than clarity of one-way communication about content.

If the church administrator, who is growing in number, should pay no attention to the personal and religious needs of those involved in the administering, he too would cease being a minister in the full sense. Any good teacher or administrator will do shepherding as the need arises, even though, rightly enough, his dominant attention may be placed elsewhere, on communicating and organizing respectively.

Since every minister must be a shepherd, among other equally important things, it follows that his education must deal in some fundamental way with shepherding. The recent study sponsored by the American Association of Theological Schools makes it clear that the past few years have witnessed a great expansion of activity along these lines.[6] Clinical pastoral training, some types of supervised field work and other supervised experience have been expanded to more students in training. Classroom courses have become more numerous, and their teachers are better prepared. There is also a growing number of refresher courses, conferences, and workshops for ministers in the general area of shepherding.

Although the study report by H. Richard Niebuhr, Daniel D. Williams, and James M. Gustafson wisely notes "that the development of pastoral theology as a theological discipline is still in process," it makes some comments that are wholly in line with our own conclusions.[7] Without attempting a formal definition of pastoral theology, the report asserts nevertheless that the drawing of theological conclusions from reflection on functions is vital for every minister and student in training. The report declares:

The student needs three contributions from his work in pastoral theology: first, an interpretation of the care of souls within the church and his pastoral office; second, an interpretation of the meaning of the data and scientific understanding in this field for Christian faith and theology, and third, growth in self-knowledge both as a person and as one who is to be a channel for the healing promised in the Gospel.[8]

The first of these implies in our terms the need to understand shepherding in both its contemporary and its historical dimensions. The second is similar to our understanding of pastoral theology. The practical dimensions are important, but even they can remain important only if the study of actual events and functions leads to fundamental theory, that is, to a pastoral theology whenever the perspective involved is shepherding. The third need, which the report puts in terms of "self-knowledge," is certainly one to the meeting of which shepherding and pastoral theology should make an important contribution. This is especially true where, as the report suggests, "healing" is the focus.

We believe there is, and must be, an interrelationship among these three needs acutely set forth by this impressive study of the education of ministers. The proper study of shepherding presupposes and leads to deeper understanding of the faith in a particular way, that is, pastoral theology. In turn pastoral theology stimulates shepherding and compels the rethinking by the shepherd of himself, his self-understanding, and his own place and function in the processes of shepherding. Rightly viewed, each of these three is evocative of each of the others.

In contemporary American shepherding and the training for it, it is the contribution to understanding the faith, the pastoral theology, that has been most neglected. We believe that this—along with the actual study of and experience with shepherding, and the movement toward self-understanding—is a concern not merely of the specialist but also

33

of every minister regardless of his particular occupation within the ministry.

The Specialist in Pastoral Theology

The tendency to use the term "theologian" only in relation to the specialist theological scholar is regrettable. For it implies that other ministers and other Christians have no obligation to be theologians. Yet if being a theologian means thinking through the meaning and implications of the faith, every Christian must be a theologian in some degree.

It is good, however, that we do have some specialists in the several branches of theology, both for the instruction of theological students and for carrying forward the necessary work of theological inquiry and scholarship in its various dimensions. It is important to understand, however, that the specialized scholar in any branch of theology does not simply engage in more and more minute and detailed investigation of the Bible, or of doctrine, or of church history, or of shepherding. He does have an obligation for such detailed investigation. But he has an equal obligation to relate his investigation to the other branches of theology and to theology in the more general sense. There may be a kind of technical scholarship that is unconcerned to relate its conclusions in this way. Such a scholar would thereby forfeit any claim to being a theologian. What makes any scholar a theologian is the combination of specialized scholarship with theological relatedness and relevance.

We regard it as impossible for anyone to be an expert in theology in general apart from careful and specialized inquiry through the several branches of theology. By theology in general is meant that understanding of our faith to which any branch of theology tends, each in its own way, to point. It is not a separate field or area, but rather the realm in which discourse is possible among all varieties of theologians. The road of any theologian, be he scholar or general practitioner, toward theology in general must be, therefore, in part one of familiarity with several branches of theology in some degree. Even if he is to be a specialist in one, he cannot be ignorant of the others. Integration is important, but it cannot be achieved by the renunciation of specialized knowledge and inquiry.

Like any other specialist in a branch of theology, the pastoral theologian must, therefore, know something more than pastoral theology. Otherwise he cannot bring the result of his investigations to the general arena of understanding the faith, and by so much he fails to be a theologian at all. And since pastoral theology in our definition is an operation-focused branch of theology, it is peculiarly important for the specialist in pastoral theology to know something about the other branches of theology that are focused on operations and functions. Although there has been no attempt as yet to name these, it is believed that they will emerge from studies of communicating and of organizing as pastoral theology emerges from inquiry into shepherding.

Many of the specialist scholars of the nineteenth century saw clearly that one could not be expert about one area of operations without knowing something about the others. Some of them, however, fell into the error of believing that the way to avoid lopsidedness was to avoid detailed or genuinely specialized investigation of any particular area. We see such a tendency continuing today and regard it as mistaken. Investigation may and should be as specialized and detailed as possible. What prevents the evils that may attach to specialism is the return to the general realm of theological discourse.[9] We make special investigations to get light on general problems and not only on the specialized problems peculiar to the specialized inquiry. Where that is done, specialism is wholly positive and not disintegrative.

Where any form of specialized theological inquiry has steadily before it the aim of illuminating theology in general, then its specialism is to be praised rather than deplored or mitigated. This point is not widely understood and accepted even in theological schools, especially in relation to the operation-focused branches of theology. The professor of preaching or pastoral care or religious education is likely to contend that he is not interested solely in something which is then narrowly defined. His intention is correct. His data can and must be applied beyond narrow confines. Eventually they must bear upon theology in general. But this cannot be a means of saying, "Don't fence me in. Don't limit me." The data should be pursued in specialized fashion. Their significance should be brought to the theological village green.

This issue is not confined to theological faculties. Whether he knows it or not, every minister confronts it also. Each of us finds one or more perspectives, or ways of inquiring, that bring home to us the meaning of the faith more deeply than do others. Such "bents," properly heeded and pursued, are forms of specialization, whether they involve much book learning or not. To neglect them, under the mistaken notion that the general practitioner is a specialist in no sense at all, will mean impoverishment of any ministry. Provided they are pursued so that they eventually shed light on theology in general, they are positive, integrative, and indispensable. On the other hand, if these bents should be used to defend one against exploring certain other things for which he feels less kinship but which are still necessary, then specialism would be failing in its proper function.

Every minister must be concerned about shepherding. For some ministers, apparently a goodly number, the perspective of shepherding is peculiarly their personal bent. Things come alive to them more deeply in shepherding than elsewhere. Whether they know it or not, therefore, they are, incipiently, specialists in pastoral theology. To the extent that they can reflect on work done from the point of view of this bent or perspective, they are at least beginning scholars in a branch of theology that certainly needs more specialized inquirers than the faculties of theological schools can supply.

There is one more fact we may note about specialism in pastoral theology—that there is currently no one who is a specialist in pastoral theology who is not also, at the same time a specialist in something else. This is due to a peculiar combination of historical conditions, of which my own experience typifies that of several other specialists as well. I became interested first (my bent) in the light that modern psychology, psychiatry, and psychoanalysis could shed upon the practical work of the minister. But it soon became clear that one could not simply take insights labeled "psychology" and apply them in ministerial work. Something in the whole setting and context of the minister's work affected what was relevant and could be appropriated. In addition this context promised a creative contribution. So pastoral psychology came to be seen as more than the application of psychology to ministerial practice.

Further, the insights coming out of the inquiry continually broke through beyond merely practical considerations and led to matters of basic theory. The conviction grew that the systematic exploration of psychology in its more comprehensive sense, with theological questions in mind and with theological conclusions drawn, was vital to our understanding of the faith. Such a field of study is "logic-centered," as I have used that term, and hence is of the same type as biblical theology, doctrinal theology, historical theology, or moral theology. This field of theological study—known in my school as "Religion and Personality"—has psychology as its data, but asks theological questions and gets theological answers. While related to pastoral theology, to some extent both its data and its perspective are different. Nearly every specialist in pastoral theology, as defined here, is also at the same time a specialist in something that may be variously named "psychology of religion" or "psychology of personality" or "pastoral psychology."

Perhaps this fact that there are no existing specialists in pastoral theology who are not also specialists in something else may cause the reader to ask in a new way why pastoral theology is alleged to be so important. The answer is that the body of divinity, as the general structure through which theological inquiry proceeds, is not a series of pigeonholes into which persons are placed, one to a hole. Perspectives and inquiries may and do overlap. The body of divinity is to help the organization and advancement of theological knowledge and wisdom, not to compartmentalize those who would advance the knowledge and wisdom. The structure is made for man, not man for the structure.

The primary impetus for our current reconsideration of pastoral theology has been the contact in many forms between theology and the growing knowledge of personality. This is leading to the development of a branch of theology of which the logic-centered focus is psychology or personality in the comprehensive sense. But it also makes imperative, we may contend, the development of a pastoral theology as the theological theory resulting from specialized inquiry into the shepherding perspective upon the functions and operations of minister and church. In shepherding more is involved than psychology and personality. And as the discipline matures, these other dimensions will become plainer.

The Layman as Pastoral Theologian

The discussion of the person in pastoral theology has so far concentrated on ministers as ordained clergymen who have had formal theological education. Certainly there need be no apology for reflective investigation of the work of the minister as professional man. But is pastoral theology a concern *only of the clergy*? Is there no universal pastorhood to go along with the universal priesthood of Protestantism?

This question is not so easy as it looks, and we do not help answer it by sentimental ascription to any or all laymen of capacities that can emerge only from special education. There are aspects of shepherding with which no one is equipped to deal, regardless of his good will and intentions, unless he has had such training. But there are, on the other hand,

37

aspects of shepherding for which participation in the faith, good will, common sense, and general ability in human relationships are the needed requirements. The two ought not to be confused.

There are many shepherding functions that can be performed by laymen who have no special professional preparation. But there is no aspect of shepherding that may be assigned indiscriminately to laymen in the sense that the minister ceases to feel any responsibility. Our study of ministry to older people, for instance, suggests that even here, where the need is so often for sheer genuine friendliness and therefore laymen may have an important part in this ministry, this tends to work effectively only when the pastor assumes some responsibility for general oversight. The minister in such forms of ministry becomes a "bishop" in the original sense—overseer of the flock.

If laymen who are not experts in shepherding are to have their interest genuinely aroused in the ministry of shepherding appropriate to them, something more than "inspiration" in the derogatory sense is needed. If imaginations are touched and brains set moving over a ministry such as calling upon older shut-ins, more will be accomplished than if they are simply told to be friendly. Elementary instruction in the ways of individual shepherding can be intellectually as well as spiritually exciting.

There is, however, a surpassingly important fact about laymen and shepherding in the church. This is that many laymen are not amateurs in shepherding. They are professional persons who spend most of their professional time healing, sustaining, or guiding other people. They are psychiatrists, pediatricians, clinical psychologists, vocational counselors, teachers, social workers, occupational therapists, and many others. They are professional personal helpers, and many of them are Christians and church members.

Pastoral theology should be interesting to this growing body of men and women who are both professional helpers and committed Christians. Their professional focus lies properly in their own discipline, whatever it is. But pastoral theology should be able to help them orient themselves and their discipline to the church, and help them to bring their Christianity and their work into fruitful relationship.

In contrast to ordained ministers, they are laymen. Seldom, unfortunately, has their professional training included anything about theology. But they are not laymen to shepherding. They can and should play an increasing role in the total shepherding activity of the fellowship.

For the church does not operate solely within the walls of the building on Main Street. It is at work wherever the cup of cold water is being given in the name of Christ. Indeed, these fellow Christians not only will be interested in pastoral theology; they will be increasingly among its creators.

CHAPTER 3

History

THE TEXT OF THIS CHAPTER CONSIDERS ONLY THOSE POINTS IN THE DEVEL-
opment of Protestant pastoral theology since the Reformation that are
felt to be indispensable to a grasp of the constructive thesis of this book.
The reader interested in further details may consult the notes.

"In matters concerning the cure of souls the German Reformation had
its inception." [1] So begins John T. McNeill's account of the important
place held in early Protestantism by what the Germans called *Seelsorge*.

McNeill's words refer to the position held by Luther and others on
indulgences as formal assurances of pardon from sin. Their indignation
was partly against the commercialization that had grown up around the
sale of indulgences, a type of misuse that was later corrected by the
Roman Catholic Church. But the protest was also religious in nature.
The very existence of indulgences implied that men, in the form of the
pope and his agents, could determine when sins were and were not forgiven. Such an assumption, however, was a libel on God's love as well
as his freedom. For when Jesus Christ told men to repent, he testified
that God was ever ready to forgive and that forgiveness came from God's
love, not from man's merit. Luther held that even the faith by which
alone man can become righteous in God's eyes is a gift freely given by
God, not something man can earn.

It followed from this early Protestant reasoning that the sacrament of
penance, as then commonly understood, was mistaken at both ends. To
the parishioner it seemed that the acts he performed after his confession
were what satisfied God and made possible his forgiveness. To the priest
it appeared that his office gave him the power to give or to withhold
forgiveness on behalf of God.

The difficulty was not with confession as the sincere acknowledgment of sinfulness, whether made directly to God or through a fellow Christian. For such acknowledgment, the Reformers held, is itself a sign that faith is at work. Only those who have been granted the new can rightly see the horrors of the old.

Nor was the trouble with absolution, when that is understood as the confident assurance that God has already granted forgiveness when there is true repentance. To an overscrupulous woman who continued to feel guilty because of some unseemly words she had uttered while angry, Luther wrote:

> Certainly it was not Christ who put into your mind the notion that you belong to the devil, for Christ died in order that those who belong to the devil may be released from his power. . . . We preachers absolve and free you in Christ's name and at his command. . . . Therefore, be content and confident. Your sin is forgiven. Rely resolutely on this.[2]

Because the Lutheran objection was not against either confession or absolution as such, but against apparent control of God by man, many Lutherans have retained some form of confession and absolution in their practice. Most other branches of Protestantism, except the Anglican, while sharing the basic point of religious conviction with the Lutherans, have felt that the formal context of confession becomes associated too easily with the very ideas that must be set aside. They have tended, therefore, to deal with confession and assurance of forgiveness on a more occasional and informal basis.

For all Protestants conviction about how the true cure of souls is wrought was central. "The grace which Protestants believe to receive from the 'word' is . . . the divine assurance of the forgiveness of sins which freely given by God through Christ makes possible a new personal relationship between man and his maker." [3]

The means by which man receives faith through the power of grace are, Protestants held, the Word and the sacraments. The Word is the revelation of God in Jesus Christ, which is both an actual historical event and a continuing message evoking belief and faith. When this Word is received, the man becomes a Christian and a new being. He lives then by faith rather than works. For most Protestants, as Wilhelm Pauck notes, "the sacraments which Protestants celebrate add nothing to the 'word'; they merely bring it, as it were, directly and personally to the believer." [4]
This function of driving home the truth and power of the Word made

41

the sacraments enormously important in Protestantism. It was for this reason that early Protestantism regarded the sacraments, especially the Lord's Supper, as the principal means of the care of souls.

The church on earth, said the Reformers, is to be understood primarily as a "fellowship of believers." In this sense believing is more than an assent to propositions. It is the mark that God's grace and forgiveness have brought new life. Those who so believe as a result of God's favor turn naturally to one another: to praise God, to uphold and help one another, and to proclaim the Word to fellow humans. So it is the man's soul is cared for in the church. The Word, the Sacraments, and the church continue through his lifetime to be the instruments by which his soul is cared for.

Man's regenerated condition through Christ is, it follows from these Protestant principles, not dependent upon a special priesthood, if priesthood is understood as a class of men serving as necessary mediators between God and man. Instead, in Christ there is to be a "universal priesthood of believers." As Pauck indicates, "everyone who has come under the lordship of God through faith in the gospel of Jesus Christ and thereby become a free man, subject to God alone, can be a priest who through his words and deeds brings the liberating gospel to his fellowmen." [5] This did not imply, as all the Reformers made clear, the renunciation of ministers. But they were to be ministers by virtue of their specially assigned functions, the ministry of the Word and sacraments, and following study, competence, and dedication needed for the proper performance of those functions. In God's eyes they were not different from other men. As some later Protestant books put it, ministers were to be an "order" but not a "caste."

Pauck's summary of the essence of Protestantism is that it

is a spiritual attitude, grounded in the living faith that God has made himself known in the person of Jesus of Nazareth and expressing itself ever anew in ways of life and thinking which reflect this faith as a proclamation of the glory of God transcending all human limitations and sufficiencies. [6]

Both aspects of this statement are important for our inquiry into the development of pastoral theology. On the one hand, our subject has its roots in basic convictions central to Protestant Christianity. On the other hand, the way in which this is worked out in one age may not be the same in form and details as in another.

The Early Centuries of Protestantism

The first use of the term "pastoral theology" in Protestantism appears to have been only in the middle of the eighteenth century.[7] Even in Germany, where all the works called by the name "pastoral theology" were first published, this does not seem to have become a recognized theological discipline until after the publication of the book by Klaus Harms in 1830.[8] The first American book on pastoral theology came in 1847.[9] There have been few attempts in the twentieth century to set forth a pastoral theology. This means that, historically speaking, attention given to a discipline called pastoral theology occurred only over a period of a hundred and fifty years, and that this was a fully recognized discipline for a period of less than a century. From such considerations it is plain that our historical inquiry must transcend the term "pastoral theology."

As pastoral theology has been defined constructively, its history is intertwined with that of *Seelsorge*, or the care and cure of souls; but the two are not identical.[10] Much of *Seelsorge* is devoted to "discipline," and it shall be argued later that this is not a direct part of pastoral theology as such, even though it is an important function of church and minister. The history of *Seelsorge* tends to be weak on precise and detailed information about how our predecessors went about many aspects of shepherding. The most detailed information of this kind that we possess from a previous century comes from Ichabod Spencer, and all the later chapters of this volume will draw heavily upon his reports.

Neither Luther nor Calvin wrote special treatises on *Seelsorge* or on shepherding, but both Huldreich Zwingli and Martin Bucer did so.[11] Zwingli tried to distinguish between the true shepherd and the false, and held that proclamation of the gospel must be followed up by instruction of and service to the people. Bucer's was the first systematic structuring of the ministry in Protestantism and contained five categories:

to draw to Christ those who are alienated; to lead back those who have been drawn away; to secure amendment of life in those who fall into sin; to strengthen weak and sickly Christians; to preserve Christians who are whole and strong, and urge them forward in all good.[12]

He held that this is to be done both in public and from house to house. Much of it is the duty of all Christians and not merely of ordained ministers.

Martin Luther's writings relating to *Seelsorge* were collected and published.[13] Like the related writings of Zwingli and Bucer, it is the shepherdly attitude set forth that has perennial value. For instance, writing to a minister who had a reputation for overemphasizing the law as against the gospel, Luther wrote:

Perhaps you hope in vain that all will hear and love the Word, or perhaps you center attention on the Law to the exclusion of the Gospel, so that the people think that they are listening to you instead of to God or feel that they are being subjected to compulsion. . . . Be gentle with those who are gentle, and let those who resist your preaching of the Law quarrel with God about it.[14]

What the sixteenth century did for pastoral theology was motivational and attitudinal. Shepherding first required the shepherd to be a Christian—with all that that implied. The shepherd was to be tenderly sensitive to those whose need required it, even though he might be severe to others. Like any Christian, but especially because of his calling, the minister was to follow up his proclamation of the Word and administration of the sacraments with personal contact and good counsel or instruction.

The great event of the seventeenth century in pastoral theology was Richard Baxter and his book that came to be known as *The Reformed Pastor*.[15] A Calvinist in doctrine, Baxter was an Independent on church polity; but he had a positive feeling toward the Church of England and sometimes attended its services, until he was forbidden. In 1656 he published his long, unsystematic, and repetitive book for his brother ministers. It called for a reform of the ministry, mainly in the form of systematic house to house calling within the parish. Although it did not succeed in its immediate purpose, it became widely known throughout the Protestant world and has been read down to our own day.

The reason for the universal appeal of Baxter can be seen in even a cursory reading of his book. He appealed directly to every minister's sense of responsibility for his people. Ministers without such a sense were reviled strongly. Much of the book is exhortation first toward serious spiritual preparation of the minister himself and then toward his spending himself upon his flock without stint. The exhortations are vivid and timeless, for they touch a minister in any age precisely at the point of some of his greatest spiritual temptations. To look to Baxter, however, for help on the structure of pastoral theology, or on the ministry generally, as has sometimes been done, is fruitless. That was his weak point. Baxter seemed to have an ability to move into any type of situation with an attitude that enabled him to meet the needs he found there. Sometimes the dominant need was for shepherding; sometimes, for instruction; at other times, for reproof or correction. His attitude seems to have been the same in all situations. Beyond the practical ability to recognize different types of need, he was unconcerned about theory. Generally speaking, this was true also of the other works of the seventeenth century, the best known being by George Herbert and Gilbert Burnet.[16]

The Later Centuries of Protestantism

From the time the term "pastoral theology" appeared in the middle of the eighteenth century until the first use of "practical theology" almost a century later, there was a certain unity in the meaning ascribed to pastoral theology. Broadly speaking, this was regarded as the theory of what the minister does except for preaching, which was set apart in a study known as "homiletics." The adjective "pastoral" was used as referring to the person who performs all the functions, usually excepting preaching. Thus the theory of the ministry in this period would ordinarily be regarded as falling under two heads: homiletics and pastoral theology. Apparently with no exceptions before Schleiermacher pastoral theology was a "theology" simply because it attempted to apply theological truth in practice. The early work on a structured discipline known as pastoral theology was done by Germans, and only in the nineteenth century do we find this in Britain.

If we ask about the history of shepherding—as against the history of a theoretical discipline known as pastoral theology—the situation is somewhat different. The outstanding fact of the late eighteenth and early nineteenth centuries about shepherding was the influence of pietism. The Methodist class meetings are an important illustration. Some of the pietists and evangelicals rated pastoral care as very important but felt they had to stand against theology in doing so. Perhaps some of the split that was recognized later on, and that is not gone in our own day, between shepherding as mere practice standing against systematic theory is finally part of our heritage from pietism. For these general reasons, and for understanding Ichabod Spencer in later chapters, it is important to get the essence of pietism. James H. Nichols says:

Here we mean an individualization and internalization which takes for granted or ignores the structure of church and state, seeking to build within it the significant religious fellowship. Pietism often expressed a reaction against orthodox formalism. The concern was not so much for new institutional expressions, as for personal appropriation of religious truth, subjective religious "experiences," and personal devotional and ascetical discipline. The larger relations of church and state and culture were discounted, sometimes because of apocalyptic expectations, or as religiously neutral. Or sometimes the pietist was himself a rationalist in these matters, accepting their emancipation from the church. In some way pietism involves the segregation of a certain sphere of life as peculiarly "religious," and concentration on it.[17]

The German literature on shepherding and on pastoral theology until the middle of the nineteenth century tended to represent either the formal orthodoxy or the pietistic reaction against it. Toward the end of the eighteenth century some "practical advice" books for the minister began to appear. A minister should possess many qualities such as prudence, knowledge, piety, prayer, and self-denial. He should visit his people, since this practice has "so greatly fallen into disuse in many places."[18] John Smith continued the Baxter tradition in words like these:

If we love our people, we may speak to them with freedom and boldness. Even when our faithful reproofs wound them to the quick . . . and when our pointed representations discover to each his own character, and make him clearly perceive that he is the man, even then they will listen to us with attention, generally love us, and bless us as their friends. Let us, by all means in our power, cultivate this reciprocal love between pastor and flock, on which the success of our ministrations, in so great a measure, must depend.[19]

A British textbook for theological students at the end of the eighteenth century organized the minister's work as follows: preaching, praying, administering the sacraments, visiting the sick, conduct toward people in general, and conduct toward people in particular.[20] The last three contained little particularity.

The study of pastoral theology came into the nineteenth century through the Germans and was taken up systematically by the the British and Americans only after the Germans, beginning in 1837 but pre-eminently with Friedrich Schleiermacher a little later, had developed what they called "practical theology."[21]

Practical theology to Schleiermacher was the "method of maintaining and perfecting the church." [22] To him practical theology was the larger discipline examining the acts and operations of the church, and pastoral theology was a part of this. He also held that the pursuit of doctrinal and practical understanding should go together. Indeed, the more progress made on the first, the more necessary to pay attention to the second. There are some hints that he believed the proper study of the reception of Christian faith would give reliable clues to the nature of the message itself, that is, that the proper study of practice would illuminate theological understanding itself.[23] Unfortunately, Schleiermacher's monumental work was never translated into English, and such influence as it has had in Britain and America has been small and with little relationship to the points noted above.

Following Schleiermacher there were several comprehensive works on practical theology, ending with a large and discerning work by the Dutch scholar J. J. Van Oosterzee.[24] All these writers held that pastoral theology is only a part of the study of the total work of minister and church, which agrees with our own thesis. Except for Schleiermacher they held that practical and pastoral theology are theological because they apply theological truth in practice, and not also because the study of practice contributes to basic theological understanding.

By the early part of the nineteenth century the offices of the church and the ministry had become fixed with slight variations in a pattern with which we are so familiar as never to have thought seriously of alternatives. In 1827 F. B. Köster divided "pastoral science" into four offices: liturgics, *Seelsorge*, homiletics, and catechetics.[25] The same general kind of position was taken later in the century by W. G. T. Shedd of Auburn and Union theological seminaries, who regarded pastoral theology as study of the minister's visiting, his catechizing, and his personal and prayer and intellectual life; while practical theology included these plus homiletics and liturgics.[26] A similar conception of pastoral theology as a catchall discipline was enunciated by James M. Hoppin of Yale.[27] It excludes homiletics but "includes all that the other branches do not teach." [28] The widely influential work of Van Oosterzee mentioned the following offices: homiletics, liturgics, catechetics, and poimenics, although an appendix dealt with "halieutics," the study of missions, and with apologetics.[29] He regarded pastoral theology as the study of poimenics and this as the "theory of pastoral care." [30]

During the latter part of the nineteenth century an influence like that of Richard Baxter was exercised by the work of Alexander Vinet, a Swiss pastor of a small free church, whose lectures on pastoral theology were edited and published by his students after his death.[31] In terms of structure Vinet like Baxter was not original. To him pastoral theology dealt with "all the kinds of activity to which the pastor is called, except public preaching and catechising." [32] Practical theology, of which pastoral theology was a part, simply applied usefully the knowledge gained in the "purely scientific" branches of theology.[33] It is Vinet's attitude—of intellectual discernment, sympathetic tenderness, and general humanity—that has won him deserved fame.

In the United States the production of systematic works on pastoral theology took place over a period of just sixty years, from 1847 to 1907. The first came from Enoch Pond, of Bangor Theological Seminary, in the earlier year.[34] Pond was full of common sense and practical wisdom. He made no effort at systematic definition but simply felt pastoral theology related to a minister's "more private intercourse with his people." [35] More systematic works were written by Cannon, Shedd, Hoppin, Walther, and Murphy.[36] None altered the basic structure of practical theology and pastoral theology as these have been discussed above. In 1874 William S. Plumer published *Hints and Helps in Pastoral Theology*, an unfortunate forerunner of much writing in our own century.[37] The notion of "hints and helps," implying the right to dispense with structural and theoretical considerations, to set aside scholarship in this area, and to appeal to the more degraded forms of practicalism, had helped to drive most systematic books out of this field by the turn of the century.

Two Americans of the latter part of the nineteenth century deserve special notice in even this brief history, Gregory Thurston Bedell, Episcopal bishop of Ohio, and Washington Gladden, of Columbus, Ohio.[38] Although Bedell had no new theoretical principles, he had a rare combination of feeling for the conditions peculiar to his place and time, and a scholarly background from which he drew basic principles.[39] Gladden wrote about the "working church." In the conditions of our time, he wrote in 1898, "it is a large part of the pastor's business to find work for the members of his church, and to secure their general and hearty co-operation with himself in teaching and shepherding and saving men and women and children." [40] The history of a basic theory of group work in the church in the contemporary sense virtually begins with Gladden. From the point of view of the thesis of this book Gladden's defect is in believing that "theology, in any proper sense of the word,

48

is not connoted" by the term "pastoral theology." [41] The study of practice and of the working church is, instead, "applied Christianity."

Of later systematic American works one was by G. H. Gerberding, the first American Lutheran to do a systematic work in English, and T. H. Pattison, the first Baptist to write a systematic treatise.[42] Gerberding developed no new structure, and Pattison demonstrated little or no concern for theoretical principles.[43]

When we examine these scholars of the past two centuries from the point of view contained in the present volume, we are struck especially by one fact about their method. Except for Schleiermacher in some respects, none of them, not even Gladden, explicated the actual method by which he had derived his principles from the study of practice as well as of the tradition. As we would see it, since most of them were teachers, the logical thing to do, with our gift of hindsight, would have been to present sample concrete situations to their students or readers, and to indicate how principles might be derived from examining the situations in the light of the tradition. Students or readers might then learn how to continue to derive and to correct principles from further experience and reflection upon it. We should not minimize the importance of the advantage we now have in this regard, due to no virtue on our part but to the availability of certain intellectual tools and models that have emerged in this century.

Pastoral Theology in This Century

With the advent of the twentieth century came an almost complete cessation of attempts to put together systematic works on either pastoral or practical theology. Replacing these was a growing amount of material of the "hints and helps" type. Such books, lectures, and courses seemed to have vitality, while the older analytical and theoretical works appeared dry. An example of such a work is *How to Be a Pastor* by Theodore L. Cuyler.[44] He called pastoral work his "passion," and his is an impassioned plea to ministers not to neglect their direct work with people.[45] The shift to a consideration of pastoral work demonstrates an impatience with any type of structural theory.

The Ministering Shepherd by Charles E. Jefferson was similar to the appeal of Cuyler for more pastoral work.[46] Jefferson attempted to analyze the analogy of the shepherd with the resulting list of functions: watchman, guard, guide, physician, savior, one who feeds, and lover of sheep. Since Jefferson's purpose was not the creation of a basic theory, he was not concerned that these functions were of different orders and hence not properly a list.

The most famous and perhaps most influential work of the turn of the century was John Watson's *The Cure of Souls*, first presented at Yale.[47] Watson was stimulating in a "hints and helps" fashion, demonstrated skill and common sense, but represented an additional move away from concern for systematic theory. Right into our own time we find many works of this kind. They commonly contend that they are "practical" and ordinarily regard theory as something irrelevant standing off against practice. Except in some Lutheran circles serious use of the older systematic works on practical or pastoral theology has been out of fashion for half a century.[48]

In Europe use of the nineteenth-century type of systematic works on practical or pastoral theology seems to have continued to a limited extent, and a few new volumes have been written in this century. Those with which I am familiar seem to contain nothing that can be regarded as a new type of structural theory such as the present book tries to set forth. Because the great problem of European Christianity in our time has been the definition and preservation of the uniqueness of the faith against the new social enemies and threatened disintegration, the climate in relation to the "new psychology" has been less positive than in English-speaking countries. Among individuals and selected groups there are notable exceptions. But in general only now are theological schools and theological faculties taking a radical new look at modern psychology on the one hand and at the nineteenth-century way of viewing practical theology on the other hand.

The British Isles, and especially the Anglicans, were quick to see the potential significance of the new psychology for the work of the minister.[49] Often under the older rubrics material of this kind was brought to the attention of British clergy and theological students perhaps before those in the United States. Nor have the British been afraid to consider the possible theological significance of the new findings about personality. From an American point of view the weakness of British churchmen and theologians so far has been their failure to describe and analyze actual concrete experiences that transcend illustrations.

We believe that many forces in our own country have worked together to make possible a new pastoral theology.[50] To the religious education movement we owe the first moves toward the study of actual people engaged in a form of religious activity and the attempts to draw basic theory out of these participant observations. Subsequently we have had the broad development of clinical study, in which this country is still almost unique.[51]

In turning attention to the nature of social institutions, their effect upon human life, and the concern of the gospel for institutional as well as personal relations, the social gospel has also helped lay a groundwork for pastoral theology.[52] For shepherding transcends one-to-one relationships and moves into the organized life of groups. The pietistic separation of religious compartments from all the dimensions of human life is made impossible.

The person who has done more than any other in our century to prepare the soil for a new pastoral theology is Anton T. Boisen.[53] He was not only one of the founders of clinical training for the clergy; a quarter century ago he set forth the thesis that there was a similarity in process between some forms of religious experience and some forms of mental disorder. In studying "living human documents," even those in deep disturbance, one was not, he held, merely studying psychology or psychiatry, but also theology. For it is out of just such experiences, he contended, that great religious insights have emerged in prophets and mystics of the past. Boisen's radical thesis is gradually gaining the recognition it deserves. Behind the particular form of his thesis, we should note, is the assertion that the study of actual and concrete forms of human experience, especially where ultimate issues are at stake, is theological if we bring theological questions to it. It is not merely psychology or psychiatry incorporated by theologians. It is a point in theological method. Boisen has not himself been concerned to work out a systematic pastoral theology, but the basic clue to the systematic construction of this author has come from Boisen.

The renewed interest in theology, the richness of the potential contributions from the personality sciences, and the increased interest in shepherding all suggest that a systematic pastoral theology may have a future far more significant than its past. This reformulated pastoral theology must be grounded, like anything Christian, in Jesus Christ as historical event and continuing saving reality in the lives of men. But its form and its details are to be wrought out by relating our shepherding work and thought to these eternal verities of the faith.

PART II

Transition

CHAPTER 4

Perspectives

THE CONTENT OF PASTORAL THEOLOGY, IT HAS ALREADY BEEN ARGUED, comes from theological reflection upon pastoral operations seen from the shepherding perspective. This perspective never exhausts the meaning of an event. The whole meaning of the event demands that it be examined from other perspectives as well. These perspectives are of the same order as shepherding.

Even before we attempt to set forth the content of pastoral theology, it is necessary for us to consider briefly those operational disciplines that are co-ordinate with it because they arise from reflection on perspectives of the same order as shepherding.

Our constructive proposal is that there are two, and only two, perspectives cognate with shepherding. When these perspectives are brought to bear upon pastoral events, with theological questions in mind and with theological conclusions drawn, they will lead to operational theological disciplines of the same order as pastoral theology.

The two perspectives cognate with shepherding are what will be called "communicating" and "organizing." The terms are used in their present participial form, communicating and organizing, rather than in the noun form of communication and organization. This is to show that the perspectives they define are active and in process. This should help us keep in mind that such branches of theology do not merely examine bodies of subject matter already drawn from observation, but also are constantly engaged in such investigation.

The reader may ask why we contend that the application to any pastoral or church event of the perspectives of shepherding, organizing, and communicating can exhaust its meaning, if rightly done, especially when we make no mention of worship or of religious education. The answer is that these are categories of a different order from the three we have mentioned. Shepherding, communicating, and organizing have both a vertical, God-man, and a horizontal, man-man, dimension, and are not being understood properly unless both dimensions are made explicit. If we added worship as a fourth category, it would imply that the God-man relationship becomes explicit only in the encounter of worship. But this is patently not true. Worship is primarily and properly emphatic about the vertical dimension, but even worship is also horizontal. Religious education, too, we hold, is of a different categorical order from shepherding, communicating, and organizing. It is involved in each of the three. Of course the meaning of shepherding, communicating, and organizing as we understand them will become clear only as discussion proceeds. It is only necessary now for the reader to understand that the absence of worship and religious education from our major categories is in no sense or form a depreciation of them as types of activities of the church and minister.

Communicating the Gospel

As a perspective upon the operations of pastor or church, communicating deals with the functional goal of getting the "Word" into the minds and hearts and lives of people, individually and collectively, regardless of the amount of such understanding they may have had prior to the event.[1] Thus communicating deals with both individuals and congregations, with those inside as well as outside the faith or the church whether by their own definition or by that of the pastor or church.

Communicating deals with the Word or the gospel or the Christian message. Its focus is not just on any truth, however true, but upon "saving truth," upon the truth of the message or gospel. Yet even though this is its focus, it can hardly be the entire area covered by the communicating perspective. If this person is impeded from receiving the saving truth of the gospel by a marriage problem or a neurosis, then communicating the gospel must proceed through some kind of dealing with those areas before it can become genuine. Or if that Christian congregation or church is caught in a political or economic situation that weakens its corporate existence, communicating of the gospel becomes effective only if it works through the problem area. That the gospel does, ultimately, contain such answers is our faith. That they can be reached directly, effortlessly, or without the painful inquiry into the impediments is, however, quite a different point and one we plainly reject.

To suggest the relationship, in communicating the gospel, between the gospel as saving truth and other knowledge that may be necessary to make that communication effective, I have already drawn by implication upon a modern scientific metaphor or "model" usually known as "field theory." [2] In the realm of the sciences the simplest illustration of this is the magnet and iron filings. If we ask where the force is and where it is not in terms of simple spatial location, we cannot answer the question of the magnet and filings. The filings converge toward a point (or two points); but if placed at a considerable distance, they still seem affected by the magnet in some degree. If we conceive the center of the operative force as a "focus" and the whole sphere of influence as a "field," then we immediately have a more accurate model for describing what is going on. The focus is the point or points at which influence is greatest. The field, for practical purposes, may extend but a short distance; but theoretically its extension is indefinite. Thus the place within the field, relative to the focus, becomes the important question—not the misleading question as to whether there is or is not influence. A categorical yes or no is seen to be irrelevant to the problem.

It is not the purpose here to try to indicate the immense number and detailed nature of the refinements in field theory that have been made by the several sciences. Our immediate task is more simple, to suggest that a model or metaphor of this type is of immediate utility in its general form, as we attempt to describe those perspectives from which pastoral operations may be examined. Even in the simple magnet and iron filing form what we should note is that this theory, while initially harder to grasp than a theory of simple location (for example, the force is here or it isn't), is more adequate to the facts. It provides a mode of thinking about these particular facts which, once grasped, makes them more comprehensible than they would have been by other theories.

We have made this notion of field theory in its simplest form explicit in order to suggest the kind of relationship that the saving truth of the gospel bears to other truth or to human knowledge in general or to what Tillich calls "preliminary concerns" as against the "ultimate concern" of the gospel.[3] Perhaps the relevance is now clear. If we used the model of simple location, we should ask: Where is the saving truth? Is it here, or is it there? Caught in such an inadequate metaphor, any answer we should give to the question would be misleading. For if we said that just this is the gospel and that is obviously something else, then we should be well on the way to an "encapsulated gospel" likely to be divorced from the means of access. If the gospel *is* the realization of our salvation through Jesus Christ, but is *not* our marriage problem, for example, it may be only a step to a categorical separation of an encased and "sacred" gospel divorced from "secular" or "profane" knowledge as of the marriage problem. On the other hand, if we use the simple location metaphor and attempt to minimize the difference between saving knowledge and other knowledge, we are likely to wind up with a humanism that has forgotten the awe and majesty and transcendence of God and the overwhelming and ultimate significance of Jesus Christ. Thus, it is not enough to work out intricately the right answer to the question. The question itself must be changed, and for that purpose a new "model" is required.

If we approach the question with the field theory model in mind, in the simple and preliminary form in which we are using it, we then alter the question. It now becomes: What is the *focus* of the gospel or of the saving knowledge, and what place in the field is occupied by this or that point or area of knowledge in general? In this form the question is much more capable of an answer. Not only need not the focus be blurred, but we can also see how we may approach it, have genuine knowledge of it, and yet in its essence it must remain "clothed in mystery." And so in traditional terms this model protects the transcendent character of the gospel. At the same time it becomes clear that the focus cannot be viewed by us except in relation to the field. Rightly viewed, the field points to the focus. Anything within the field, if we rightly understand it, has a certain degree and kind of relationship to the focus. Thus theological immanence is also preserved in principle. If the right model is used, there cannot be inherent contradiction between transcendence and immanence; one is unthinkable without the other.

When we approach communicating the gospel in the light of this new model, we have immediate and practical assistance. At any time the true focus of the gospel is forgotten or replaced by something from the field, there is distortion or idolatry. But it is impossible for the gospel to be encapsulated. It may be precisely the realization of something about a marriage problem that enables this person to move toward the focus in the gospel. Further, this model makes it impossible, as it is in fact, to approach the focus by ignoring the field. Saving knowledge and other knowledge cannot be seen in compartments; and yet their relationship in fact must not lead to their apparent merger, as if ultimate and saving truth were of the same order as any other.

When communicating the gospel is viewed in this way, two things become possible. First, that which is distinctive, unique, saving, and ultimate about the message can and must be emphasized, albeit with a humility fully aware that any man's knowledge and assimilation of it is limited. Second, all true human knowledge (and ways of securing knowledge) can and must be examined for the possible light they shed upon our reception of saving truth over and above their own autonomous significance.

With such a theory students of the perspective of communicating are, therefore, at one and the same time compelled to rethink and rework that which is essential and distinctive and focal about the gospel, and are driven to examine anew the findings and methods and conceptions of all areas of human knowledge for the light they may shed upon the processes of communicating. In the process of inquiry they must move toward theological depth and operational breadth.

There have been, especially in recent years, many studies bearing upon aspects of "communicating" in the general sense. A great deal of the work in education is to this end. More recently studies in semantics, in psychology, in anthropology, and in psychiatry have borne directly upon the processes of human communicating.[4] Very little of this work has so far been assimilated, at least to the depth available, in Christian theories of communicating the gospel. With a model or metaphor like the field theory it is now possible to absorb these insights and this knowledge without qualifying in any way what is unique about communicating the gospel. Because the gospel and saving or ultimate truth are involved, the resulting theory will be theological in character, hence no pale reflection of the general studies of communicating.

Because the understanding of the content of pastoral theology requires at least a preliminary understanding of the content of its cognate operational theological disciplines, we shall devote a later chapter to a branch of theology that should emerge from study of operations from the perspective of communicating. Here we have simply desired to give a brief overview.

But even at this point one or two other things must be said about communicating the gospel. For one, communicating is not confined to the preaching office of the ministry, nor to the preaching and teaching offices viewed jointly. These may be crucially important for understanding communicating, as pastoral care is for understanding shepherding; but the study of communicating must involve all types of pastoral operations or events.

Another thing to note is that communicating cannot be regarded solely as instructing, nor alone as making real through emotional impact. Certainly instruction and education are involved in any communicative process. Certainly the heart of communicating the gospel is a realization within one's whole being, not the absorption of this or that bit of doctrine or knowledge. And certainly implications flow immediately when communication has been achieved. It would seem important not to identify communicating with one aspect at the expense of the others, but to keep all aspects in mind as provisional subgroupings of the functional goals within the communicating perspective.

So viewed, it is clear that communicating the gospel and shepherding the flock are perspectivally different, yet proceed through the same types of pastoral operation. It is not that this pastoral act aims exclusively at communicating the gospel and that one at shepherding persons. Every pastoral act, rightly understood, includes both. In this instance shepherding may be the dominant perspective and functional goal. In that one it will be communicating. The difference will lie in the nature of the need, reflected in the dominant perspective of the pastor but not in his basic attitude.

Someone may ask at this point: What is the use of all this? Suppose we grant your reasoning, what good is the result when you deprive us of compartments? If both shepherding and communicating are involved in all pastoral operations, do you not complicate things for us? To which might wistfully be added: Why do you not find the master perspective that subsumes both shepherding and communicating?

To all these questions the answer is: We are attempting to move toward a more adequate theory, just as we did with the magnet and the iron filings. If that theory at first seemed to complicate things, remember that the complication is in the material; if it is also in the theory, and if the theory is accurate so far as it goes, then it is better prepared to represent the actual complexities of the situation than is a previous theory. If a compartment or "office" theory of pastoral operations does a completely satisfactory job of representing those operations theoretically, then much of our reasoning and work would be unnecessary. While admitting the continuing utility of this type of thought, however, we have denied its exclusive adequacy and have indicated that it has failed to provide a theoretical foundation upon which fundamental inquiry may proceed.

As to the wistful yearning for the master perspective and the economy of mental effort it would appear to promise, we can only assert that the human mind does not work that way. Communicating and shepherding are each indispensable perspectives upon the operations of church and pastor. To attempt to reduce one to the other would not only deny the finitude of our mental processes, but impoverish the actuality of those operations.

Organizing the Fellowship

We shall turn now to a preliminary word about the second perspective, in addition to communicating, that it has been alleged is cognate with shepherding, namely, "organizing." By this is meant that perspective upon the operations of pastor and church that makes the fellowship cohere and that determines its relationships as a fellowship with everything that is not of the fellowship. That is, in the operational sense organizing has two aspects, or perhaps better, two phases. The first is that of centering, or to use our field theory metaphor, that of bringing the field to focus in a human fellowship. The second is influencing or being influenced by the relation of the fellowship, as focus to the field— to the world in all its aspects.

Organizing is the perspective of social embodiment. It implies, therefore, more than ordering or structuring. The very use of the metaphor "body" implies an organic rather than a mechanical process, as, indeed, the most ancient tradition has stressed by referring to the church as the "body of Christ." To study organizing is, consequently, to study those processes by which the fellowship is brought to focus, and in turn those operations by which the church as a body is related, positively or negatively, to other bodies such as social institutions, conflicting ideologies, the political and economic orders, and the like.

When so identified, it is plain that the function we are discussing has been recognized and performed from the beginning of the church. But it was seldom, if ever, recognized as a separate perspective, as has been done here. Very often the function was subsumed under shepherding, as for instance, by Richard Baxter. The reasoning followed was like this: Shepherding means oversight of the flock; oversight of the flock includes making an embodied flock out of the sheep; hence the embodying or cohering function is a part of shepherding.

There is much that is attractive about this argument. If followed, it would leave shepherding and communicating as 'he two great perspectives upon operations, and that case could then be strengthened by reference to Jesus' commission to "preach and to heal" (to communicate and to shepherd). If this course is followed, however, something of immense importance, especially to the modern world, is likely to be lost sight of. Shepherding may become a kind of catchall, as it has been in the past, instead of the more precisely defined perspective that shall presently be elucidated in terms of healing, sustaining, and guiding.

More important, the difficulties of getting the fellowship embodied or cohered in our world could easily be minimized by considering only the shepherding and communicating perspectives. Still more dangerous, the organizing perspective could enter sub rosa and thus not subject itself steadily to the judgments of the gospel.[5] It is this last that we believe has happened widely in the modern Christian world and nowhere more than in our own land. In the conduct of a finance campaign, or a membership drive, or a meeting of a refractory board of deacons, a purely pragmatic criterion—Will it work?—may be substituted for principles wrought out in the same fashion as would be those for shepherding or communicating.

If Christ is Lord of all life, then his gospel must have something to say about how a finance campaign is run, or a meeting of the deacons. In the institutional and social complexities of the modern world it is more than ever necessary to define the focus of Christian organizing operations. At the same time any wisdom of the world about organizing and cohering and embodying is tested and used to point to the focal Christian perspective on operations.

Even the rural pastor and church point out that today they are more organized than a few years ago. In part they simply mean that there are more formally organized groups in the church than was once the case. But they also mean that more explicit attention now has to be given to the embodyings, more time devoted to them and principles called upon explicitly that in another day might have remained implicit. The fact is of course that some organizing principles have always been present, whether made explicit or not. One has only to recall any church controversy to see how quickly such principles (often competing) have emerged when their previously implicit security was threatened. Today the principles need to become explicit not so much because a competing group questions them as in order to get things done. Much of today's competition in organizing the fellowship is not with competing churches or with churches holding different theories about organizing, but with a multitude of nonchurch agencies and institutions setting a pace that must somehow be acknowledged. Because of this, as well as for other reasons, intellectual work is required from the organizing perspective of a complexity never previously demanded.

It is my contention, then, on both practical and theoretical grounds that organizing should be understood as a distinct perspective upon the operations of pastor and church, cognate with shepherding and communicating.

In a brief and preliminary way I have now indicated what I believe to be the three perspectives from which the operations of pastor and church may be studied most fruitfully. I have admitted to some pragmatic motives for setting forth these three but have also defended the choice on grounds of basic theory.

Shepherding and communicating have biblical and historical warrant that enables our modern ways of structuring the problem to have obvious continuity with our tradition. As we have noted, the situation is different in regard to organizing, where we simply have to declare that conditions of the modern world have made it necessary to lift this up for special study in a way that may have been unnecessary in earlier days. But we cannot get at the gospel's relevance, through the operations of pastor and church, to the modern world without taking it seriously. It is our contention that taking it seriously means recognizing it as a distinct perspective from which all operations require to be examined.

Remembering that our focal concern is with pastoral theology, not merely with shepherding activities but with a shepherding perspective leading toward a theory, so our concern with the cognates or relationships of pastoral theology is not alone with communicating and organizing, but also with theological disciplines that should emerge from inquiry undertaken from these perspectives. What such disciplines should be called is something I am not here prepared to argue.

There is an inescapable humor in thinking of a communicating theology or a theology of communicating, or of an organizing theology or a theology of ecclesiastical cohering. But the reason for the humor is itself illuminating. We are endeavoring to link ancient concerns, which were differently organized, with a new type of structural theory. With "pastoral theology" the merger does not present terminological incongruities. With the two other perspectives it does. The chances are that we shall have to live with the content of the merger for a time before we can find terms that do not seem to confront us with verbal monstrosities. But the vital point is that, just as study of pastoral and church operations from the perspective of shepherding should result in a *pastoral* theology, so study of the operations of pastor and church from the communicating and organizing perspectives should result in branches of theology cognate with pastoral theology. However difficult or humorous it may appear when we attempt to name these twins, they are already members of the family demanding legitimate theological recognition.

Shepherding Persons

In this section I shall present a preliminary account of the content of pastoral theology. It is, as it has been defined formally, the theological theory of the shepherding perspective upon the operations of pastor and church. It remains to be more specific about what shepherding connotes.

As a perspective upon pastoral operations shepherding must be regarded as a unity. But we have tradition behind us in believing that subgroupings within that unity are useful. The traditional aspects of shepherding have been three: discipline, comfort, and edification. The most inquired into and what we know most about in the tradition was discipline. About comfort we know something, but mostly by inference. Edification in the tradition shaded into what has been called here the "organizing perspective." As a perspective on operations, it received little if any study except under offices of the church such as religious education or catechetics.

Despite the ambiguities surrounding edification the first question we confront is whether we shall make use of this traditional tripartite notion of the function of shepherding: discipline, comfort, and edification. Our answer will be negative; and we shall propose the substitution of: healing, sustaining, and guiding.

First I shall indicate the reasons for rejection of the old trinity and then present those on behalf of the new.

Of the old trio of discipline, comfort, and edification we reject edification because of its ambiguity. The term was sometimes used as correlative with evangelism, edification being for those within the faith and evangelism for those outside. It was also used to refer to the routine shepherding ministries as against those involving special need. In the first instance the reference is not relevant. In the second the distinction is a superficial one. So edification disappears because of its ambiguity in contributing to our understanding of the meaning of shepherding.

With "comfort" we need less change than with the others. In most respects what will be intended by our word "sustaining" is the same as what was meant by "comfort." Yet there are unsatisfactory aspects of the word "comfort." Its derivation, "with fortitude," tends to be forgotten. The defection becomes more serious when we move to "comfortable," whose connotation now is "with ease," or "without effort." If the original meaning of "comfort" were still extant, "with courage," and especially "with courage" when nothing about the situation could be changed except the attitude of the persons concerned, we could use it handily. But since common speech has lost this, we must use another term.

Our difficult problem comes with "discipline." Originally this came from the same root as "disciple" and meant schooling or training oneself. Christian discipline at one time was the exercise of one's discipleship, training in Christianity. But it has long since meant something quite different.

John T. McNeill's great book *A History of the Cure of Souls* is primarily a history of what came to be known as Christian discipline—what the pastor or the church did, in order to keep itself pure and to correct the sinner, to those who offended against the Christian community. At first such discipline was administered in the group, then individually. Rules for its administration became codified, first locally, then over larger areas.

Judging from Paul's letters, it seems very likely that the original intention of Christian discipline was *equally* to bring back the offender and to preserve the church. Whether Paul saw the bringing back of the offender as the one possible way of preserving the church may be a moot historical point. What is certain is that with the growth of the church as a social institution the emphasis swung heavily to discipline for the sake of the church—with the assumption that what was good for the church was bound to be good for the offender. When what was "good for the church" acquired associations of power over people, plainly that function of discipline originally concerned with the care of the offender for the sake of his soul's salvation took second place.

The Protestant Reformation altered the fundamental theory upon which such a conception of discipline had come to rest, but in practice changes came slowly. Thus there is much to the charge that the church of Calvin's Geneva was as harsh toward offenders as were the Roman Catholics of its day. Church discipline which made "examples" of offenders (thus betraying the motive as purity of the church, automatically identifying this purity with the good of the offenders) gradually became less severe. The general tendency since the Reformation has been toward mildness, with certain exceptions of which bars on the remarriage of divorced persons have been the most consistent.

So in skeleton outline the history of discipline has been like this. First, welfare of person and church were both kept in mind. Second, more attention was given to welfare of church with person's real welfare assumed automatically to follow (seen in most extreme form in the killing of heretics presumably for their own good). This moved from medieval Catholicism into Protestantism, despite the inherent repugnance to it of Protestant principles. Third, there was the application of Protestant principles in the form of gradual relaxing of discipline in areas in which it had once been exercised. Today for the most part the exercise of discipline, barring bruited scandals, has disappeared. There are still museum pieces, often of immense importance for individuals; but in contrast to the broad areas in which the church once exercised discipline, they are Wedgewood or Chippendale.

A brief note on the other two contexts in which discipline has been historically important is relevant. These are child care and penology. The old child care apparently proceeded on a spare the rod and spoil the child philosophy, although tempered by human leniency and often, as Tom Sawyer proved, successfully but quietly upset by the use of guile. A generation ago this was condemned. There were reasons for the child's behavior; therefore, help him but do not discipline. More recently discipline has been altered in meaning. It is not the arbitrary exercise of parental will over offense done to parents, but the protection of the child from that from which he is not yet equipped to protect himself. As such it sets limits which are themselves parts of the child's security base. So there are now strong attempts to root discipline in the good of the child, but to suggest that parents have rights too and can be offended. That is, the former trend was toward a one-sided *laissez-faire* policy, from which there seems to be emerging a more conjunctive notion of discipline as involving the welfare of both child and parents.

Humanitarians in all ages have sought to ameliorate conditions in prisons and in the last century or two have been more successful at it on a larger scale. Yet humanitarian services until quite recently were admitted to penal institutions as concessions. It is only within recent times that one has heard this principle so expressed—that the best possible protection of society consists in the best possible rehabilitation of the offender. Lip service is now paid to this principle and by many penal workers something more too. But we now know better than ever that the sentimental type of person who identifies himself wholly with the welfare of prisoners and believes the welfare of society can take care of itself is not the successful agent of rehabilitation. It is the tough-minded prison worker who cannot be fooled, who will put up with no bluster or guile, yet who will go to any lengths to help a man trying to rehabilitate himself, who makes possible the tremendous number of rehabilitations. Here again the proper understanding of the relation between the good of the individual and the protection of the group (and not one as against the other, nor the assumption of automatic harmony between them) is what works for effectiveness.

If there is any lesson to be learned from these partial parallels, it can hardly be in the form of reinstatement of authoritarian disciplines in which the good of the church is automatically assumed to dictate the good of its members. But neither can it be in a sentimental form that would deny the need for any protective function to the ecclesiastical body. The first is impossible if for no other reason than the taking over by civil law of many functions once performed by church courts. But the second is impossible too. Even the most liberal of churches, one finds at times with bitter experience, has certain offenses for which it exercises discipline upon the offender. And it may be precisely in those churches that do not regard themselves as having a discipline that treatment of the offender may become most arbitrary.

So we shall, while arguing completely against any authoritarian-type discipline, argue in favor of intelligent discipline within the church for the welfare both of individuals and of church. We shall argue not for more discipline, but for more carefully thought out premises upon which discipline should proceed and with a proper relationship between the purity of the church and the good of the offender.

But so viewed, discipline is not shepherding; or better, not all that is involved in discipline is shepherding. It may be a necessary function of the church from the point of view of the purity of the church; but it more properly belongs under the organizing perspective, as that has been defined here, than under the pastoral. As we noted, most of what is meant here by organizing was placed traditionally under shepherding.

This is not to say that the church should not discipline. What I am saying is that, wherever the purity of the church is in the forefront, the perspective involved is not shepherding but something else.

Discipline, then, involves two notions which under ideal conditions become united. The first is of a shepherding character, part of what shall be called "guiding," in which what is dominantly intended is the welfare of the person involved. The other is of an organizing character and is part of the organizing perspective. I am not advocating no relationship between these, but I believe that the most meaningful unity will emerge when each is seen rightly. Where this point is not seen, the result tends to be either a false notion of automatic harmony or the imperialism of one over the other.

What we seek above all to retain for the shepherding perspective is the quest for the good of the person or persons involved—temporarily, if need be, without thought of the larger good of larger groups or institutions. It is simply the good-Samaritan principle in operation.[6] It is not the only thing necessary for the community. Suppose that the victim, healed of his wounds and back in Jerusalem, joined his local ecclesiastical Gestapo and went out after the Samaritans? If it is properly serpent as well as dove, the church should be alert to such a possibility. But it is not in the forefront of the mind when the poor victim is lying wounded at the side of the road. The dominant perspective is bringing help now. In simplest terms that is our parable of shepherding.

Of the three old terms used to indicate aspects of shepherding, we can accept wholly the intention of "comfort" while eliminating the word, we reject "edification" as ambiguous, and we discard "discipline" as carrying some connotations which, while needful to the purity of the church, are not shepherding in our understanding.

Central to the content of shepherding is the shepherd's solicitous concern for the welfare of the sheep. The most basic attitude of the pastor does not vary from one situation to another although it assumes different forms from the point of view of others in the situation. To the notion of shepherding as solicitude in the pastor, therefore, we must add the necessary presence of some degree of recognition of need in the parishioner and some degree of receptivity to help. The need, we might say, is always specific, although the recognition of its nature need not be clear and distinct. A sheep, if lost, is lost in one part of the field or forest, not in all. The point being made is that, when shepherding is the dominant perspective in the pastor's operations, there occurs a particular combination of attitudes in pastor, parishioner, and the relationship between them, and not merely in the attitude and intention of the pastor. Where some other attitude is dominant in the parishioner, the pastor still has a solicitous intent; but the dominant perspective may be communicating or organizing as those terms have been defined here.

How shall we view the content of these total situations (pastor, parishioners, and relationship) in which shepherding is the dominant perspective? My proposal is to use the concepts of healing, sustaining, and guiding.

"Healing" in this connection means binding up wounds in the precise sense of the good-Samaritan story. "Sustaining" means "comforting" in the original sense of "with courage," upholding or standing with one who suffers even if the situation cannot be altered except perhaps by change in the person's attitude. "Guiding" within the perspective of shepherding means helping to find the paths when that help has been sought. When guiding is being done from the dominant perspective of protection of the church (which may be legitimate and important), it belongs under the rubric of organizing rather than of shepherding. One presumes the attitude of the hundredth sheep to have been such that it sought the shepherd's help.

So viewed, healing, sustaining, and guiding are plainly all of a piece; and yet each of them is necessary to do justice to the full dimensions of the shepherding perspective. If we had only healing, it might wrongly be assumed that all wounds could be bound up, would heal, and that the focal infection in any situation could always be cured or changed in essence, which plainly is not true. If we had only healing and sustaining, we should be tempted to think of the shepherding function solely as removing obstacles and not also as aiding the person to find a path.

We need all three terms, therefore, in order to indicate fully the content of the shepherding perspective: healing, sustaining, and guiding. The content of pastoral theology is, then, the theological theory resulting from study of the operations of pastor and church approached from the shepherding perspective and studied under the subheadings of healing, sustaining, and guiding. To have shepherding as the dominant perspective (remember that those of communicating and organizing are never absent) in any situation, there must be a certain attitude (by no means always clearly conscious) in the sheep as well as in the shepherd; at a minimum the parishioner or parishioners have some sense of particular need and some receptivity to being helped.

CHAPTER 5

Cases

AT THIS POINT IN THE INQUIRY WE SHOULD NORMALLY MOVE TO THE description of one or more contemporary situations in which shepherding is the dominant perspective, describe these as concretely as the data permit, and then attempt to draw theory of a theological order from reflection on these observations. And as the discussion proceeds, we shall attempt to meet this obvious requirement.

But we stand in a peculiar historical situation which demands that we do something else as well. To a greater degree than in any other theological discipline, we lack in pastoral theology a sense of identification with our pastoral roots and heritage. This is true for those of us who have had the benefit of the best modern training in shepherding methods, but it is also true of those who apparently continue in old ways. In the case of the former group there is an important and legitimate conviction that some important new knowledge has been discovered; and since this new knowledge cannot be found in the tradition, one regrets this but must face the facts. Those contemporary ministers who have not assimilated the new insights to aid their work of shepherding may believe that they are using traditional methods. But what they identify as the tradition is ordinarily recent, like the "old hymns" that are relatively very recent. Both groups tend to lack a sense of positive identity with what is great in the long pastoral tradition.

We regard this lack of identification with the pastoral tradition as a basic part of the problem to be solved. Unless such identification is present, it will be difficult to develop a systematic pastoral theology for our day. The issue is not whether pastors have a theological interest. We take that fact for granted. The question is whether this interest extends to the pastoral and shepherding dimensions of the theological tradition.

This situation demands that we inquire into some significant orders of shepherding data from the past as well as from the present. If we should find in doing so that everything our modern shepherding experience has shown to be valuable is missing from the past practice and theory of shepherding, then we shall have to acknowledge such a fact. If we should find, on the other hand, matters of importance in past practice and theory that are being neglected in modern work, then we should have to judge critically the modern. In any event, we shall have to be critically discriminating.

My study of Christian shepherding of the past has made me conclude that I cannot identify with most of its methods when viewed *literally*, but that my sense of identification increases enormously the minute I cut through literalism to something more basic. Far from destroying my objectivity, some sense of identification of this sort is necessary if I am to feel my way into what these ministers of the past were about. It is not necessary for me to attack or to defend them. I can try to understand them, being alert to essential but currently forgotten truths of which they were aware, and drawing judgment upon them wherever our modern knowledge exposes their ignorance.

There is one tremendous handicap to this aspect of our task of studying shepherding of the past in the lack of appropriate records. As John T. McNeill makes clear, there is no lack of records about certain aspects of shepherding in the past. On discipline the records are massive. On comfort there are mainly letters written to sorrowing persons. There is some literature on "spiritual direction," but it tends to be general in actual content. The difficulty with nearly all of it is that it does not go as far as we should like in revealing the concrete nature of shepherding acts and operations.

The distinction is not a black and white one between the concrete and the abstract. Even if some shepherding event should be on an electronic machine or a color and sound film made of it, not all the concreteness would be captured. And yet the distinctions among degrees of capturing the concrete event may be extraordinarily important. In modern psychiatry and clinical psychology case histories were first presented in the words of the therapist who, when he got to paper and pencil, was chiefly interested in an accurate history of his patient. When later on he also became more interested in the history of his relationship with his patient and then in studying his own attitudes as they affected that relationship, he began to realize the advantages of recapturing more

71

of the concrete situation. This led to the report of dialogue rather than merely of indirect discourse and by various devices to attempts to capture more of the total concrete situation. That no device or no record is a perfect reproduction of the whole concrete situation must be taken for granted. But some forms of presentation are closer to the concrete than are others. And that difference may be vital in speaking to the point of our inquiry.

Except for scattered excerpts here and there, there seems to have been no pastor before the middle of the nineteenth century who wrote out in direct discourse what happened in specific contacts between himself and his parishioners. Our inquiry in its historical dimension will concentrate on that pastor of the mid-nineteenth century who wrote out his experience in dealing directly with his people. Being closer to the concrete than are indirect discourse recollections, his reports will give us a chance of penetrating further into the whole situation than would otherwise be true.

Ichabod Spencer's Cases

The nineteenth-century pastor was Ichabod S. Spencer, a Presbyterian minister whose last and long pastorate was in Brooklyn, New York, and after whom the Spencer Memorial Church in Brooklyn is now named. In 1851 Spencer published a book entitled A Pastor's Sketches and in 1853 issued a second volume under the same title but with new sketches.[1]

These sketches were what we should call "cases" or reports of Spencer's dealings with individuals and families. With the exception of a few, which are mere vignettes, they are all recorded in direct discourse. The human memory being what it is, one may well question how much Spencer actually got on paper of what took place. Yet our modern experience shows that one who really tries can recall more about a conversation than he believes he can and that practice in doing so improves the memory. A strong attestation to Spencer's competence in recording may be found in his inclusion of things critical of himself. The fact that he must have practiced such recording over a period of years also stands behind his relative accuracy. The accuracy can of course be only relative, but the accounts bear the inner marks of authenticity.

I shall first give a brief overview of Spencer's sketches and then a general picture of his concern and his approach. After that it will be possible to draw upon his sketches as concrete material from the past for purposes of our inquiry in pastoral theology.

In the two volumes of more than four hundred pages each, Spencer presented seventy-seven sketches. A few of these are but two or three pages in length and are more anecdotal illustrations of a point than concrete data. But thirty-five of the seventy-seven are ten pages or more in length, and less than twenty are so brief that they are relatively useless for our inquiry. The median length of the sketches is about seven pages, which means nearly three thousand words. With the vignettes excluded, the median length is probably closer to 4,500 or 5,000 words. One sketch is sixty-four pages and three others more than thirty.

Each of Spencer's sketches focuses on an individual person, but other people are frequently involved, especially other members of the family. In 60 per cent of the sketches women are the leading characters, over against the 40 per cent of men. In the overwhelming majority of the sketches, about 85 per cent, success with the leading character is finally achieved by Spencer's standards. But nine clear failures are recorded.

The subtitle of both Spencer's books is *Conversations with Anxious Inquirers, Respecting the Way of Salvation.* "Anxious inquirers" were those who were concerned and seeking. There was basically one "way of salvation" to Spencer, but he recognized many varieties of approach to it. Thus, to put the subtitle in modern terms, we might say that Spencer sought to record his efforts to help those who were concerned enough about their salvation and ultimate destiny to be receptive to a minister who sought to help them in relation to it.

Spencer himself had no particular pattern of organization in putting down his sketches. Two or three about prayer or about despondency may appear consecutively, but there is no overarching attempt to classify them.

When we attempt to organize them from the point of view of Spencer's implicit categories as represented in the term "anxious inquirers" (concerned and seeking), we find the sketches falling approximately under the following headings. Persons who are both anxious about their souls' salvation and seeking it number twenty-two, a little less than a third of the total number. Those who are indubitably anxious or concerned but are not really inquirers (because of feelings of hopelessness, bitterness, and the like) number eleven. Those who are inquirers or seekers but who do not exhibit anxiety in Spencer's sense number twenty-nine. Seventeen of these Spencer felt to be dominated by emotion or emotionalism, as in the young woman who wanted a sign or in the other who wanted to be converted again for the third time. Eight of them simply did not have enough anxiety in Spencer's view. Four, however, were people who did not need anxiety in the usual sense. They were, therefore, to be sharply distinguished from the twenty-five others who were seekers but without the right kind or amount of anxiety.

Two cases are about the faithful who exhibit now neither anxiety nor seeking because they show the fruits of both. Eight persons manifested (at least at the beginning of Spencer's dealings with them) neither anxiety nor seeking; four of them were openly resistive to him, and the other four were apathetic.

To sum up (we have excluded five of the sketches as not relevant to this question), we find the following:

Anxious and inquiring 22
Anxious but not inquiring 11
Inquiring but not anxious (bad) 25
Inquiring but not anxious (good) 4
No current anxiety or inquiring needed 2
No open anxiety or inquiring (resistive) 4
No open anxiety or inquiring (apathetic) 4

From Spencer's statements in the leads of his stories, describing the basic attitude presented by the person at the beginning, we can get a slightly different list. The first group is characterized by anxiety as either present or absent, increasing or decreasing, mild or frantic, or absent despite a clear readiness to receive the faith. It seems to be this kind of consideration that led Spencer initially to compile his book.

But there are two subsequent groups that soon stand out in his mind: those preoccupied with emotion in some way or those puzzled over doctrine. The emotional leads include people who are overemotional, those who seek a sign (one admitted she would believe if an angel appeared to her), those who are fearful about some particular thing (one woman feared her husband if she became a Christian; a mother feared being baptized before her family), those who want religion merely as a cult of reassurance, and those who are not emotional enough or not sufficiently capable of feeling.

Those who were stopped by doctrine mostly had trouble with election and predestination, and their relation to human freedom; but one young man wanted to be baptized by immersion. In this last case, after becoming convinced of the young man's sincerity, Spencer proposed to take him privately to the river. When the man demurred, Spencer suggested that he wanted to make a stir in the church. Soon afterward the ideas on baptism changed.

Then there is the group who had deep negative feelings for which illness or circumstance was plainly, in part, responsible. Finally there were the insolent, impudent, or otherwise openly resistive persons.

What Ichabod Spencer wrote about his approach to a young mechanic of thirty is in many ways typical of and fundamental to his thought and work. "With the Law of God on the one hand, and the Gospel on the other, his conscience to condemn him and Christ to invite him, I hoped his heart would be brought to surrender in faith." [2]

When in his judgment law and conscience were laid so heavily upon the person's heart that he could not receive the gospel despite all efforts, Spencer was tenderly compassionate. When, on the other hand, he felt that a person was moving in anxiety to consider seriously his own sinfulness in the light of the mercy offered by Christ, he did not hesitate to add a push to the arousal of anxiety.

A favorite statement of Spencer's, which recurs, appears when some seeker is moving toward anxiety and says, "I feel that I have a very wicked heart." He invariably replies, "It is a great deal more wicked than you think it." [3] In Spencer's mind this was not being severe, not even drawing judgment himself upon the person. It was designed to elicit the experience described by one young man afterward, "You drove the arrow deeper, when I expected you to do just the contrary; and I could find no relief, till I gave up all into the hands of Christ." [4]

To us Spencer's attempt to stimulate the emergence of anxiety appears at first as cruel, as it did sometimes to his parishioners. A teen-aged boy came to Spencer after a morning meeting of prayer and asked him what he should do. Since Spencer had just been telling the group what sinners ought to do, he pointed this out, indicating that he could say nothing new. The boy declared his distress, but Spencer said, "I cannot relieve your distress. Christ alone can give you rest." [5] The boy went away downcast. Soon, however, he was back to say his burden had been lifted. After Spencer had "cast him off," he reported, he had lost all hope and "had nowhere else to go but to God." [6] He concluded, "I do not believe I should have gone to God, if you had not cast me off." [7] Spencer took very seriously the idea that at a minimum he should not interfere with the work of the Holy Spirit. To relieve anxiety at a time when it was pushing the person to confront his ultimate condition would constitute such interference. When anxiety was working in this way, it was not to be relieved but sharpened; for only then would Christ and the gospel become relevant to the sinner's real need.

One day a young woman who was "gloomy" and "had no hope" in Christ sent for him. She talked mostly about the magnitude of her sins and finally said she had committed the unpardonable sin. What was it? asked Spencer. She was unable to specify what it was but indicated that God would have forgiven her already if she had not committed it. Spencer, who felt that "pride" and "self-righteousness" were what blocked her, said, "Very well, I suppose you want nothing more of me, if you are unpardonable," and left.[8] Next day she sent for him again, but her attitude was the same. She asked him if he denied there was such a thing as the unpardonable sin. Spencer said No, he did not deny it, then added, "But you don't know what it is. And you don't know enough to commit it." [9]

A young woman who was ill and thought she was going to die sent for Spencer. She admitted that she was looking for a "witness" in the form of a "great light." [10] When she asked Spencer why she had not had this witness, he replied, "For three reasons; first, you are not nervous enough; second, you are not imaginative enough; third, you are not quite fool enough." [11]

When once dealing with a young woman who indicated herself as ready to listen to him but not to say anything about herself, Spencer reported, "I told her that at present I had no time for any other than religious conversation." [12] This was not bluff; yet having spoken thus, Spencer asked to be permitted to call once more. In this case it turned out that the girl's mother had been hard after her, and Spencer had at first seemed to her to be doing the same. When, however, he said he would not bother her if she did not wish to talk, this broke the barrier, and she found "she was opposing God." [13] Spencer does not directly discuss the (to us) obvious way in which he here helped the girl toward autonomy in relation to her mother. How much he recognized it, we can only conjecture.

From Spencer's own point of view his ordinary approach to people, even the resistive, was not "severe." In calling upon one whom he called "The Obstinate Girl," she was "insolent" to him. Thinking at first he could draw the barbs, "The more impudent she became, the more polite and gentle I became." [14] In this instance it did not work; and when Spencer returned home, he meditated upon it, decided he had made an error, and reached a "fixed conclusion" about what he would do on his subsequent visit. Next day, "I told her there was not much truth, and not an item of sincerity in all she had been saying,—that I knew it, and she knew it herself,— . . . that she was just wickedly acting out the deep-seated and indulged wickedness of her heart against God." [15] Soon she cast her eyes down and then wept. Spencer continued along his muckraking line and, having finished, started for the door. She begged him to stay. He did and "wept with her." Spencer concluded later, "This is the only instance, save one, in which I have ever ventured upon such a course of severity. I do not know as I should do it again." [16]

His more general conclusion, drawn from the case just cited, was, "There can be no question but the power of the gospel lies in its kindness and love, and that through such affections, rather than the opposite ones, souls are to be wooed and won to Christ. But kindness and love can censure as well as smile." [17] In a moment I shall indicate the sense in which Spencer was kind and compassionate. But we should note the profound insight in the idea that "love can censure." We have redis-covered in our own day that the most profound sense of judgment a person can feel comes not out of another's plain misunderstanding of him, but precisely when, despite all he has done that must make the other misunderstand and reject him, there are both understanding and acceptance.

Spencer's compassion is much in evidence whenever he believes the person has anxiety and is trying to wrestle with it. With one woman of middle age, who had been reserved but finally became quite emotional, Spencer wrote, "I dared not leave her. I said nothing, but remained till she became more composed." [18] A younger woman came once to talk with Spencer, after he had preached on church discipline, and asked if he intended to discipline her. Spencer saw her as "agitated," which he regarded as a condition to be soothed (unlike anxiety or concern), and wrote, "I soothed her agitation all in my power." [19] He found eventually that this girl in her religious opinions "was entirely an infidel." She was open to instruction, however, and had an "uncommon mind"; so Spencer had no hesitation in instructing. "I proposed to reason with her; and would not blame her but commend her, for overthrowing every argu-ment, if she could." [20] Since she hesitated to tell her views lest they give pain to Spencer, his active encouragement to her to tell just what she did believe seems to belong under "compassion."

On another occasion Spencer wrote in a situation of poignancy, "I could not have uttered a word of censure, even if my principles would have allowed it." [21] A little later, when cobwebs were being removed from an old family Bible, Spencer wrote, "I could not but weep too." [22]

Spencer was not out of sympathy with Christians who hesitated to speak about Christ to others, although he wanted this done in due season. "Many times they are afraid to say anything to them on the subject of religion, lest they should do them an injury by awakening opposition or disgust." [23]

With those who were plainly victims (as, for instance, of "despondency") or whose suffering was obviously real but did not lead to peace and joy in Christ, Spencer was tender. With such a girl, who was dying, "it was enough to melt any one's heart, to hear her cries for mercy." [24]

Spencer never let up on anxious inquirers as long as he felt his persistence would help and would not stand in the way of the Holy Spirit. With two girls who were wavering, "they were scarcely left a day to themselves." [25] Yet his persistence was also exercised even when he was himself most puzzled about what to do. One fine woman, a true anxious inquirer, had talked with him many times.

She came to me so many times, and I had so many times told her all that I knew about the way of salvation, and so many times presented to her every motive of the gospel, and invited and urged her to cast herself upon Christ, that I did not know what more to say or do; and time after time I was half sorry to see her come into my house, and then ashamed of myself because my heart had such a feeling.[26]

But long afterward the woman said to Spencer, "If you had been discouraged with me, I should have been discouraged,—and should have given up trying to be saved." [27]

At times Spencer seemed forthright with a shrewd kind of perversity. When talking with one "man of science" who was a religious seeker but felt that the caliber of his own mind required "views of truth adapted to its calibre," Spencer did his best to be as plain and simple as possible.[28] When a married woman of thirty who became frantically anxious and then despondent about her salvation finally declared that she would perform her religious duties "and go to hell at last, as I deserve!" Spencer replied, "You will find it hard work to get to hell in that way." [29]

Yet Spencer's restraint is often surprising. With one young woman who seemed to him to have the faith right, although she had not yet found peace and joy, "I was afraid to say much to her, lest my words

should diminish her impressions, instead of giving them more depth." [30]
Once, traveling on his horse, Spencer met a taciturn farmer with whom
he had been discussing religion who was "serious" but had not taken the
step. As they spoke together on the road, the farmer in his wagon and
Spencer on his horse, the pastor saw a "brown jug," which he rightly
suspected of being taken to fetch liquor. What should he say or do?
It was, wrote Spencer, "an awkward business. I did not know how to
begin. I would not insult him, and I did not wish to injure his feelings." [31] Finally the subject was broached, but with great restraint.
Spencer would not duck an issue; but except to help sharpen up emergent
anxiety, he would not say a judgmental word, as he saw it.

Spencer certainly had no hesitation about talking, most of the time.
In some of the dialogue reports there are speeches and arguments by him
that run to four or five pages. And yet the so-called Young Irishman,
Spencer's longest case, who received the largest barrage of Spencer's
theological reasoning, finally said, "You have done what few men could
do; you have seen the heart of me rightly, and have indulged me in
having my own strange way in talking about religion." [32] This must not
be taken to mean that Spencer thought as we do about what should be
listened to. What he was prepared to listen to was any sincere opinions
about religion. He was a bit apologetic, in reporting the Young Irishman, that he had listened so attentively to his views on the corruptness of
England. [33] So far as we can tell, Spencer did not believe that an acceptance of negative feelings, regardless of their content, would lead
in the direction he wanted. But if they were about religion, as he understood it, then he was patient. A moment's reflection will show that this
is, at root, a philosophical difference, having to do with the kind of relation that religion and theology are believed to bear to culture—within
the individual psyche in this instance. At such a point Spencer was a
child of the idealism and pietism of his day.

One of Spencer's most endearing characteristics was his honesty when
he did not know what to do. With one woman he had tried various
things. "I had hoped, that by conversation with her I might get a
glimpse of her heart, that the peculiarity of her state of mind would
casually become manifest; and thus I should learn what it would be
best for me to say to her." But this failed to work, and "after several
trials I was still in the dark." [34] So "I called upon her, one day, and
frankly told her my embarrassment about her." [35]

Work on the doctrines of religion, Spencer felt, "is only the benefit of defence, or, at most, only *clearing the way*, in order to get at the position and real work of religion." [36] He was an advocate of "experimental religion." Each man must decide for himself, for "nobody else can choose for him." [37] It was partly this conviction that caused Spencer to write his sketches about individuals; for whatever preaching and groups may do, receiving the faith was finally a matter of "experimental religion" and "decision." "One word to a sinner is often more effectual, than a score of sermons," and "how much more efficacious is a message than a proclamation." [38]

In meetings Spencer had no hesitation in preaching, for each hearer might take what applied to him. But when speaking later with this individual and that when others might be within earshot, Spencer was often troubled. He wrote about one such occasion:

I should greatly have preferred to converse with each one alone; as there would have been less restraint on their part, and on my own, more certainty, that what I was saying would be truly applicable and would not be applied by any one, for whom it was not intended.[39]

When anyone seemed hesitant to speak to Spencer about something plainly important, he offered the "most inviolable secrecy." [40]

Even for his own day Spencer indicates that many regarded him as strict and even rigid. Yet he was far from being without a sense of humor. In writing about a smart young girl who was being insolent to him, he said, "And in her abuse, I believe she made some capital hits, as she drew my character." [41] To a fearful woman who had written him about her fears of hell, of thunderstorms, and of much else, Spencer wrote along with words of understanding and guidance:

I am not willing to speak evil of anybody, but I can assure you, that these same creatures, called *nerves*, are the greatest liars in the country. Do not believe them, when they tell you that you are a Christian, or when they tell you that you are a reprobate. They will tell lies on both sides, and they don't care which.[42]

Spencer's conception of the relation among faith, feeling, and intellect is interesting. Although we may today regard it as based in part upon a faulty psychology, some of its points are still worth pondering. For instance, he wrote, "Faith is one thing, and feeling is another. It is the faith that saves. It is the feeling that comforts." [43] In Spencer's experience with bereavement few people had come to Christ as the result of the "seriousness" brought by the grief; instead, they had been comforted too quickly, he thought. Today we might attribute a similar result to a different line of causation, that the grief was never really "grieved out." He feared any feeling that would seem to obviate the need for faith, which in turn meant jointly the recognition of the depth of one's own sinfulness and the breadth of Christ's mercy. As to intellect and reason Spencer was somewhat more ambiguous than he believed himself to be. He warns himself against the possible misfiring of "direct demonstrations addressed to the intellect." He warns a doctrinal inquirer lest he think he have the answer to the problem of the relation of God's sovereignty to man's freedom; what we do know, avers Spencer, is that each of these is so. He considers it speculative to try to go beyond demonstrating the truth of each. Yet, especially in the long case of the Young Irishman, he resorts to arguments of the most rationalistic character concerning matters such as the existence of God. The statement to which he recurs most often in respect to knowledge is, however, "We know in part."

A large number of Spencer's sketches stress surrender, release, or ceasing to struggle, as the turning point while the person moves toward faith. Yet when he confronts those who will take no thought about their faith on the ground that, if it is to be done, God will make it happen, he senses the error and states in no uncertain terms that "salvation is to be sought." [44]

There were certainly some respects in which Spencer was limited; and the closer he comes to basic theory, the more those limitations become exposed. What is extraordinary about him, perhaps above all else, is his attitude of inquiry about his dealings with people. If there is any reader who wishes to brush this off lightly, let him go and write up from memory the next pastoral contact he makes. In referring to a certain subject but applying throughout his pastoral learning, Spencer wrote of his days as a young pastor:

> By conversation with older and more experienced pastors, I aimed to get some instruction on this subject; but all I could learn did not satisfy me, indeed it did not seem to do me the least good. *I found I must teach myself what nobody appeared able to teach me.*

Spencer does well to italicize his method of learning from reflection on his own experience; but he might just as well have italicized the previous sentence also, in which he had the courage to admit that in this realm his authorities were no authorities at all.

In the introduction to his first volume Spencer wrote, "The particular religious experiences of individuals are not guides for other people." [46] And he meant it. The pastor respects the individuality of the way in which various people may come to Christ. But this does not mean that what anyone happens to believe is the best way for him, since "convicted sinners are very poor judges of what 'will do them good.' " [47]

Comment on Spencer

In presenting an overview of Ichabod Spencer's approach to his pastoral operations, I have intentionally put as much of this as possible in his own words and have tried to move from his reflections on what he did to the theory upon which he rested. I elected not to begin with an account of his systematic theology, of his view of the Bible's authority, of the sometimes concealed philosophy upon which his intellectual premises rested. In following this approach, it is hoped that a fairer picture of Spencer has been presented. And by inference, if not at all points by explicit statement, we can see that his doctrine, his view of the Bible, and his philosophy were the ordinary accompaniments to the form which the pietistic Calvinism of his day had assumed.

In certain specific sketches by Spencer that I shall be using later, I shall attempt to deal more explicitly with that which we can yet learn from him as against that which was time-bound and local to him. Yet even here a few evaluative remarks may be made.

Perhaps above all else, one is impressed with the work Spencer did with people and with that involved in reflecting upon and improving the work, including the writing of his sketches. We admire his intention in taking almost unlimited time to talk with any who were prepared to consider religion seriously, even though we cannot accept his compartmentalized notion of what it is to talk about religion as against talking about other things. He brings no cult of easy reassurance, does not talk to please, becomes suspicious when people seem to think too much of him and not enough of Christ and the Holy Spirit.

Although he concedes, even contends, that the particular form of a religious experience is not necessarily normative for another, yet he seems to us to be highly literalistic about what is legitimate among the varieties. At the same time he is attempting to testify to some kind of fundamental process, beneath all particularities of form, that involves the very depths of each person. Whatever this is, and we may well believe Spencer partly mistaken about his knowledge of what it is, if it exists at all, it is something that cannot be bypassed. Whether we believe Spencer identified it or not, or in what degree, it is vital that the question about such a basic process be seriously asked. For this is the salvation corollary to the doctrine of God as creator and sustainer.

Spencer as a man was extraordinary. Although bearing the marks of a deep piety, there was never a trace of unctuousness. He would if he thought the situation warranted it, say the word that would "drive the arrow" of anxiety deeper; yet he wept more with sorrowing parishioners than do most pastors of our day or his. He was plainly indefatigable in calling upon his people. In his mind there was no basic difference between his calling upon a parishioner and a parishioner's coming to see him. The former was not duty and the latter not flattering. He was extraordinarily singled-minded in concentrating on the need of the person as he understood it.

To be sure, in his day there was no basketball team to provide for, no nursery school, no committee on committees, no special program for older people. When parishioners were ill, they were cared for at home. The minister stood for the way of salvation. Some might disbelieve in it and others ignore it. But it had, in a sense, no competitors. Such things were different from our own day. In his assiduous work with individuals and families Spencer may well have failed to recognize the power of group work in the church. It is certain that his detailed schedule cannot be ours. Yet he gives hints that we do well to note and reflect upon seriously.

What strikes the modern eye most critically about Spencer is his compartmentalization of religion. His work with anxious inquirers was to get a sincere and inward verdict for Jesus Christ. His complete single-mindedness on this, we must recognize, would have been regarded as one-sided by the Anglican tradition and as partly distorted by most of the Lutheran tradition. With this emphasis Baptists and Methodists would have had little quarrel, but they would have regarded Spencer as too rigid and doctrinal. There is some truth in all such perspectives upon Spencer.

This sharp pietistic focus on religion as a thing apart can hardly be accepted by pastors of today who are accustomed to deal with marriage problems, alcohol problems, sex problems, money problems, and problems of many other kinds. We are inclined to say that there is a religious dimension to any problem if pursued deeply enough. Spencer did not see it that way. He reported two alcohol problems, with one of which he succeeded and with the other failed; but the jug and the bottle were mentioned almost with reluctance. He reported one problem of ethics in business, but this was rapidly cut through. Even concerning family relationship problems, the most pervasive of all, Spencer paid little attention to this aspect of his stories, only enough to give the right context to the process of salvation. Husbands might be drunk or derelict; but if they would not come to Christ, Spencer felt there was nothing he could do for them. On several occasions Spencer indicated that someone had had a sore trial or a bitter experience, but he could not tell the nature of it. In the story of the young woman who felt she had committed the unpardonable sin, the modern reader will strongly expect a sexual indiscretion eventually to be brought forth. But not so. The sin turned out to be entirely religious in nature. By not so much as a hint is sex ever referred to in these volumes, even in relation to husband and wife. In learning from Spencer the much that he has yet to teach, we do well to guard against identifying this continuing contribution with the localisms and literalisms.

At this point the reader may well ask why we are devoting such attention to a man who wrote entirely about his work with individuals and families, since the operations of the minister and the church do not stop there. That is correct, for they do not stop there. But we do have to start in some particular place, and there is much merit in beginning with the more easily analyzable situations. All the operations are relational in nature. By starting with, in effect, the study of one-to-one relationships, we may more easily reach principles that, to be sure, must also be tested by study of other orders of relationship.

There is still another great virtue in beginning our study with Spencer's work with individuals and families. This is because Spencer did not bring the shepherding perspective to bear upon his work either in an exclusive or even in a dominant way. In fact, according to the three operational perspectives set forth here—shepherding, communicating, and organizing—Spencer concentrates or focuses more on communicating than on either of the others. How, then, is it a virtue to study shepherding through Spencer?

It is a virtue because the shepherding perspective does not operate in Spencer as a bias to condition the choice of material. As we have seen,

Spencer is not without biases. But if his concerns are of the nature I have indicated, then anything we may find through him about the shepherding perspective may be doubly valuable precisely because that was not what he set out to emphasize in the first place.

In selecting contemporary material (and we always do select and abstract), the danger is that we shall use only that material in which shepherding operates in dominant or uncomplicated form. This has its good points, but it may obscure the actual nature of most pastoral situations. Remember that we are here concerned not merely with this or that kind of pastoral operation, but with the shepherding perspective upon all pastoral operations. Spencer is more valuable to us as he is, therefore, than if his perspective had been exclusively or dominantly one of shepherding.

In what follows I shall draw upon current material. But I shall also draw upon Ichabod Spencer. Having given this brief account of him, I may treat his sketches to some extent as if they were contemporary. Through these contributions of Spencer's, it is my conviction that we shall advance in emotional identification with our own pastoral history and gain also in our understanding of the value of the unique tools and instruments which the modern world has made available for pastoral theology.

PART III

Content

CHAPTER 6

Healing

HEALING MEANS BECOMING WHOLE. IT IS A TERM NOT APPLICABLE TO things or processes below the level of the organic. With suborganic processes there may indeed be movements toward integration, but we do not think of these as healing.

Healing implies, further, that the becoming is actually a rebecoming, a restoration of a condition once obtaining but then lost. It does not necessarily imply that the result of the healing will be the same in its particulars as the condition that previously obtained, except for the one characteristic of wholeness. A man who has lost one kidney is healed when the other kidney so alters itself as to perform the work of two. In structural details the new wholeness is not the same as that pertaining before one kidney was lost. But in the terms of functioning of the whole body, including the performance of the kidney functions, wholeness has been restored.

Thus healing is to be understood as the process of restoring functional wholeness. Structure is not unimportant to it. Some structure is needed. But the details of the structure may be different after the healing than they were either in the preceding stage of unwholeness or in the still earlier form of wholeness, provided only the wholeness of function is restored.

This wholeness of function is to be viewed primarily from the point of view of the organism as itself a functioning whole. Some functions of the parts are essential to the whole organism's existence; others are not. Healing is to be seen as taking place mainly from the point of view of the whole organism, so that a failure to restore function of a kind not essential to the over-all function of the organism is not ordinarily thought of as a failure in healing, but as a functional handicap. If the remaining kidney did not succeed in doing the work previously performed by two kidneys, there would be a central failure in healing. But if an arm is amputated and the remaining arm cannot quite perform all the functions once performed by two, we speak of functional handicap, in this instance accompanied by structural loss.

Can we speak of healing in reference to the emergence of a wholeness that had never previously been actually present? For instance, was it healing when the man blind from birth received vision and, disdaining causal questions, exclaimed, "One thing I know, that though I was blind, now I see"? [1] Yes, this may be regarded as healing on two grounds. The first is simply the tremendous importance of vision to the function of the whole organism, not indispensable but without which many functions cannot be carried out. The other is that this man's absence of sight, even from birth, was not, so to speak, in line with the general intention of nature. The loss of wholeness came early, in the womb or perhaps even in the genes. It came so early that the later emergence of vision was plainly not a restoration of a previously existing actual state of ability to see, but the putting right of a direction which without the impairment would have led to the earlier emergence of vision.

Thus, to understand the meaning of healing as restoration of functional wholeness, we must dispense with simple substantive metaphors (either he sees or he doesn't—not relevant to the fetus) and utilize some model or models that permit us to think of the restoration directionally, that is, in terms of the emergence of a dominant process (as against a previously existing but different dominant process, for example, the maintenance of blindness) that permits vision. What is restored is not, theoretically, a vision that once actually existed "full-grown," so to speak. It is restoration only in terms of process and direction. In its emergence it is a new whole.

The term "healing" is not appropriate, however, when the emerging whole is "on schedule." When the baby first learns to focus his eyes to fix on a bright color, a new whole is emerging; but this is not referred to as healing because no redirection has been necessary. If the child were five or ten years old before this function emerged, then the process could be referred to as healing. Thus healing is inseparable from timing.

A formal definition of healing, taking the factors noted into account, then becomes: *the restoration of functional wholeness that has been impaired as to direction and/or schedule.*

Such a definition applies plainly to healing of an organism as body. For from the bodily point of view direction and timing are generally

90

given by nature according to any definition of nature that may be used. Even here, however, the matter is not so clear-cut as it appears. But when healing is applied to the human being as spirit or total being, a new order of problems emerges. What constitutes wholeness is both more variable and more culture-conditioned. It is not arbitrary nor infinitely variable; nature by any definition is still involved. But a new order of complexity has appeared.

When we think what the condition is from which healing is the rescue, it is not difficult to use "illness" and "disease" when we are thinking of the organism from the bodily perspective. Especially "disease" suggests that certain direction-impairing processes are at work and that these must be deprived of force if healing is to take place. A dramatic illustration is found in those new drugs that do not kill harmful bacteria but simply prevent them from reproducing. The healing process will become dominant if the disease process is arrested or rendered sufficiently powerless.

"Illness" in contrast to "disease" is often used to refer to the whole organism's experience, while "disease" refers to the chemical and physiological processes of impairment. When used in this way, "illness" attempts to link the fact of the underlying processes of impairment with the subjective experience of impairment.

"Disease" seems at first glance a singularly inept term for describing organismic impairment of the psychic and personal kind. For it suggests that the trouble lies in some subterranean process, probably physiological in nature, and therefore should be approached only from such perspectives. "Illness" seems not much better, for it assumes that the foundations of the subjective experience are of a different order from the experiencing. Some persons concerned with psychotherapy or some other form of helping the whole personality overcome its impairments have for reasons like this eliminated the words "disease" and "illness" and even "healing." We shall not do so, but we warn against the unsatisfactory connotations that "disease" and "illness" have acquired.

Healing from What?

What are the factors that produce the conditions that make healing necessary? Specific causes are of course usually complex. But there seem to be four broad types of causal factors: defect, invasion, distortion, and decision.

Defect may be seen in the idiot, in the man born without arms, possibly in the person experiencing severe swings of mood from his earliest days, and perhaps to some extent in the so-called psychopathic personality incapable of responsible social relatedness.

Invasion covers the bacteria and viruses and poisons. It also describes accurately those social conditionings in which, for example, one person so invades a second that the second feels insecure and impaired unless he has one like the first on whom to rely.

Distortion can come from foot-binding or high heels, from too many calories or too few vitamins. It can also come from the acceptance of false or inferior goals and methods of living, on the representation of those persons who are trusted and who have themselves been similarly distorted.

To defect, invasion, and distortion I have added decision. This will prove frequently misleading if regarded as a conscious choosing in the light of clear and distinct knowledge of all major factors involved. The young girl invaded by her mother's dominating personality does not choose with a clear view of factors and consequences to become dependent or even masochistic. The adolescent boy who is violently antisocial was probably aided to this by the absence of affection or respect, by slum living conditions, and by other factors he did not create. Yet in all such instances there is some factor of choice which, however small in this or that instance, may nevertheless prove decisive. As many theologians use the terms, there is "history" as well as "nature" involved. Such terms are useful so long as they are not used to suggest categorically two different realms.

To many peoples in early stages of cultural development, all the conditions for which healing was required came about through their own decision, which offended the gods, who then invaded them. Medicine and the other healing arts made their great progress in understanding and dealing with those minor impairments in which decision was' a relatively minor factor, and in finding specificity in the forms of defect, invasion, and distortion. Indeed, the supposed separation of body and mind into two realms is relatively recent and is now rapidly being set aside in favor of the organismic theory that regards body and mind as two basic perspectives upon the organism.

With many primitive people the medicine man was also priest, and healing was thereby symbolized as an undifferentiated unity. Healing lacked specificity and a base of scientifically acquired principles. When specificity came to the fore, the movement was toward differentiation and away from the unity that was felt to be synonymous with primitivism. Each form of impairment, it was hypothecated, had its specific cause or causes. We know how fruitful with many types of impairment this notion has proved and doubtless will with others.

For some years past, however, there has been widespread recognition that a new level of unity is necessary for healing. It is not just any unity, certainly not a primitive type of unity resisting any differentiation. It is a unity built up out of the experience of many differentiations. Thus one well-known physician refuses, for example, to speak of a "psychosomatic approach" in medicine; for this term tends to perpetuate, as he sees it, a dualism that was the creation of faulty theory to begin with.[2]

The minute such a position is taken, then the factor we are calling decision can be reconsidered, not as fate nor as the single explanation of everything for which healing is needed, but as a factor of importance in many impairments and perhaps of decisive importance in some. The more specific and differentiated the knowledge of defect, invasion, and distortion, however, the more it becomes necessary to be specific also about decision. It may be of small importance in the healing of this infected vermiform appendix, but of cardinal significance for the healing of this person who claims to know all about himself but to have no idea what to do with his life.

The connotation of "disease" that we wish to retain is of the movement of some inexorable process at such a level that "wishing won't make it well." Such are the ravages of tubercle bacilli and equally those of having learned to be overdependent (or overindependent). There can be nothing but symptomatic healing that does not find differentiated ways of affecting this disease process. Such a way may be psychoanalysis as well as drugs or surgery. But the process must be reached, its force negatively affected, and this requires differentiation in the form of specific knowledge.

The connotation of "illness" that merits retention is emphasis on the painful reality of experiencing impairment, whatever its causes. Used in this way, it may deal by proper differentiation with defect, invasion, and distortion, and also with decision. When used, as both it and "disease" sometimes are, to eliminate any possibility of the factor of decision, it is false and misleading.

93

Healing and Sin

We are now prepared to consider the question as to whether healing in its most basic sense is from sin.[3] As we noted, among many primitive peoples that from which healing was needed came from acts they had committed that had offended the gods, who then invaded them, so that it was the result of the invasion that required healing. The type of act considered offensive to the gods was felt to be from the human point of view arbitrary. Especially from our modern knowledge of the unconscious, we know there was a psychic connection. But the nature of man's offending acts was not felt to be equally offensive to the gods and to the fulfillment of man's own nature. Thus, if we regard sin, generically, as that part of man's alienation from God (and from his own true being) for which he is himself responsible, we see that the first notions of sin were highly legalistic, were related to act rather than to motive, and were undifferentiated.

Historically, it took a tremendous effort of the religious imagination to transcend such notions of sin, and they always threaten to break through more adequate conceptions. If one can regard *this* act as the sin, in such a way that the characterological matrix from which it springs may be ignored, an economy of psychic effort is achieved. If he can regard this or that type of act as something for which he is wholly responsible, he may repent of that—but retain reservations and defenses about just that total complex of psychic conditions that will lead again to such acts. Just because he has not differentiated that for which he is responsible from that for which he is not, he avoids dealing with sin as a holistic phenomenon.

With the rise of differentiated methods of healing from differentiated forms of impairment, it became impossible to regard sin in the primitive sense as *the* efficient causative agent. "Who did sin, this man, or his parents?" The conception of sin behind these questioners of Jesus was primitive, and the question itself was therefore rejected. If one linked illness or disease with sin in its primitive sense, then one was arguing automatically against differentiated study of the causes and very likely also against mercy for the sufferer. If one wants a simple modern illustration of this, think how many good people of our day deeply regret the effectiveness with which the antibiotic drugs destroy the syphilitic spirochete.

Let us be clear that the disassociation of sin and sickness has been a good and positive thing in so far as a connection with sin in the primitive sense was being renounced. This is thoroughly in line with Jesus' rejection in the case of the blind man of any primitive sin notions of causation.

But the separation of sin and sickness has been premature if sin is regarded in a different sense—in our rough definition as that aspect of man's alienation from God and from his own true fulfillment for which he bears responsibility.[4] This then becomes what has been called above "decision" when the decision is wrongly or perversely made.

To see what this means, let us examine the apparently simple case of a person who is seriously overweight.[5] Our differentiated knowledge enables us to reject flatly any notion that this comes solely and simply from repeated and perverse and clear decisions to eat too much. We know that this person's glandular and other physiological apparatus may so operate as to convert into fat for him what will be discarded by another, that he may suffer in part from a defect. We know also that he may have been rejected in terms of affection and that food may have to him a symbolic psychic meaning that it does not possess for others, that he is, therefore, in part the victim of distortion. And since such processes, once initiated, act with circular effect, we know that he may also be in part the victim of invasion. Each of these three types of factor in his case works with a certain automatism. He was not responsible for any glandular defect. He did not choose to be deprived of affection. He did not decide that the food would so operate within him as to make poundage impairing. He is in very fundamental respects, which are tremendously important for healing him, a victim not directly responsible for his plight. Any conception of his predicament that would deny the importance of these factors should be rejected.

All the same, defect, invasion, and distortion do not account entirely for the impairment. Let us suppose that, when he first passed a certain weight, he consulted a physician and that this physician suggested a diet of a certain kind, and let us further assume that our man tried it. After the first meal he felt unsatisfied and because of the obsessive character of his craving was therefore able to think of nothing else, until the next meal, except mashed potatoes, whipped cream, or avocados. For the rising up of such obsessional thoughts, let us note that he is not (at least for purposes of our point) responsible. Then comes the second meal, which we shall assume is a lamb chop, lettuce, and rye-crisp. Since the last meal he has thought of nothing but the next. With the next arrived, suffering is enhanced. And this may be made still rougher for him if his wife eats mashed potatoes and retains a sylphlike figure. At any rate, what I am describing is a situation in which there is real although not complete compulsion, but in which the movement toward relief of suffering destroys that element of control that could be exercised. From the point of view of eventual healing of the seriously excess weight, nothing finally will take the place of exercising that amount of responsible control that exists. Did sin cause the weight? In any primitive sense, no; for such an alleged explanation is mistaken and likely to impede healing. Is sin in a normative sense uninvolved in the situation? No, sin is there and emerges most obviously at the point of failing to exercise that element of control that is possible despite immediate suffering. And from the point of view of healing, the element of decision, while it may be quantitatively small in the causation of the disorder, may be prognostically all-important.

Let us examine an utterly different kind of impairment, Parkinson's disease, or "shaking palsy." The onset of this is an uncontrollable shaking, usually of the limbs, slowly followed by a growing rigidity of all the body's externals. It is like the growing of a shaking shell between oneself and the world. Its causes are not thoroughly understood; but once the disease process is initiated, there is no doubt that the bodily structure itself is altered. There are few illnesses that give their victims such a sense of inexorable invasion as this, like the drip of water wearing away a stone. And so far there seem to be no pharmacological ways of arresting, not to say healing, this disease, although its ravages may be slowed and its symptoms partly relieved. At first glance there would seem to be nothing at all but invasion in this disease.

While all this is true, it is not the whole truth at a deeper level. If we can believe the psychiatric investigators, the Parkinsonian has had a deep and secret longing to be dependent, to be taken care of, although in overt behavior he may have seemed unduly independent or detached. He tends to have been a "good man" in the conformist sense according to the particular standards of his class and community. All these and related characteristics operate automatically, and he cannot in any easy or simple sense be regarded as responsible for them.

Let us suppose, however, that the disease has begun and our patient sees his physician. The physician may explain the slowly progressive course of the disease, prescribe medication to alleviate symptoms and help arrest the progress. He may also, if he believes the psychiatrists are right, suggest that the longest possible attempt to maintain function in all parts of the body despite some suffering will itself hold back the progress of the disease. In line with this advice, our patient may make a valiant effort to continue penmanship with his shaking hand. This may, however, become impossible. He may then simply stop trying to use this hand—instead of moving to using it for some exercise less fine than handwriting. Or he may suddenly refuse to go out walking not because of the suffering in his limbs but because someone ignorantly jokes about his affliction. A hundred daily decisions are made that have much to say about the progress or arresting of the disease process.

Confronted with decisions of this sort, a person of aggressive character would act quite differently from our Parkinsonian. The latter, precisely because of the concealed psychic wishes, unknown and unassimilated by his conscious self, has the cards stacked against him in reference to such decisions. Yet the fact remains that some Parkinsonians have delayed for many years the most serious ravages of their illness; and others, learning of the psychic factor involved, have pursued psychological therapy—and by gaining increasing insight into their character, have enhanced their power to make the daily decisions that slow up the disease. When understood in any other than this subtle sense, decision is meaningless. And yet, so understood, it may prove decisive.

The greatest progress of modern medicine has come in the realm of infections, of acute diseases. It has made least progress on the so-called degenerative diseases. If our reasoning is correct, it is precisely in the degenerative diseases that the factor of decision, however subtle, is most prominent. Yet it is just here that decision is also most difficult. The Parkinsonian lacks just that element of character that would enable him to sustain the immediate sufferings produced by keeping his muscles functioning. The fat man, reducing, is willing to give up anything but food. The man with high blood pressure struggles excitedly to avoid becoming excited. For each of us, it may be added, the factor of decision is likely to be weakest just where putting it into operation is likely to do the most good. But this simply increases the subtlety of decision; it does not destroy it.

Let us put the general principle prospectively in this way. That impairment from which a man most needs healing (because it most affects his functional wholeness) is likely to be just that which seems most inaccessible to decision, and yet it is precisely to that area that decision must be applied if there is to be healing. This is the reason we must retain words such as "illness" and "disease," and yet not so define them as to eliminate any connection with "decision." This is why in a subtle and profound sense we must regard sin as crucial in many forms of serious impairment.

In the Christian gospel the word about sin is good news, not bad. This is true for two reasons. First, if the condition is in fact serious and all-embracing, then a recognition of this is a necessary prelude to liberation; while soothing syrup or aspirin tablets could lead one to the brink of destruction by destroying the finger-pointing symptoms. Second, one who is capable of acknowledging not only his lack of central wholeness but also his own share in its production has already, whether he knows it or not, in part transcended his impairment. For the "he" who can see deeply the nature of his impairment is more than the impairment. As the tradition has said in many ways, only the faithful know the depth of their sinfulness. The emergence of a genuine conviction of sin is itself an indication that healing is in process.

Healing of the Spirit

The arch impairment from which healing is most necessary, the tradition has declared, is sin, the most pervasive of all degenerative diseases. Yet its healing at the same time presents the greatest difficulties just because it is so central and therefore so crucial.[6] At this point resort has usually been had to spatial metaphors. If the entire person and character are impaired (sinful, corrupted, or depraved), then the healing agent is from "outside." As one who is in process of being healed feels it, the metaphor is correct. But it is theoretically inadequate, since "inside" and "outside" are analogies of simple location and hence unable to do justice to the complexity of organism in social relatedness. Too much reliance on the spatial metaphors gives the impression of healing by invasion, which then produces a lot of unnecessary and unfruitful theological complications.

Healing or salvation of the soul would not run counter to our argument if "soul" was used in its earlier sense of animating or enlivening principle, unless, as often happened "soul" was set against a supposedly inert and peripheral "body." A dichotomy of this kind runs against the Christian conception of "spirit," which is close to our modern use of an expression such as "whole person." But it is true that the constant temptation to see "soul" as a thing apart, instead of as a useful abstraction from the functioning of the organism, often resulted in a notion of "soul healing" that ignored both body and culture.

Thus Ichabod Spencer in the middle of the nineteenth century had a mental picture of the healing or salvation of a soul that made its relationships to the organic body and to culture merely extrinsic, external, or peripheral. In discussing depression or despondency, he was ready to state, "Despondency originates from physical causes more than from all other causes." [7] In his view, therefore, such a despondency was not to be treated as if it came from a sin-sick soul. But having put the matter in this way, he had then to ask if there was a difference between the despondency of a believer and that of an unbeliever; to which the answer was that the believer "still has faith," which "only needs to be brought into lively exercise, and his despondency will melt away." [8] He has "lost sight of the objects of faith," whereas the unbeliever "never had any faith." [9] Thus Spencer put himself in the position of asserting that where the "objects of faith" were still properly viewed, there could not be despondency, which can be clinically contradicted. He had also to divorce physical causes from soul causes, feeling no responsibility, as a pastor, for the former. If in fact they are related, as we believe, Spencer relieved himself of responsibility prematurely.

As he disassociated healing of the soul from that of the body more or less categorically, so he did with what we have called culture. His reasoning was of the same order as in relation to the body. If someone had marital problems or grief, too bad; but move toward the salvation of his soul. Would this take care of the grief or the marital problems? Probably, but if not, the most important thing had been done anyhow. Thus Spencer did believe in one-way communication between salvation of the soul and salvation in the several orders and circumstances of life and culture, from the soul to the relationships and problems. In his theory, however, the relationship did not also run the other way.

In the usual connotations, therefore, we must simply deny that what our faith is concerned to heal is the soul. It may be that this term can be rejuvenated, its original intention as "animating center" restored, and that it may operate in a more adequate intellectual context instead of encouraging dualisms; but this seems unlikely. To the extent that that is true "soul" will only confuse and not help. What is most important to have healed is man's spirit, his total personality, his sinful (because free) self. But all healing is of a piece. There is a continuum from the whole personality at the focus to a cut finger somewhere out in the field. No aspect of the field is categorically separated from any other or from the focus. But to try to deal with the focus without serious attention to the field is to speak of an abstraction without recognizing its abstract character.

Spiritual healing, then, from the point of view of the pastor and the church is related to all other healing by physician, rehabilitator, or re-educator. There may indeed be a division of labor. The more prominent in the particular healing are technical means the sharper must become such a division, as when we refrain from giving clergy the right to remove diseased gall bladders. But the nearer we come to focus in the whole personality, the less possible it becomes to draw sharp lines.

If healing is all of a piece, all in the same field although not all equally important or central, then there can be no categorical division between secular and religious healing, between salvation for another life and for this, between healing by religious means as against those of the world, of nature, or of science. Any healing, brought about by whatever means, may have religious dimensions or move toward religious depth. It is its effect upon the production of functional wholeness that indicates the degree and kind of its religious dimension and depth.

"Impairment," which I have used as the general term for that which requires healing, whatever else it may be, is preoccupying. It is equally difficult to fix one's gaze on the finer things of life when one has a tooth-ache or a sense of guilt. Because of the common factor of preoccupation each may impair one's functional wholeness. The healing of the tooth-ache is not very likely, however, to lead directly to a reconsideration of one's over-all functional wholeness; thus it may be some distance out in the field from the focus of the processes needed for central healing. But the healing of a toothache could perform this function. In contrast the healing of a sense of guilt may very easily lead to a consideration of factors that are central to the personality. But if done in a certain way or if not healed on the mistaken ground that any feeling of guilt will make one an anxious inquirer, it can lead directly away from central healing.

The healing that the pastor and church seek to aid, therefore, has a clear focus in what is felt to be central and fundamental in relation to functional wholeness. The nature of that wholeness cannot, it is believed, be defined in itself but must include reference to the fellowship of the church and the person's connection with it, and to connection with God and Jesus Christ. But these necessary aids to defining the nature of func-tional wholeness from the Christian point of view are not such as to mark off some realm or area of healing and call it Christian, as if healing this direction could not come through various channels. To put it bluntly, the movement toward Christian healing may come through profane channels. And to state the corollary, exclusive concentration on alleged Christian means and modes of healing may impede healing in the Christian sense.

Such a position, it should be carefully noted, does not make Christian healing or salvation synonymous with ideas such as adjustment, maturity, or any possible content definition of functional wholeness. Because of the field model we use, it enables us to get a precise notion of the focus or center of Christian healing or salvation. Whatever is distinctive, therefore, can be stated without having to protect distinctiveness by an artificial and misleading separation from just those unexpected sources that may press movement toward healing in the Christian view. Distinctiveness is protected without denying enriching relationship.

In this discussion of healing it is well to keep in mind the place to which it has been assigned among the perspectives upon the operations of the minister and church. Healing is not everything; it is not even all there is to shepherding. It is that aspect of the shepherding perspective that is dominant when there is need, when that need is in some sense recognized, and, it may now be added, when the nature of that need involves impairment that can in some measure be made whole. When the nature of the need is such that the new whole cannot emerge or must be postponed, then the sustaining aspect of shepherding is in operation. When the need, and in some measure the desire, require redirection (or change in direction of the whole), then guiding is the aspect of shepherding that becomes paramount.

One of Ichabod Spencer's longest sketches concerns his pastoral dealing with a young married woman whose need and desire, he finally discovered, were for what I have called healing.[10] Spencer for a long time had regarded the need as something else and castigated himself for mishandling when the real nature of the need became clear.

Spencer does not give this young woman of twenty-five a name, but let us call her Mrs. N. so as to avoid repetitions of "young woman." Spencer's opening characterological description of her was as follows:

In the discharge of pastoral duty I have never been more deeply interested or more perplexed, than I was in the case of a very affectionate and intelligent woman, whom I knew with great intimacy for several years. She was a married woman before I became acquainted with her. She was young in life, I suppose not more than twenty-five, and her husband was probably about thirty—not a religious man. I visited her as her pastor, soon after she had removed from another part of the country, and taken up her residence in the place where I lived. I was much pleased with her. She was a woman of refined manners, of excellent sense, of trained mind, of gentle and affectionate disposition, but withal of unusual firmness, having a mind and a heart of her own. Few women, as I believe, have ever adorned their station more than she adorned hers. As a wife, mother, friend; as a neighbor, as a daughter, (for I became acquainted with her parents and knew her demeanor towards them,) she was a pattern of propriety. A stranger to her might have deemed her manner somewhat reserved and cold, (as indeed it was to strangers,) for there was no forwardness about her. She was modest, unassuming, unobtrusive. But her reserve wore off by acquaintance; and though she never became imprudent, and never lost a just sense of a woman's dignity, she became peculiarly confiding and companionable. However, she was rather taciturn than talkative. Like a woman of sense, she took care whom she trusted, and what she said.

By this time it is plain that Spencer likes Mrs. N.'s type of woman in general and her in particular. He then gives his preliminary statement of the characterological problem.

But there was a shade of melancholy which seemed to hang around her, quite noticeable to a keen observer, and yet not so distinct as to be visible, perhaps, to most of her acquaintance. Her half pensive look gave an additional interest to her intelligent countenance, (which had no small claims to be denominated beautiful,) and indeed there seemed to be a cast of sadness thrown over the very movements of her tall and graceful figure.

Now Spencer begins his account of his pastoral dealings with Mrs. N.:

When I first became acquainted with her, I noticed this tender melancholy which hung around her like the shadow of a cloud; and I supposed that the twilight of some affliction still lingered around her heart, or that some secret grief was buried deep in her own bosom. After a more intimate acquaintance with her, I came to the conclusion that she had some trial of which she never spoke, but which preyed in secret upon her heart. I thought her appearance indicative of a concealed grief, which, like a worm in the bud, was preying upon her life.

Let the reader be warned at once that, if Mrs. N. had ever borne an illegitimate child, been beaten by her father, or been in prison for forgery, no such fact ever comes to light. Spencer next begins his account of his religious conversations with Mrs. N.:

I aimed to mention the subject of religion to her, in the most delicate and affectionate manner possible. I called upon her for that purpose. I found her alone. After a few moments of conversation I said to her,—

SPENCER: I have several times mentioned the subject of religion to you, Mrs. N., but you have been quite reserved; and I have called upon you to-day to converse with you upon that subject, if you will allow me such a favor.

MRS. N.: I am glad to see you, sir.

SPENCER: Allow me to ask you whether you are a member of the church?

MRS. N.: No sir, I am not.

SPENCER: And do you think you are still living in unbelief, after all your opportunities?

MRS. N.: I suppose, sir, I have no reason to think I am a Christian (with a look of mingled solemnity and sorrow).

SPENCER: Is it wise for you to neglect your salvation?

MRS. N.: I know it is not wise, sir. My own heart condemns me (with much emotion).

SPENCER: Then, madam, do not neglect it any longer. The favor of God is within your reach. He calls to you in His gracious kindness, and invites you to turn to Him for pardon and peace, freely offered to you through the great Redeemer of sinners. But how comes it about, Mrs. N., that you have neglected salvation so long?

MRS. N.: I do not know, indeed, sir. I suppose I have been too worldly, and too much led away by my own heart, though I have thought about religion a great deal all my life.

SPENCER: I suppose so too. And I know you ought, instantly, to "deny yourself, and take up your cross and follow Jesus Christ," and not suffer your heart to be led away any longer.

She was much affected. I asked her some questions which she did not answer, because (as I then supposed), of a conflict in her own mind, betwixt a sense of duty and the love of the world. I therefore urged her as solemnly and affectionately as I could, to give her attention to religion without delay, and left her.

Of Spencer's next call upon Mrs. N., the following is an excerpt.

SPENCER: Have you been giving your attention to religion since I saw you?

MRS. N.: I have thought of it very often, sir.

SPENCER: And have you prayed about it very often?

MRS. N.: I have tried to pray (sadly), but I do not know as it was true prayer.

SPENCER: Do you feel your *need* of God's blessing, as an undone sinner, condemned by the law of God, and having a wicked heart?

MRS. N.: Sometimes I *think* I feel it; but I suppose I do not feel it as much as I ought to.

SPENCER: Do you feel that you need Christ to save you?

MRS. N.: I *know* it, sir; but I am afraid I do not feel it. My heart seems hard, very hard; I wonder at myself, my stupid self.

Such discussion continued, Mrs. N. became emotional and "wept bitterly" although striving "hard to control her emotions."

MRS. N.: Pardon my infirmity, sir. I do not know why it is, but I cannot restrain my feelings. I hope you will not think me *quite* a child.

I assured her of my entire respect for her, and my attachment to her as a friend; that I was unwilling to say one word to make her unhappy, but that I wanted her attention to a happiness unequalled and everlasting.

MRS. N.: I know it, sir, I know it; and I thank you for all your kindness to me (*with tears*).

We may pause at this point to remind ourselves that Spencer is like a lawyer who has come upon a will giving rich treasure to a close friend, if she will but come and claim it, the will also containing a codicil that, if she fails to do so, her final punishment will be dreadful. Thus he would not say one word to make her unhappy, but he felt bound to mention the treasure and the punishment.

In the subsequent period Spencer had several interviews with Mrs. N., "in all of which she was solemn and much affected, but ordinarily her words were few." Several months passed, and Spencer went over the plan of salvation, recommended texts of Scripture, and otherwise sought to touch or instruct her. But "still she found no peace of mind, no hope." Spencer says he had expected at first that she would "come out of her darkness into the light of faith"; but when months passed and she failed to do so, then he feared that she would become "less solemn or less studious or less tender in feeling." But that did not happen either. At every pastoral call Mrs. N. would "be melted into tears in spite of all her efforts," but would express gratitude to Spencer.

Spencer became more and more puzzled. He "soothed and comforted" her. He "reasoned with her." He "aimed to reach her conscience." He taught her "all God's truth, which I thought adapted to her state of mind." She listened to it all. "She never uttered an objection, complaint, or excuse." But she remained "uncomforted." Spencer "blamed *myself* very much, for I supposed I must have failed to instruct her appropriately."

On his next call Spencer attempted to make up for any possible previous instructional deficiencies. He minced no words.

SPENCER: And certainly, madam, I can tell you nothing new,—can preach no new gospel, can tell you nothing different from what I have told you before. If you do not obey the gospel, nothing can save you. The gospel will not change. You must change.

Soon afterward Mrs. N. said:

MRS. N.: I wish, sir, I could tell what hinders.

Spencer in questions went down a long line of possible "hinderings," but as before, on each one Mrs. N. was without reproach. For instance,

SPENCER: Do you think you can make your heart any better?
MRS. N.: I am sure I can do nothing for myself. . . .
SPENCER: Do you seek the Lord with all your heart?
MRS. N.: I suppose not, sir; for if I did I should not remain in this miserable condition.
SPENCER: Do you rely upon any righteousness of your own to save you, or commend you to Christ?
MRS. N.: I have no righteousness. I know very well there is nothing in me but sin and misery. . . .
SPENCER: Don't you love the world too well?
MRS. N.: The love of the world *tempts* me, I am afraid, sometimes; but I feel that I am willing to forsake all for Christ.

Finally Spencer ran out of specific questions.

SPENCER: Let me ask you, my dear friend, with all respect and affection, don't you indulge in some sin (sin of enmity, or envy, or discontent, or something else), some sin that keeps you from peace of conscience and peace with God?
MRS. N.: No sir, I am not conscious of any such sin. I know I sin all the time. I struggle against it, but I do not *indulge* myself in any sin that I know of.

That was certainly the right answer, as were those to Spencer's other questions. But still her "peace" did not come. Still perplexed over what was happening, Spencer made some calls in which religion was not mentioned, hopeful that he might "have a more perfect knowledge" of Mrs. N.

"Several years" passed from the time of Spencer's meeting Mrs. N. until the incident next to be recounted. In those years she had "been called upon to pass through some severe trials, in which I had sympathized with her and aimed to lead her to improve them rightly." Just what these trials were, Spencer does not say. But she certainly relied on Spencer. "She appeared to repose in me the most perfect confidence, told me her sorrows, consulted me in her difficulties." But she "continued without hope."

One day Spencer called on Mrs. N. He wrote, "I did not know but I was making her unhappy by my constant solicitations, and perhaps doing her harm." So he said:

SPENCER: My dear child, I will not press this subject upon your attention any more, if it is unpleasant to you to have me mention it. I have loved you, and aimed to do you good; but I have failed. I do not wish to make you unhappy. I will leave you hereafter entirely to yourself, if you desire it, and never say a word more to you on the subject of your religion.

As perhaps Spencer had expected, she wept and invited him not to leave her. "She demanded a promise" that he come again.

In another call, which turned out to be crucial, Spencer asked:

SPENCER: Is it not strange that you do not love such a God?
MRS. N.: (*Greatly to Spencer's surprise*) I think I do love God, sir.
SPENCER: How long do you think you have loved Him?
MRS. N.: Ever since I was a little child. I cannot remember the time when I did *not* love Him. It has always seemed to me, as well as I know my own heart, that I did love God.
SPENCER: (*With amazement*) Why did you never tell me this before?
MRS. N.: I was afraid you would think me better than I am.
SPENCER: And do you hate sin?
MRS. N.: I have always hated it, (if I can judge of my own feelings,) ever since I can remember.
SPENCER: Why do you hate sin?
MRS. N.: Because it offends God, it is wrong, and because it makes me unhappy.

106

SPENCER: Do you desire to be free from it?

MRS. N.: Yes, I do, if I know anything at all of my own desires.

The conversation continued in this manner about prayer, reliance on Christ, trust in him as Saviour, resting in God's hands, reconciliation to God, loving God's people. All her feelings now, Spencer saw, were authentic evidences of the faith.

SPENCER: Don't you think that these feelings, which you have now expressed, are evidences of true religion?

MRS. N.: I *should* think so, perhaps, if I had not always had them. But I have never been sensible of any particular change. I have *always* felt so since I was a little child, as long as I can remember.

At this point the truth hit Spencer like a ton of bricks.

I was utterly amazed! Here I had been for years aiming to make conviction of sin more deep, instead of binding up the broken heart! I had been aiming to lead a sinner to Christ, instead of showing her that she was not a stranger, and an outcast! I was ashamed of myself! I had often talked to this precious woman as if she were an alien from God, and an enemy; and now it appeared as if all the while she had been one of His most affectionate children, her very anguish consisting in this,—that she loved Him no more, and could not get assurance of *His* love towards her. It was true she had never told me these things before; but that did not satisfy me. I ought to have learnt them before. I went out and wept bitterly! I felt as if I had been pouring anguish into the crushed heart of the publican, as he cried, "God be merciful to me a sinner!"

Later on Spencer found out what the "secret grief" was that preyed on her mind, as he had surmised from the beginning. "I may not here record what it was." But it was "cause enough, I am sure, to excuse all the melancholy which so long held possession of one of the noblest hearts that ever bled."

Knowing as little as we do about the factors, trials, and tribulations in Mrs. N.'s life, the psychological account of her must be partly conjectural. She may have been a person, in the language of our day, of limited ego strength, who needed a bit of assurance that she counted. Or she may have had a rather severe conscience that did not much mislead her in content but made certain that she enjoyed nothing. Whatever the specific explanation of her character structure, she was able, on the one hand, to face the problems of life (including Dr. Spencer), and on the other hand, she lived in an aura of slight but pervasive "gloom."

Spencer had no hesitation with Mrs. N., as with others, in recording the nature of his primary perspective. This is communicating the gospel in such a way that the Holy Spirit will make persons into anxious inquirers, and they will then turn to God and Christ and find peace, joy, and solemnity in the faith. To describe his encounters with people from this perspective was the aim with which the sketches were begun. And so he began with Mrs. N.

Yet at the time of the crucial call, he saw that he had misdiagnosed the situation. Far from needing more anxiety, Mrs. N. needed support. Instead of needing more "conviction of sin," she actually needed to have her "broken heart" bound up. She was, so to speak, whole already if only she knew it and could approach her impairment (the despondency) in that conviction. She needed not a fundamental change in what was central, but support to what was central in order that the part that was impaired might be attacked.

What came to Mrs. N. finally was healing in the precise sense in which I have defined it. Reading between the lines, we can see that Spencer helped her to distinguish that part of her impairment that was defect, invasion, or distortion from that which came out of decision. Unlike us, Spencer was not interested to describe that aspect of his work. Indeed, he was hesitant to do so; for once people had reached the anxious inquirer stage, and the nature of the faith had been made clear to them, one should be careful lest the working of the Holy Spirit be impeded. Spencer was just a little afraid that the work of healing might smack of playing God. Perhaps this is a good warning.

At any rate, we see in his dealing with Mrs. N. that he had, so to speak, two conceptions of healing, each applying to a particular kind of situation. In Mrs. N. as he described her through most of the contacts, he was like a surgeon urging a patient to have an operation. Later he was the postoperative surgeon dealing most tenderly with his patient, all the more because he realized he had made a wrong diagnosis. Whether the first type is to be understood as healing in our definition is dubious. It is certainly more aptly described under "communicating" as I have defined that. But from Spencer's point of view these two views were simply two stages in the whole process. His recognition of wrong diagnosis was, therefore, a reconsideration not of the whole process but of the stage at which this or that individual was. Spencer wisely comments after his account of Mrs. N., "If we think . . . that all true conversions will come within the scope of our favorite patterns, we have much yet to learn."

Two other sketches of Spencer's, which may be presented briefly, are useful in helping us to understand his view of healing. The first concerns a mother who was ill.[11] Spencer called upon her and found her mind "shrouded in darkness and gloom." He came again, and her attitude was the same. "She wept in agony." Spencer tried several approaches. He treated her as a "backslider," as a "believer under a cloud," and as an "impenitent sinner," but still there was nothing but "gloom." But some months later he called and found her hopeful and glad. Thereafter he found her sometimes up and sometimes down. Finally it dawned on him that she was glad in the morning and gloomy in the afternoon. He drew the conclusion that her gloom came entirely from "her physical condition" and explained that to her.[12] A few weeks before her death the gloom lifted.

In this story we may note Spencer's persistence, his trying various specific approaches designed to get at the cause of the gloom, his sharp observation about the ups and downs. When the cyclical nature of the moods had become clear to him, he no longer felt it relevant to try to have "religious conversation" with her when she was gloomy. His explanation to her of the cycle, which she herself had noted, was an attempt to heal the ravages of the gloom through insight.

At no point was Spencer prepared to settle for dealing with symptoms. He was, as we would see it, wrong in making a sharp demarcation between religious and physical causes; but until it became clear that the cause was not religious in his sense of the word, he was going to attempt to reach beneath the surface to find its nature. From his own point of view, and no doubt that of his patient, this was done tenderly.

In another sketch Spencer dealt with a woman by correspondence.[13] She first wrote him that she had long wanted to give herself to Jesus but had never really been "willing to go to perdition."[14] Spencer regarded such an interpretation of doctrine to be extreme and in error. The correspondent also indicated that thunder made her fearful and ill, even to the point of vomiting. Her plea was, "Oh! tell me, if I cannot bear a little storm, how am I to view the terrors of the last great day?"[15]

Spencer saw this letter as "melancholy proof of the unnecessary perplexity and torment of spirit, which false theological principles will sometimes produce."[16] In his report, but not to the correspondent, Spencer quoted another minister who had been approached by a woman willing to be damned for the glory of God, "Well, Madam, if you are willing to be damned, and God is willing you should be, I don't know as I ought to have any objections." [17]

Spencer began his letter in this way.

The only thing, beyond the ordinary range of strictly religious matter, which (as I judge from your letter), you have any special need that I should write to you, is a few words to call your attention to the *influences of physical condition upon religious sensibilities*. "Thunder" will sometimes kill goslings, turn milk sour, and spoil the tanner's calf-skins, when they are at a particular point in the process of being manufactured into leather. And it is not a miracle, if "thunder" sometimes makes you sick. Though it may be a very humiliating idea to us, that we are sometimes under the influence of external physical causes in the sacred sensibilities of our religion, yet it is true.[18]

The "physical causes" are wholly external, categorically different from "strictly religious matter," although they may affect it. In another letter Spencer wrote, "That condition of nervous excitability, which forbids your sleeping, or forbids your loving 'thunder,' is not to be fostered or indulged." [19] Still more explicitly, " 'Thunder' has an inexplicable effect upon some such things, with which religion has nothing to do; and if it has an inexplicable effect upon you, you need not link that effect with your religion." [20] At the conclusion of the correspondence the woman wrote to Spencer, "The last thunder shower we had I did not feel *half* so much afraid as usual." [21]

We can see that from Spencer's point of view it is as if this woman were wringing her hands over a small thing, such as a corn on her toe and neglecting direct examination of the large thing, such as a cancer, that was eating her—on the ground that the small thing must be healed to give her courage to study the large. Note that Spencer did not tell her that her feeling about the thunder was of no importance. What he did try to convey was that she should not use her fear of thunder as an excuse for not examining directly the soul salvation matter. We cannot accept his categorical separation of the orders of causes. And for this reason we may believe that a serious examination of the factors involved in one should lead to consideration of the other. Yet Spencer certainly sensed the mental automatism that uses one thing as a defense against the other. In a dim way he sensed that the fear of thunder may be a sign pointing to needed healing at another level, if rightly understood.

Today we know one fact about healing, in general and comprehensive form, that Spencer did not know in this way. He recognized it in limited form, but so limited that the result is from our point of view distortion. The general principle may be stated thus: Where impairment is due to negative feelings, whatever their nature, healing begins by acknowledgment, acceptance, understanding, and assimilation of those feelings, and not through encouraging bright thoughts, verbal encouragement of the right feelings, and the like. The special form of this principle understood by Spencer was that, when a person had religious or doctrinal problems or questions, he should be encouraged to state them rather than keep them to himself. This, then, enabled Spencer to accept the integrity of a person holding such views, but to proceed at once to demonstration of the falsity within them. The failure to generalize on the specific form of the principle is something Spencer held in common with virtually all Christians until this century. Its discovery is something genuinely new.

Today we believe that genuine acceptance, which is not approval, and undertanding, which is not agreement, of negative feelings will aid the person to assimilate these as facts of his psychic life; and that, having done so, the positive forces and feelings, without which acceptance could not have been achieved, will begin to emerge into the open.[22] This therapeutic doctrine is founded in part upon the phenomenon of repression, as first set forth by Freud, and in part upon experience with recuperative psychic powers of the organism when aided to assimilate and accept what had previously been present and influential but unacceptable. The even more general significance of this principle (loving the unlovable, in traditional terms), theologically speaking, has been stated by Tillich as "acceptance in spite of unacceptability."[23] For purposes of pastoral efforts in healing, what we recognize is that movement away from the negative feeling before it has been assimilated is untherapeutic, even from the religious perspective. This is very much like Jesus' injunction first to become reconciled with your brother and then to take your gift to the altar.[24] What is new is our understanding the specific processes necessary for reconciliation, either within one's self or with others, proceeding through painful processes of assimilation of negative feelings. Otherwise the apparent healing that results is symptomatic and hence not holistic.

Taken in conjunction with the field theory model of the organism, the full implications of this negative feelings principle would come close to spelling out the one great new discovery in healing since Spencer's day, apart from the specific and differentiated discoveries in medicine and the related arts and sciences. For these implications are tremendous. Had Spencer believed that something in the field (for example, grief), dealt with in a certain way, would lead toward consideration of more ultimate dimensions, he would have proceeded somewhat differently. His timing would often have been changed. He would have given religious arguments less often and at somewhat different places.

On the other hand, as we have seen, Spencer may suggest a corrective to us. We may stop too soon, as if it were not our task, as it was Spencer's, to help the person move beneath the problem area to its religious dimension. Our acceptance of negative feelings, he may remind us, is not to be a mere passive business of playing silver screen; to the extent that we do this, it is because we believe finally that it is the best way to aid the operations of the Holy Spirit. Above all, Spencer points us to healing as needed change of fundamental direction. If we believe that he identified prematurely and overconfidently the underlying processes of healing and impairment (or salvation and sin), we may nevertheless be profitably reminded that the general picture is true and correct, and should never be wholly out of our minds. To Spencer any day might be judgment day. And so it may. If we interpret the signs differently from Spencer, we nevertheless do well to be as alert to the emergence of healing and as assiduous about dealing with it as was he.

Even an introductory or prefatory chapter on the healing aspect of the shepherding perspective cannot be concluded without brief reference to the modes of pastoral ministry today in which healing is dominant.[25] A great change in the institutionalization of many forms of healing in our society has brought consequent contextual changes in the exercise of the healing aspects of ministry. Even in Spencer's day, just a century ago, hospitals were small, few, and for the poor. We are now rapidly approaching the point where anything regarded as illness in the ordinary connotation is treatable in a hospital.

For a time hospitals and related institutions, although the church was vitally involved in their development, did not take cognizance of the new contextual problem thus presented to the ministry of shepherding. In more recent years there has been a tremendous development of chaplaincy service, of pastors especially set aside to bring ministry to those temporarily or permanently away from the usual ministrations of the local church and its pastor. This contextual change has compelled new work and thought about the nature of the healing ministry. Working side by side with others, each interested in healing the whole man but working with differentiated equipment, the pastor has had to develop a differentiated method for his own task and at the same time to keep in sight that he is present to restore a wholeness that had been impaired by his absence from the healing team. He cannot do this by a categorical parallelism, whether of soul and body or of religion and secularism. For that ministry which begins with the most secular content may turn out to have the most religious significance, and that which proceeds from considering the body may prove decisively important for the soul. This task of definition is not new, but its complexities are greater than ever before. This is not, however, a disadvantage but a challenge; for it is compelling a way of rethinking the shepherding function that is proving fruitful with those not only in hospitals but in the shepherding ministry in general. Indeed, much of the stimulus to our study of shepherding and healing has come from just this circumstance.

Summary

In concluding this chapter, let us remind ourselves of its purpose. That was to give preliminary consideration to the healing aspect of the shepherding perspective upon all the operations of the pastor and the church, to the end that a way might be seen, although not spelled out in detail, for the construction of a pastoral theology in its healing dimensions. And since a part of our current problem is a lack of emotional identification with the past ministry of shepherding, we had the added historical problem of examining instances of such past ministry to test out the possible grounds for such identification.

Accordingly I began with a consideration of the meaning of healing. It was defined as the restoration of functional wholeness that has been impaired as to direction and/or schedule. As to that for which healing is needed, I retained that aspect of "disease" that indicates the direction and movement of certain inexorable (if not redirected) processes disrupting functional wholeness. I retained that aspect of "illness" that attempts to link such processes with the subjective experience of impairment. I rejected the primitive conceptions of sin, but indicated that, more adequately understood, sin is the most ultimate and important and difficult condition from which healing is required. The efficient causes of impairment were classified under the headings of defect, invasion, distortion, and decision. I suggested that attention to differentiated knowledge is essential to healing, but that when this knowledge is brought to a new level of unity, the scope of healing greatly increases. We saw healing and the impairment from which it emerges in a continuum. From the Christian point of view we saw the religious dimension of healing as focal, but all healing as a part of the field.

We turned then to Ichabod Spencer in order to see how a minister of the past approached healing. We examined one of his pastoral efforts in detail and others more briefly. We were impressed that there was unity in Spencer's own attitude, that the dominance of a healing perspective came not from a change in his attitude toward the person but from his perception of the nature of the need within the situation. We saw him deal with a parishioner on the assumption that the need for healing was not dominant, and later discover that it had been. From the point of view of attitude, however, we saw no pastoral chameleonism.

We saw in Spencer also a cutting through of everything felt to be superficial or merely symptomatic, in order to reach that which was believed to be causal or basic, even though we criticized the form and method of this. We noted too that Spencer saw healing in its most basic sense as a change in life direction, that the depth and elusiveness of this were great, and the variety of its appearances many. It is our conviction that these and related things in Spencer give very considerable ground for our emotional identification with him. If we had had data of this order from an Anglican, a Lutheran, or a Baptist, there would of course have been differences from Calvinistic pietist Spencer. But especially on the points where we have found common ground with Spencer and been suitably warned by him, the differences would have been slight.

On the other hand, we have found things in Spencer we cannot possibly accept. We cannot agree with his categorical separation of soul and body, religion and culture. He did not understand in general form either the dynamics or the therapy of negative feelings. While rightly testifying to the depth of both sin and salvation, impairment and healing, we regard him as having made a premature or overconfident identification of their nature.

Yet we saw too that Spencer had both courage and sensitivity, persistence and yet restraint, confidence and yet humility, solemnity but not humorlessness. He was dedicated but without unctuousness. In our assessment of his potential contributions to us, we cannot ignore such personal characteristics. They are the stuff of pastoral character in any age.

We have noted briefly the social changes that have brought demands

114

of a new complexity to the modern ministry in its healing aspects. In none of this have I professed to deal with all the significant aspects. To do so would require an entire book. The purpose here has been more modest, more prefatory, and more structural in nature, such that the many studies now being made of healing aspects of the ministry, when their data are in, will find their place in a systematic context and will bear upon the construction of a pastoral theology.

Two brief questions remain. First, I have dealt here mainly with one-to-one operations, and the reader must be warned that this choice does not mean that there is no healing in sermons, in religious education, in group work, and the like. For a complete study of pastoral operations from the healing aspect of the shepherding perspective, all these and others must be examined. We may defend our choice on the grounds not of exhaustiveness but of relative analytical simplicity. And especially where healing is concerned, this has reminded us forcibly of individuality, of the superiority, as Spencer put it, of a message to a proclamation.

Second, I proposed at the beginning to discuss the healing aspect of the shepherding perspective so as to move toward a pastoral theology. The reader may ask where the pastoral theology is. The answer is that I have already done so with some small degree of system but not to the extent desired or needed. Among others I have attempted to present answers to questions like these: What is the relation between sin and illness? In what sense is salvation a form of healing? From the point of view of the Christian faith is it only sin from which we require healing or something else as well? Whether the reader has liked or disliked the answers given to these and related questions, some answers have been suggested. And it is just such material, when emerging out of the examination of pastoral operations, to which initially theological questions have been brought, that constitutes the content of pastoral theology. The system that begins to emerge is not the same as that of doctrinal theology, although it is in no necessary contradiction to it and indeed ought to aid and support and correct it. But by no other method of theological examination is it possible to get answers to questions of this order. Above all else, what I have sought to demonstrate is the *method* by which a systematic pastoral theology can be constructed.

CHAPTER 7

Sustaining

BY "SUSTAINING" IS MEANT THAT ASPECT OF THE SHEPHERDING PER-
spective that emphasizes "standing by." Unlike healing, in which the
total situation is capable of change, sustaining relates to those situations
that as total situations cannot be changed or at least cannot be changed
at this time. The simplest illustration is bereavement, in which no
amount of change in attitude can bring back the total situation in the
form of restoration of the deceased person. Sustaining is the ministry of
support and encouragement through standing by when what had been a
whole has been broken or impaired and is incapable of total situational
restoration, or at least not now.

We must include the "not now" phrase for important reasons. In the
instance of bereavement it is impossible for the whole situation to be
reconstructed through the return of the deceased. A young person may
have had a serious lover's quarrel, the response to which is like bereavement, so that he is for the time being incapable of being healed. Conceivably the breach may be healed in time. But even if this should be
both possible and desirable, the ministry in the time of crisis may have to
be sustaining in the same basic sense as in bereavement. Whether healing
or reconciliation should eventually be possible, if reconciliation were desirable, might depend upon whether sustenance had been given when
needed.

As the noun form of the word implies, "sustenance" is that which
keeps one alive. When one is healthy and hungry, he does not ordinarily
refer to the approaching gastronomic performance as "sustenance." He
anticipates savory tastes. But if something happens to remove all interest
in the taste and smell and feeling of food, then anything from sirloin
steak to canned baby food would be the same to him. His mind would
be elsewhere. Sustenance might even have to be forced upon him, even

116

though his swallowing and digesting apparatus might have none of its parts incapable of operation. This is just what happens literally in the case of some mentally ill people in a stuporous or withdrawn state.

As we have already noted, the basic attitude of the pastor does not differ from one situation to another. But the dominant perspective with which he approaches a situation and the aspect of that perspective that he places at the forefront depends upon the nature of the situation. If "aspect of a perspective" seems a confusing notion, think of a perspective by analogy with a beam of light going through a prism and then lighting up this or that object. The beam is all one; but for clearest vision of an object of this color or that, one may move the beam toward either the red or the blue ends of the spectrum. When the situation is such that, at least for the time being, change is not possible, one stands by or makes sustenance available. The situation is one of sustaining, not because the pastor decides here not to aid healing, but because, so far as his knowledge and skills are concerned, healing does not seem possible, at least not now.

Broadly speaking, the ministry of sustaining becomes dominant in two types of situations: when there is shock or loss and when some irreversible process of impairing or degenerating is at work. Shock and loss are illustrated by bereavement or by a lovers' separation. The process of impairment that cannot be reversed is illustrated by an inoperable cancer, by the slow loss of vision, or by arterial degeneration affecting mental functions. In neither type of situation is it possible, at least not now, to restore the previous actual situation. Nor is it possible to change the direction of the impairing process. It is as if the person in such a situation stood facing the turbulent ocean. Either he is terrified (in case of shock) because he had previously been elsewhere, or the ground on which he stands is gradually being eaten away by the force of the surf (in the case of degeneration). He who is shocked may eventually (but not now) build a dike, or move to the mountains, or buy a boat; but in some situations he and his friends may simply have to stay there and do nothing. Where irreversible impairing is going on, the man's friends may protect him from spray or may delay the erosion of the ground on which he stands; but building a dike, so to speak, is impossible. And this analogical ocean is not the fountain of youth.

Like the ministry of healing, that of sustaining is not confined in the intention and availability of the pastor and church to those who are officially of the faith. It is offered to any who need and want *this service,* whether they want the whole faith or not. Or so goes the goal and intention, whatever the deficiencies in its execution. Whether the cup of cold water heals and restores him whose sole problem is thirst or merely soothes the one with a rising fever, the cup is offered to all even if they are unprepared also to eat the bread and drink the wine.

Comfort and Sustaining

We can now see why there is only a small change from the traditional ministry of "comfort" to our ministry of "sustaining." For our purpose in sustaining is to "enhearten," to help the person find courage with which his situation may be confronted. Had "comfort" not so radically changed its meaning in common speech, we might refer to it instead of to "sustaining."

Yet there is one connotation of "comfort," even in its original sense, of which we need to be wary. This is well illustrated in the "letters of consolation," which established their pattern in the pre-Christian era, as McNeill has shown, which were given Christian content in the early church, and which flowered in the relatively early days of Protestantism. Such a letter, written to one who was grieving, for example, did stand by and attempt to indicate the comforting character of one's presence beside the sufferer. But the letter tried also to do much more. It detailed the consolations, whether in crude or subtle form. The departed one might be pictured as blessed in heaven or as simply safe in the hands of a loving God. The sufferer might be exhorted to attend to the responsibilities of life, or he might be told that this too shall pass. Crude or subtle, the timing was wrong. When in the crisis period, what comforts is not consolation but silent companionship. Later on, the crisis past or assimilated and emotion down, consolation may be thoroughly relevant. To try to do it all at once is to be insensitive to the pressing character of the immediate need. One cannot imagine the good Samaritan, while pouring oil on the wounds, indicating to the victim of the attack that his sojourn in a hospital would help to strengthen his character or to heal the breach between Jews and Samaritans. Such things may be true, but at this time they becloud what is needed.

The goal of sustaining is certainly to comfort and enhearten. But this does not mean that the road to a result of enheartening and comforting is through words and actions that are about enheartening and comforting. The reason we can think of the functional goal of enheartening is because we are not in our own person suffering in the same way as the other. Not preoccupied to the extent he is, our view can be longer and broader, perhaps even deeper. But his situation is precisely such that he cannot at this time attain such a broad perspective. If we attempt to have him do so, we shall interfere with the very processes that will eventually help him to such an end. The surgeon does not try to teach his patient how to use an artificial limb until the wound has healed.

The trouble with comfort is, then, that it may become so preoccupied with the functional goal of enheartening that it foreshortens the steps necessary to move toward that goal and thus interferes with the very processes by which the goal could be approached. "Sustaining" is a more neutral term and applies equally well to various stages of the move toward the goal of "enheartening." It is, therefore, superior for our purposes.

There is, however, one possible poor connotation of "sustaining" that should be noted in order to be eliminated. This is the notion that the efficacy of sustenance lies wholly in the sustainer, that all the strength lies with the shepherd and none with the sheep, that one who has gives to one who has not. This implication becomes even sharper if we use the word "supportive."

Such a connotation is misleading as to the actual nature of the situation. Characterologically speaking, the sustainer may be no whit stronger than the sufferer. If he were in the same situation, he might be far weaker. Besides, in so far as he succeeds in sustaining, it is not by giving something like strength, but by aiding the sufferer to draw upon the resources of strength that are potentially available to him. The function is "obstetrical" rather than "presentational." In our use of "sustaining" this must be kept in mind, or the deficiencies of the metaphor will render it useless.

Methods of Sustaining

When we ask how sustaining is actually accomplished, many of our best insights now come from study of ministry to the sick, the dying, and the bereaved.[1] We shall examine briefly such a situation. A young man of twenty-five, whom we shall call George, had got a serious and continuing but not fatal illness in his late teens. Its handling was a difficult business and required both care and perseverance on George's part. Over a period of years he had been moving toward functional wholeness. Although some handicap remained, he had planned his education and his

119

life in the light of it. He had become engaged to be married and had just embarked upon what promised to be a successful occupational life.

What appeared to be a small complication brought George to the hospital for a checkup. There the physicians found that the original condition had recurred and in a form less easy of access. With much time and effort on George's part and the physicians' something could be done, George could live for an indefinite period, but the remaining functional handicaps would be much greater than before. The planned career would be out and probably the marriage.

When George was first seen by the pastor who was working as a student chaplain in the hospital, he had been admitted only a day or two before, tests were still in process, and he was confidently expecting that the small complication would be quickly repaired. The first call was brief. The chaplain gave a brief explanation of his interest, and George told a little of his history and expressed appreciation to the pastor for calling on him. The pastor said he would return.

When he returned on the following day, the physicians had told George that the complication might not be simple and rapidly repaired, but the full extent of it was still unknown to them. Following is the crucial part of this second call.

GEORGE: It looks as if I might have to stay here a little longer than I had figured on. I hate to have my mother use her money for this, although I guess she can help me all right if it doesn't take too long.

PASTOR: It's a bit of a setback to you, I gather.

GEORGE: Yes, I guess it is. But I'm not really worried. They said they would know more tomorrow. But even if it takes longer than I had planned, I guess I can take it all right.

PASTOR: It isn't easy but can be managed?

GEORGE: Sure. I've had a long climb of it, and I certainly ought to know how to handle it by this time.

When the pastor made his call late the following day, the physicians had already talked with George. They had explained the nature of the condition they found, indicated to him that he could live and retain some functions, but that even greater patience and effort on his part would be needed than before. When the pastor entered, the following took place.

PASTOR: (George's eyes are closed, but he is obviously not asleep.) It's Chaplain Ray, George.

GEORGE: Oh! (*He seems exhausted.*)

PASTOR: I gather you've had some bad news?

GEORGE: (*Begins quietly but emotion mounts as he talks.*) Yeah. Bad news is right. My G—, it's . . . it's . . . (*He sobs silently.*)

PASTOR: Take it easy, George. I'll just sit beside you.

GEORGE: (*After two or three minutes*) They tell me I've got to do it all over again—only worse.

PASTOR: That really hurts.

GEORGE: (*Bitterness creeping into his voice*) They say I'll live. . . . But that won't be living!

After a little time George's bitterness became more sharply focused. He reviewed his struggle previously, this time not in the easy conversational way of recounting past history as he had done on the first call. He was slow and halting, alternating bitter outbursts with silent tears and expressions of solicitude for his mother. His occupation would now be ruined, and his fiancée—What could he do about her? As in the preceding excerpts, the attempt of the pastor was to respond more to the negative feelings of George's total outlook and predicament than to this or that segment. The whole call took more than a half hour. At its close the pastor said he would return and then added, "I'm going to offer a little prayer, George." He prayed:

PASTOR: O Lord, when our days are dark and our affliction is very great, let us know that thou understandest our anxiety of spirit and our loss of hope. Let us know that thou art with us, that it is thy hand that upholds and sustains us. Even when we do not see and feel thy light, let us know that thou art by our side. Through Jesus Christ our Lord. Amen.

In the subsequent ministry to George no miracle was achieved, medical or religious. But George's bitterness and his anxiety were expressed, and through this expression in a context of understanding George was able to assimilate or domesticate some of the feelings. He was able to do some working through of his feelings toward his mother, on whom he would now again be dependent just when he had been counting on exercising a long-sought independence. About job and fiancée the going was slower. When George left the hospital, problems of attitude were still severe. Yet the bitterness did not stand corruscatingly alone. Difficult and long as George knew the trials would be, he was ready to face them with at least 51 per cent of himself. When last heard of, he was still engaged in the heartbreaking task of recovering what could be recovered and adjusting to what could not.

We may regard this as mainly a ministry of sustaining. George could not be healed in the sense that the status quo ante could be restored. In addition, since George had already struggled for years, he knew poignantly just what was in store for him, except that it would be worse. It would be more severe, and its functional end would be far more restricted. He felt like a man who has sweated through a dank and narrow cavern toward the light; and just when the exit is reached, he begins to fall into another cavern longer, danker, and narrower than the first and with virtually no light visible.

In such situations it is human for us to place ourselves empathically in the position of the sufferer, perhaps as a result to be temporarily speechless, but then to ask ourselves, "What can I say?" Human as it is, this question reflects more of our own empathic suffering than it does attempted sustaining of the sufferer. In one sense, sometimes a literal one, there simply is nothing we can say at such a time. The smaller the rays of light in the gloomy sky, the more tempted we are to attend to them than to the clouds. All this is human, but at this time it is mistaken.

What this able student pastor attempted to do was to stand by. Right then what should have had attention was the "sufferings of this present time" and not any possible form of "glory which shall be revealed." No doubt there is more than one detailed method for doing this. In this instance Pastor Ray did it by explicit expression of his understanding of the depth of negative feeling that George was expressing. But beneath the details of method were two things: first, the pastor's concern for George that was not promiscuously mixed with his own feelings about how he would feel in a similar situation; and second, the implicit reassurance given through the pastor's readiness to deal with negative feelings rather than attempt to brush through them as if they were mere preliminaries. If George was helped significantly toward sustaining by this contact, it was through the combination of these factors in Pastor Ray. Concern was not enough. Anyone short of a monster would feel concern for George in this situation. But the concern for George and the concern for oneself projected imaginatively into George's situation are not the same. Without concern of course the acceptance of negative feelings might be experienced as indifference or coldness. In combination these two are both the testimonies to hope and the channel through which it may be delivered.

We may note also that Pastor Ray's approach might have been put to even more severe trials if George had asked him, as many people do, "Don't you think I can go back to this job some day? Don't you think it would be all right for me to get married anyhow? Don't you think I should be content to be dependent on my mother?" When the sky is so black, one is tempted to paint in a silver lining or two, evanescent as he may know the paint to be. But the results are disastrous. Not clouds but only pictures of clouds will take paint. And by the act of painting, one is testifying to his own feeling of hopelessness precisely when his underlying and deep confidence can best be expressed through the renunciation of fantasy.

I have emphasized what comes chronologically first in the ministry of sustaining. This is partly because without it the subsequent stages will be built on sand. It is this stage in the sustaining process that is most often violated and hence requires our most careful attention. But there are later stages of sustaining as well. There is a "glory which shall be revealed" as well as the "sufferings of this present time." To these stages the explicit communication of the faith through Word or sacrament may indeed be relevant. But until there has been a pastoral descent into hell, the pastoral ascent will not be to a Christian heaven.

In Europe, especially during the Hitler regime, a great deal of the ministry of pastors and churches was sustaining in character. This was, and still is, difficult for us in the United States to feel in any depth. We are a "healing" country. Unless proved otherwise, everything can be repaired. Under a Hitler shadow it was quite otherwise. Thus it is not only conditions in individuals that compel a ministry of sustaining but also larger social situations.

Recalling that part of the current problem in pastoral theology is in our lack of emotional identification with our own pastoral history, we shall examine Ichabod Spencer's sketches in order to understand his ministry of sustaining, as we did with his ministry of healing.

One of the interesting stories about Spencer's ministry of sustaining was called by him "The Stormy Night: or, Perseverance." [2] By "perseverance" he was referring to his parishioner not to himself. And unlike most of his sketches, this one was presented mainly in indirect discourse. As we shall see, it was Spencer's sustaining that finally helped; but his aim throughout was for healing, and even when the healing had been successfully accomplished, Spencer undervalued what he had done to sustain during the dark days.

Spencer plainly had a high regard for Mrs. E., who lived about a half mile from his residence. He called on her one day, and her "seriousness" about religion began shortly afterward. She had then decided, although she told Spencer this only later, that she would continue to seek the Lord until she had found him. During the first conversation Spencer had said to her, "*I know*, Mrs. E., that you will be saved, if you seek God with all your heart."

Almost every Sunday evening for nearly two years Mrs. E. came to Spencer's house to talk with him about her salvation. She was during this entire period persevering in seeking the Lord but had no peace. One cold winter Sunday evening, "the wind blowing violently, the snow drifting into the path, in places more than two feet in depth," Mrs. E. walked alone to Spencer's house. When Spencer opened the door to admit her, he was quite surprised to see her and said, "Why, Mrs. E.! are you here on such a night?" This, he later found out, struck Mrs. E. a blow. Long afterward she told him:

It stumbled me. I did not know what to make of it. You had invited us there, and I thought you would be expecting me. I thought you ought not to be *surprised* to see me there, if sinners were in danger of the everlasting wrath of God and might escape it, as you had preached that day. It was a long time before I could get over that stumbling-block. I thought, if you had *believed* what you preached and felt about it as I did, you would *expect* to see me. I know it was a stormy night and I was afraid; but I kept thinking as I went, that the day of judgment would bring a worse storm.

On that night, however, Spencer was unaware of Mrs. E.'s attitude. In a parenthesis, when telling how deep the snow was, he wrote, "As I found on accompanying her home." The fact that he had walked the half mile to Mrs. E.'s house and back to his own was not to Spencer even a matter worth recording. And his human and masculine instincts, feeling a woman ought not to be out alone on such a night, had for a time confused Mrs. E.

But if Spencer's chivalrous impulses on the stormy night worked against the Holy Spirit, something else worked in its favor. Mrs. E.'s husband was an "irreligious man." He too did not like to see his wife wading through two feet of snow. But when his wife braved the elements to see Spencer, "he thought there must be *something* about sin and religion which he did not know anything about." A little later Mr. E. became an anxious inquirer.

For months after the stormy night Mrs. E.'s "deep anxiety" continued. As Spencer saw her, she was truly an anxious inquirer. "Again and again, I aimed with all possible carefulness to tell her all the truths of the gospel, and to discover what error, sin or temptation, kept her from repentance and peace with God." She seemed stuck at the point of anxious inquiring. "It was a most painful and perplexing thing to discharge my pastoral duty to this woman." This was especially so because "she was frank, she concealed nothing, she told me all her heart, she was desirous of being interrogated." Spencer was torn up.

He wrote:

At one time I was on the point of telling her that I had nothing more to say to her, and she need not come to me again. But I could not do it. She was so miserable, so sincere, so determined, docile, and confiding, that it was impossible for me to cast her off.

As we have seen previously, if Spencer had thought he detected the slightest lack of "determination" or "seriousness" in her, he would have had no hesitation in "casting her off," so that the Holy Spirit might increase her anxiety to the point where she would cast all on Christ. But he did not so interpret this situation, and "I afterwards rejoiced that I had not done it."

The situation was made all the more poignant because during this long period Mrs. E.'s husband, her sister, and some of her friends came to Christ. But Mrs. E. herself "did not advance, and she did not go back." Spencer may have been puzzled, but he was not inactive.

A hundred times I cautioned her most solemnly against putting any trust in her perseverance. . . . Time after time, the Bible in my hand, and she in tears before me, as a minister of God, and on his authority, I offered her a free salvation, and demanded her heart's faith, and instant submission to divine authority and unbounded love. Her mind, her conscience, her heart, I besieged with all the kindness of Christ.

In fact, wrote Spencer,

I have never spent half as much time with any other awakened sinner, or uttered to any other one half as many threatenings and promises of God, or kneeled with any other half as many times in prayer.

None of this, however, brought her peace.

And now in Spencer's account comes the dénouement of the story, very brief, thrown in almost casually. Referring to all his efforts with Mrs. E.,

But so far as I know, she never received any benefit from it all, unless that was a benefit which she one day suggested to me long afterwards, when she said, "If you had been discouraged with me, I should have been discouraged— and should have given up trying to be saved."

From our point of view Spencer's lack of emphasis on this last statement is truly astonishing. If he had ever over the long months seemed to be discouraged about her, as he seemed to be in part on the stormy night, she would have given up and moved backward, said Mrs. E. But his belief in her, his lack of discouragement, was what enabled her to hang on until she could move ahead. Since Spencer titled the story "perseverance," referring to Mrs. E., it immediately strikes us that the perseveration was in Spencer. It was *his* holding on, standing by, and refusal to be discouraged that finally empowered her. But Spencer himself did not put it this way.

When this seems plain to us, why did Spencer not see it thus? Part of the answer is found in his attitude toward persevering. "A hundred times" he had warned Mrs. E. to put no "trust in her perseverance," for this could be attempting to find salvation by works. If he should regard perseverance in himself as the virtue that eventually brought healing to Mrs. E., he would be in the same danger of regarding his function as producing salvation by the works of perseverance. We can see this motive; but we can also see that, in hewing close to its line, Spencer failed to understand the function his own pastoral perseverance had performed.

There is, however, another reason why he did not rightly evaluate his own encouragement or sustaining of Mrs. E. Remember that Spencer, in the entire period of his dealing with her as an anxious inquirer, uttered more of the "threatenings and promises of God" than he had with any other person. Picture the situation as Spencer with Bible in hand and Mrs. E. with tears in her eyes. Almost from the beginning Spencer was satisfied that Mrs. E. had a "full conviction of all the great doctrines of the Bible," and therefore his talk was not mainly instructional. Suppose that we now had Spencer before us and were discussing his work with

Mrs. E. and that we said to him, "Dr. Spencer, it seems to us that it made little difference *what* you said to Mrs. E. or that you said anything at all. As she herself finally told you, it was your refusal to become discouraged about her that proved to be crucially important. Is it not true, therefore, that the midwife of her salvation was your standing by with her and not your discussion of the Bible or anything else?" Perhaps Spencer's answer would have been problematical. But the chances are he would have fended off the implications of our question. For if the same result, encouraging and sustaining Mrs. E. until the light broke through, could have been attained by listening to her and saying scarcely a word, Spencer would have felt ill at ease and derelict to his duty. Yet once the biblical message had made Mrs. E. a true anxious inquirer, what Spencer said thereafter had by his own admission no observable effect upon her final healing, which was brought about instead by the steady sustaining itself. The sustaining cannot be identified with particular words or acts.

Let us suppose that Spencer had been able to sit and listen to Mrs. E. hour after hour and to say only, "I am convinced that your anxiety and your inquiring are genuine. I believe that the Holy Spirit is working truly in you and that, although your suffering is now deep and genuine and difficult, he will lead you through. And I believe in this so profoundly that I am standing by." As we see it, not only might the same result have been achieved, but it might have come sooner. For we suspect that part of the effect of Spencer's much speaking was to retard the expression and assimilation of Mrs. E.'s own tortuous feelings.

But Spencer, while by no means incapable of silence or of listening, could not have done this. In this respect he was like any workman identifying himself with his tools. As the mechanic feels at home with a wrench and screw driver in his hand, so Spencer felt at home with the Bible in his hand and the words of salvation on his lips. Yet the fact is that in religion as in mechanics the tools that are most valuable are not always those that are most palpable or obvious. After examining the motor of an automobile, the mechanic may say, "Don't adjust that screw either way. She's new, that's all. Just keep plenty of oil in her and keep her running until she wears in." He has done nothing of an obviously active nature. He has not touched the obvious tools such as the screw driver. He may not "feel" that he has as a mechanic "done" anything. Yet granted the accuracy of his diagnosis, what he has done is vitally important. The automobile's owner can now keep plenty of oil in it and run it without fearing that the odd noise he hears is going to tear it apart.

There are deficiencies in our analogy with the mechanic. But even in so simple a realm as this we can see that a workman's identification with obvious tools may impede his understanding of what he is actually doing. This is our contention in relation to Spencer. As a pastoral workman he so identified himself with the Bible in hand and the Word on his lips that he failed to see the significance of his standing by. That the process by which the message of the Bible and the healing of the Word would be received and assimilated by Mrs. E. might have little or nothing to do with what Spencer would say about it, is a hypothesis we doubt Spencer could have entertained. He reported accurately what did take place, but for these reasons was unable accurately to evaluate it.

With Mrs. E., Spencer performed a true ministry of sustaining during the long period when "she did not advance, and she did not go back." Hers was not, it proved, the type of situation in which sustaining can never be followed by healing, as some sustaining is. But during this period healing proved not to be possible. Spencer's preoccupation was with the healing, and accordingly he minimized the dynamic effect of the sustaining when seen either in its own right or as the security out of which healing eventually emerged.

Faith and Doubt in Sustaining

In quite another form Spencer's ministry of sustaining is shown in a brief but moving sketch of a woman reported to be dying.[3] Mrs. M. was a member of Spencer's church and a good Christian. Word came to Spencer "in great haste" while he was speaking at an evening service. He "closed the service, as soon as I could," and went to Mrs. M.'s house. When he reached her room, "I found it filled with her friends, who had gathered around her to see her die." Mrs. M. "was bolstered up in her bed, gasping for breath, almost suffocated by the asthma; and the whole bed shook, by a palpitation of her heart, which seemed to be shaking her to pieces."

SPENCER: Mrs. M., you seem to be very sick?

MRS. M.: Yes, I am dying.

SPENCER: And are you ready to die?

MRS. M.: (*Speaking with great difficulty*) Sir, God knows—I have taken him—at his word—and—I am not afraid—to die.

Spencer wrote, "It was a new definition of faith. . . . It struck me in an instant, as a triumph of faith." Spencer then prayed "some four minutes" and "recited to her some passages of God's word," and was about to leave her when she said:

MRS. M.: I wanted to tell you—that I can—trust—in God—while—I am dying.—You have—often told me—he would not—forsake me.—And now—I find—it true.—I am—at peace.—I die—willingly—and happy.

As a matter of fact, Mrs. M. did not die. Spencer told the story mainly because "that expression of her faith has been of great benefit to me." By this he meant faith as, "I have taken him at his word." The last idea Spencer's mind would have entertained was the notion that his call may have been crucial to Mrs. M.'s recovery. Of course we have no medical report on Mrs. M. But we do know from contemporary pastoral experience that such a call in such a situation *could* have been crucial even from the medical point of view.

Consider the nature of the situation. Mrs. M. apparently has the deepest kind of sustaining faith. She believes herself to be dying, as do her friends, who are hardly contributing to her health by filling the room and bolstering her up in bed. But if she has this faith, why does Spencer do *anything?* Why does he pray for four minutes and recite some passages of Scripture? Because this is confirmatory, supportive of her faith— because he, representing both God and the whole company of the faithful, thereby demonstrates a standing by. Because it is in just such an act that sustaining lies, in a reminding and enheartening renewal of actual relationships.

But why, we may persist, is such reminding carried out? If her faith is in fact deep and genuine, and if she herself gives more succinct and poignant expression to it than any pastor can do, why does Mrs. M. have to express it and more than once? The answer would seem to lie in the interconnected and dialectical relation that faith bears to doubt. Let us assume, as Spencer did, that Mrs. M.'s faith is of the deepest and most genuine kind, that it is threatened by doubt in no serious or observable way. Still Mrs. M. now confronts a situation she has not faced before, the conviction of approaching death. The faith she has is more deeply tried than ever before. Since that faith is genuine, she has access to its depths, on which she had not had to call before. But our use of the word "tried" shows that, in reaching toward the deeper level of faith,

129

she was reaching *through* something else. Faith had always proved capable of trust before—Would it do so now? The very question shows the presence of something else in addition to faith.

Granted the depth and genuineness of Mrs. M.'s faith, then, a new level of doubt has been cut through and a new depth of faith touched. But until something else happens, that new depth has only been touched, not fully received or assimilated. Her saying to Spencer, "I have taken him at his word," seals the new depth of faith. Her statement to him is itself a vital and dynamic part of her realization of the new depth of faith. That is, it is both a testimony to a new depth of realization in her and an act of creative "incarnation" of that new depth. The ultimate reasons for this lie in the twin facts of our being symbol-using creatures and having our very selves emerge only through social interaction. If Mrs. M. had not said this, but had only thought it, it would have been less real and less deep.

It is noteworthy also that Mrs. M. made her statement to Spencer. Perhaps she had said the same words to her friends who filled the room. But Spencer represented in a focal and central way both God and the company of the faithful, in a way the friends did not. So the new depth of faith became more deeply incarnated when expressed to Spencer.

In the light of this analysis we can see better the function performed by Spencer's reading from the Bible and his four minutes of praying. These showed that *he* accepted the new depth of faith. What had been real to Mrs. M. became more real. And after Spencer had spoken, Mrs. M. told him the same thing again. The effect, which may be thought of almost as a "mobilization" of faith, was to confirm the reality of faith's new depth. This, we know, may have a healing effect even upon the organic processes of the body.

We are accustomed to think of doubt in quite a different way from the story of Mrs. M., as the explicit statement of, "I don't believe it," or "I can't believe it," or "Help thou mine unbelief." But the fact is that doubt is also the matrix in which any new level of faith is received or achieved. In itself it is not an enemy. It becomes an enemy under two conditions: when it so dominates that the desire for faith is repressed or blotted wholly from awareness; and when, to avoid the steady struggle with it, it is itself wholly repressed in the name of faith. There is no faith that is not moving through doubt and no doubt that is not linked with yearning for faith, as "I believe; help thou mine unbelief."

With Mrs. M., Spencer performed a ministry of sustaining that may have been more crucial for her healing, even in the physical sense, than he realized. He did not, however, have the equipment to analyze the psychic processes involved that is now available to us.

Another form of Spencer's sustaining is shown in his ministry to Mary Ann.[4]

She was "one of the most distressing instances of religious darkness and despondency" that Spencer had ever seen. Although still in her late teens, she had a "seated pulmonary affection" and had no hope of recovery. She turned out to be correct about the imminence of death. Mary Ann "had no hope in God" for her salvation, although she had carefully studied the Bible and given much attention to religious matters. She anticipated her death "with an indescribable anguish," as the "commencement of eternal woe."

At first in dealing with her, Spencer "felt no peculiar discouragement, on account of her religious depression." He felt she was a true anxious inquirer; and although she might shortly die, she would accept God's promise of salvation. But week after week "she continued in the same despondency." She "had not a single gleam of light." In fact, "her soul was dark as a double midnight, and seemed plunged into an ocean of horrors." Spencer was deeply touched. "No one, I am sure, could have listened to her dreadful wailings, without feeling a sympathy with her, which would have wrung the heart with anguish." Spencer visited Mary Ann often and talked to her as well as listened to her. Ever the honest reporter, he wrote, "But I never had any evidence to the last, that anything I ever said to her was the means of any benefit."

Mary Ann seemed to come occasionally to believe she had some love for God. But "at times, when she appeared to me to be coming out of her gloom, and to be standing on the very borders of a light which she could not but see; a single recurring idea about herself would fling her back into all her darkness, and she would weep and wail in despair." One day Spencer had been speaking to her of heaven.

MARY ANN: Others will be in heaven, but I shall be cast out! From the distant region of my doom, I shall behold my companions by the river of life, happy, happy spirits, perhaps I shall hear their song; but no such home for me!

SPENCER: How came they there? They were not saved by their goodness. They were not better than you. Jesus Christ saved them by his blood, and he offers to save you.

131

MARY ANN: He passes me by, sir. He called them, and they obeyed the call in due time; but he does not call me!

SPENCER: He does, my child, He does. He calls you now, "Come unto me."

This continued, but Mary Ann's "only answer was tears and groans." A little later a crucial event occurred.

SPENCER: Mary Ann, what do you want more, to convince you that you are a child of God? What do you expect? If these things do not convince you, what could? What evidence more do you want? Do you want an angel to come down from heaven here to your bedside, to tell you that you are a Christian, and shall go to heaven as soon as you die?

MARY ANN: Oh, yes (in a transport of emotion), that is just what I want—just what I want.

SPENCER: That is just what you cannot have; God is not going to give you any such kind of evidence.

On the unavailability of angelic visitations Spencer expatiated at some length.

Immediately prior to her death Mary Ann sent for Spencer. Almost literally in her last hour "she avowed her perfect trust in Christ" and said, "I am full of peace, I can trust my God. This is enough. I am happy, happy. I die happy." Spencer had to interrupt his last call on Mary Ann to go to church and conduct worship. When he returned to her bedside, Mary Ann said:

I wanted to see you once more, and tell you how happy I am. I have found out that a poor sinner has nothing to do only to believe. I am not afraid of death now. I am willing to die. . . . I wanted to tell you this. I thought I should live long enough to tell you. I thought God would not let me die till I had seen you, and told you of my joy, so as not to have you discouraged when you meet with other persons who have such dark minds as mine was.

Spencer prayed by her bedside, "and in less than five minutes more she was dead."

As in the story of Mrs. M., we can see that Mary Ann's faith was not quite fully realized until she had told it to Spencer and been confirmed by his acceptance of it. But until that point her condition was quite different from that of Mrs. M. She was deeply depressed, felt Christ had rejected her, and would accept no evidence to the contrary short of an angel visitant. Spencer was a bit abrupt about the nonappearing angel, but in all other respects full of patience and gentleness.

In his own evaluation of the case he said:

If this poor girl had died in all her darkness and fears, I should not have despaired of her. Amid all her glooms of guilt, I thought she exhibited proofs of faith. . . . The very point of her anguish consisted in this—namely, that she believed Christ to be a full and free Saviour, and yet could find no evidence in her heart that she trusted in Him. . . . She distrusted herself, but not God. She was afraid to believe that she was a believer. She was so tremblingly afraid of getting wrong, that she dared not think she could possibly be right. On this ground, I was led to believe that Mary Ann was a child of God, long before that memorable light shone on her soul in the hour of death.

In our language what Spencer saw in Mary Ann was a latent faith deeper than the constantly voiced doubt. He expressed criticism of her friends and relatives, including her physician, who believed that Mary Ann's faith began only in the hour of her death. Had it not been for her long-continued wrestle with her doubt, even in the demonic form desiring an angel visitant, her final move to faith would not have been genuine.

With Mary Ann, Spencer not only sustained while "gloom" covered her head, but did so in the confident conviction that the sustaining might be sufficient, even if the final explicit coming to faith should not take place. This shows a greater subtlety of perception in Spencer about the nature of faith and doubt and their interrelationship than we have previously seen in him. To feel no hope might indeed bring anguish, but this was not necessarily the same as to be hopeless in fact. If one was resting on Christ, faith was implicitly present, even though hope seemed nonexistent.

One more sketch of Spencer's is needed to present the full dimensions of his ministry of sustaining. This is called by Spencer "The Dying Universalist." [5] Following his custom when he names the people, we shall call the man Mr. U. Mr. U. was twenty-six, married, and father of one child. His mother was a stanch member of Spencer's church, as was his wife. Mr. U.'s father was a Universalist, and in this Mr. U. had followed him. Spencer had previously attempted to talk with the father, who always managed to disappear when he arrived. Both mother and wife had spoken with Spencer about Mr. U., but he had always been absent also when Spencer called.

133

Spencer reported this entire story with the greatest of reluctance, only, he writes, because "several of my friends have urged the publication." Even after sixteen years, he continued, he could not recall the scene "without the most painful emotions."

One day Mr. U.'s mother sent an urgent request for Spencer to call. Her son had become violently ill, and his family believed he would die, which turned out to be correct. On his arrival Spencer was met by the mother, who "did not wish him to know, that I had come at her request." As Spencer entered Mr. U.'s room, his mother told him Spencer was calling. Mr. U. "cast a sudden look at me, appeared startled, and turned away his face towards the wall, without uttering a word—as if he regarded me with horror."

Spencer then wrote, "I approached him familiarly and kindly, offered him my hand, which he seemed reluctant to take, and feeling his feverish pulse, aimed to soothe him, as much as I could." When Mr. U. became a bit more quiet, Spencer "inquired about his sufferings, and aimed to soothe and encourage him, expressing the hope that he might soon be relieved." In a voice of "intolerable agony" Mr. U. exclaimed, *"Oh! I shall die! I shall die!"*

SPENCER: I hope not by this sickness. I see no reason why you should not get well. And I think the doctor will be able to relieve you in a few hours.

MR. U.: The doctor has done what he could, my time has come! I cannot live! Oh! I shall die!

Mr. U. then covered his face with the bedclothing. Spencer again attempted to soothe him, but Mr. U. continued "still groaning as in agony."

Spencer, "thinking that he might perhaps feel embarrassed at my presence," then moved to another part of the room to converse with the wife and mother. This action "had the desired effect," and Mr. U. soon brought out his face and listened to the conversation. But he avoided looking at Spencer. After a time as Spencer rose to approach him, his mother got there first and asked him if he would not like Dr. Spencer to pray with him.

Instantly, stretching both his hands towards the heavens, he raised himself on his bed, and holding his hands still aloft, as far as he could reach, he uttered the single syllable, "oh!" with a dreadfulness of accent and a prolongation of the sound, which made my blood curdle in my veins.

This was not, said Spencer, "like the action of bodily distress." Then Spencer, "thinking it the best way to induce him to express his feelings," asked:

SPENCER: Has your pain returned?
MR. U.: (*In a tone of horror*) Oh! oh! oh!
SPENCER: Are you in great pain?
MR. U.: (*Groans*).
SPENCER: I am sorry to find you so ill.
MR. U.: (*Groans—a dreadful shriek*).
SPENCER: God is merciful. He is the hearer of prayer; and if you are—
MR. U.: (*Interrupting*) Oh! (*Shrieking*).
SPENCER: (*After the shriek had brought the entire family to the sickroom*) Shall I pray with you?

Spencer and the family knelt in prayer by the bedside, while Mr. U. turned toward the wall and covered his head with bedclothing. Spencer "aimed to pray in such a manner, that he might be soothed and encouraged by the idea of the mercy of God towards sinners, through our Lord Jesus Christ." The prayer was "six or eight minutes," perhaps longer than it should have been, reported Spencer, "had not this exercise appeared to quiet him." After the prayer Mr. U. was silent, then:

MR. U.: It will do no good to pray for me, sir.
SPENCER: (*Waiting for him to say more, but when he failed to do so*) God is the hearer of prayer; he has encouraged us to pray to him; he has not said, that it will do no good to pray.
MR. U.: My day has gone by! It is too late for me!—it is too late!
SPENCER: No, sir; it is *not* too late. If you want God's mercy, you have it. . . .
MR. U.: Mercy! mercy! that is what makes my situation so dreadful! I have despised mercy! I have scoffed at God! I have refused Christ! If God was only *just*, I could bear it. But now the thought of his abused mercy is worst of all! There is *no* mercy for me any longer! For years I have refused Christ! My day has gone by! I am lost! I am lost!
SPENCER: You think wrong, God has not limited his invitations. Christ says, "Come unto me *all* ye that labor and are heavy laden."
MR. U.: My day has gone by!
SPENCER: No; it has *not*: behold *now* is the accepted time—now is the day of salvation.

This continued until Spencer said:

135

SPENCER: God is so rich in mercy, that he pardons sinners at the eleventh hour.

MR. U.: The eleventh hour is past! This is the twelfth hour!

Soon Mr. U.'s father entered the room, telling him, "Why, you need not feel so bad: you have never done any hurt to anybody." Mr. U. turned upon his father with a long and bitter speech that included:

You have been my worst enemy! You have ruined me! You led me to disobey God, and neglect the Bible! You led me into sin when I was only a little boy! You took me off to fish and hunt, Sundays, and stroll around the fields, when mother wanted me to go to church. You told me there was no hell, that all men would be saved. . . . You have done your work! You have been my ruin! . . .

When the father attempted to speak, Mr. U. refused to permit it. Then came perhaps the most blood-curdling incident of all. Mr. U. asked that his young brother, twelve years old, be called in. On his arrival he called the boy to his bedside and, "looking tenderly upon him," adjured him to read the Bible, go to church, not to swear, obey his mother, and beware of his father. The small boy "stood by him weeping, manifestly struggling hard to control his emotions, till entirely overcome he cried aloud in a burst of grief, and rushed out of the room." Mr. U.'s wife and his mother and Spencer had become "subdued to tears." But the father and Mr. U. himself shed no tears. Mr. U.'s voice never faltered.

The doctor came soon and, while he said he had not expected to find Mr. U. in such a bad way, promised he would be better the next day. The next day, when Spencer returned, Mr. U. was far worse. He said, "Prayer comes too late now—the harvest is past!" Spencer remained in his room "for a long time." Apparently Mr. U. was delirious part of the time. After a time Spencer thought the end was approaching and so indicated to Mr. U.'s wife and mother, who called the physician. Upon the latter's arrival Mr. U. was found to be dead.

By any standards this is a gruesome story. Here was a big and robust young man in the throes of fatal illness, convinced that the "harvest is past." From Spencer's point of view the Universalists held that God would save everyone anyhow and thus prevented people from paying attention to the way of salvation. It is doubtful that the Universalists would have understood it in this way. In the literal sense Mr. U. was convinced he was going straight to a hell of fire and brimstone. Spencer was not convinced of this. "It does not belong to us to decide upon the condition of this departed man," he wrote. He was impressed with Mr. U.'s sincerity and no doubt felt, as he did in the case of Mary Ann, that there was much implicit faith here despite the open doubt and bitterness, which were not against God.

From our contemporary point of view we are rather appalled by the family implications of this story. The dying man's solemn warning to his twelve-year-old brother sends chills down our spine; we fear the traumatic effect of this in the boy's future. Behind the immediate scene we can see years of controversy within the home. Mr. U. Senior liked to hunt and fish and stroll, and built up a masculine companionship with his older son. Mrs. U. Senior perhaps talked piously against such amusements, and to the robust son his mother's piety was probably associated with femininity. So we cannot be far wrong in hypothecating a father who fled from an engulfing kind of piety to the woods and streams, and a mother who withdrew all the more into her religion to bolster her against the fact of lack of kinship with her son and husband. Just what all these family emotions may have meant to Spencer, we do not know. His concern was with the salvation of Mr. U. and of the rest of the family, viewed in compartmentalized terms. Incidentally he called on Mr. U. Senior the day after the funeral but made no impression; and so far as Spencer knew, "I never found any reason to believe that he ever became a different man."

To Spencer this whole incident was filled with horror. He failed. The anguish in Mr. U.'s wife and mother was great. In no explicit way did Mr. U. indicate readiness to accept salvation. From Spencer's point of view the one good thing was the lasting impression made upon the twelve-year-old brother. Spencer wholly minimized his ministry in this situation from the point of view of sustaining. Yet we are struck by it.

He was tenderly human throughout. He was "subdued to tears" more than once. He was often silent, never forcing Mr. U. Even the father, who appeared so culpable to Spencer, was treated with respect. And it is not without significance that Mr. U. with all his pain and bitterness was finally able to to tell Spencer precisely how he felt. Had Spencer not conveyed to him some kind of understanding, it is doubtful that he would have been so honest.

In our usual experience, and no doubt in Spencer's, the open expression of a long withheld bitterness, when received with genuine understanding, ordinarily leads through remorse to a new equilibrium. Here the situation was otherwise, as we sometimes find it in our own experience. Just why that was so in this instance, we can only guess. Not improbably, the bitterness that was expressed to Mr. U.'s father extended also to his mother, but that was neither recognized nor faced. Everyone present but Mr. U. Senior himself could have sympathy for the bitterness against him. None could have had it if bitterness had been expressed against Mrs. U. Senior. Yet this may have been present, as we know from our experience. Spencer did not actively encourage the expression of the bitterness, as we should try to do today. Here again the way in which he understood the function of negative feelings may have impeded Mr. U.

The fact is, however, that a "cathartic" theory about negative feelings is always inadequate. It is not enough to get them off one's chest. Every psychotherapist becomes wary of the people who simply go on expressing negative feelings without, so to speak, "repenting" of them and thus demonstrating that other feelings are mobilizing so that they may emerge. The "bridge" is the pastor's or therapist's understanding and acceptance, not mere expression in itself.

As we look at Ichabod Spencer's ministry of sustaining through these several sketches that have been described, we cannot avoid the impression of paradox. He minimized any ministry that did not aim at a "conviction of sin"; or if the person was in the faith, he denigrated anything he might do to sustain him in it. On the other hand, with those inside or outside the faith he was indefatigable in his solicitude, tender in his attempts not to alienate the person from the gospel, and in an amazing sense what we might call "relaxed." With an openly anxious inquirer, who needed only to feel more deeply the law of sin or the gospel of forgiveness, Spencer would wrestle verbally and mightily without hesitation. But even then, though often puzzled, he was not "tense." For profound was his conviction that the issue lay with the Holy Spirit, not with him. And when dealing with Mary Ann or Mr. U., there was something calm about him that commands our admiration and is far removed from indifference. So Spencer minimized the function of sustaining yet in some respects revealed the depths of his faith precisely when nothing could be accomplished except standing by.

Sustaining and Healing

It may be that there is a continuing truth in such a paradox, if we alter its form a bit. It might be put in this way: The success of a ministry of sustaining is greatest where it always aims at something more than sustaining, but where a failure to achieve healing does not destroy our sense of the value of sustaining and at the same time spurs further inquiry. To put it conversely, if we settle too soon for nothing but sustaining, we may lose the opportunity to bring healing; yet if we find ourselves interested only in those whose healing we can help, we become derelict.

There are striking demonstrations of this paradoxical truth today in mental hospitals. Wherever a staff, embittered and discouraged by lack of funds and personnel and public concern, have resigned themselves to giving only custodial care, that care fails to sustain much less heal. But where every failure to heal is a spur to inquiry, and a constant battle is maintained to get funds, personnel, and proper public interest, then even those who cannot be healed become sustained in a genuine sense. Humanly speaking perhaps we could go so far as to say that sustaining actually sustains only when it is attempted healing arrested by circumstances. The one danger in such a view is that the therapists may, even unwittingly, neglect those they regard as incapable of change.

In mental hospitals and related types of agencies a phrase has come into use, at times spoken with an obscurantist tongue in cheek, but intended seriously. The phrase is "tender loving care," usually abbreviated to "T.L.C." Where a hospital, for instance, knows of no specific therapy that will help this particular patient, or when its funds and personnel do not permit concentrated attention on him, still something may move in a healing direction if through the action of all who meet and serve him he is given T.L.C. If T.L.C. is alone, then the result is a holding operation although with therapeutic intent. If a part of over-all therapy, it may be much more than that. The conviction is growing that without T.L.C. few refractory cases have much chance. There must be a healing intent before there can be even a sustaining effect.

Another way to say this is that a fully satisfied sustaining does not in fact sustain. Psychoanalysis first saw this in the "positive transference" that resisted breakup, when the patient wanted to remain dependent upon the analyst instead of using his newly acquired self-knowledge to move toward the autonomy he had first professed to be seeking. Some therapeutic workers believe that the emergence of such a dependency is a mark of poor therapy. But all recognize it as a possible problem. Whether it is the therapist who unwittingly encourages dependency or the desperate clinging of the patient who dreads the unknown seas and distrusts his new boat, dependency trends may be alarm signals.

139

And yet there may be instances when life itself can be sustained only by some form of dependency; and there are certainly occasions in the lives of all, as in grief, when standing by, even of a dependent kind, is essential. One cannot say, then, that any dependency is a problem to be analyzed and resolved. But neither can he say that dependency should be regarded as a satisfying state. Again, a paradoxical type of statement seems necessary to suggest the truth.

Protestantism has tended to be extraordinarily suspicious of any human dependency. Such doctrines as the sovereignty of God and the universal priesthood of believers are in part warnings against it. If all this is taken in the light of its *intent*, it means, in the terms I have been using, that sustaining is not true sustaining but idolatry if it does not push on to receive any healing that may be needed and possible. Any dependency should, therefore, have a note of uneasiness about it. Not to move ahead is automatically to move backward. The patient with a heart condition, for instance, should move fully within the limits of his condition; if he overprotects himself, his condition grows worse. This is the kind of intent behind the Protestant push toward autonomy and independence under God alone.

In fact, of course, this intent has often been destroyed and in various ways. Any peace of mind has at times been regarded with suspicion, overlooking the fact that only one with some security can face insecurity, independence, or uncertainty. Sometimes dependence on God has been a thinly disguised transference from human dependency with nothing changed but the object—a far cry from what the psalmist or Schleiermacher meant by full and utter dependence on God.

In many ways we see the worth of the Protestant intention and the dangers of its distortions in Ichabod Spencer. Spencer always strove for healing. This made him preoccupied with change and conversion; and in spite of his own warnings that the forms of this are many, we see him as almost monolithically single-minded. The virtue of this was that he never gave up, never thought he could sustain by encouraging dependency, never felt any situation to be beyond the power of the Holy Spirit. The weaknesses, as we have seen, were in his literalism, in his undervaluing of the function of sustaining of either those in the faith or those who were not, and in his compartmentalization of a religious area away from both body and culture. We may be both edified and warned by him.

Hope

Reflection on the ministry of sustaining leads finally to consideration of hope and even to Christian eschatology. What has our pastoral theological inquiry suggested at this point? We have seen that a ministry of sustaining actually succeeds only if its intent transcends sustaining. At the same time we have seen that any depreciation of the sustaining function implies that we have identified ourselves with healing as "success," that we will play the game only if we can win. Sustaining is genuine when it is attempted healing prevented by circumstances, neither disgruntled that healing failed to eventuate, nor deflected from the unhealable—never self-satisfied (always inquiring toward healing) but never discouraged (neglecting what cannot be changed).

If hope was only in the real opportunity of healing, then sustaining could contain no hope, and circumstance could only embitter and discourage. But if hope should be made into a sour-faced kind of adaptation to circumstance, then it would cease to be real hope because its healing intention and direction would be lost. To use the more common theological terms, a Christian hope conceived as entirely within history would run the danger of becoming hopeless in the face of circumstance, of taking its marbles and going home when the game goes adversely. But a Christian hope regarded entirely as beyond history would not be hope either, for it would deny the healing intention and direction within history because of its frustration by circumstance. Directionally speaking, the Christian hope is within history; its success or realization is beyond history when any full healing is meant.

Such a view of hope has very practical consequences for the Christian life. Suppose we have a middle-aged sufferer from a heart condition. Wherein lies his hope? If he overprotects himself (in the pattern: If I can't be active as I used to be, I shan't be active at all), his condition is likely to grow worse. His hope does not lie in passive adaptation to circumstance. If he continues at his former rate of activity (in the pattern: I'd rather be dead than slow up), he will kill himself. His hope cannot lie in a hopeless defiance. If he performs the activities that are possible within the limits of his condition, he may live a long time. But this is not likely to work if he does it only as a chore, or if he secretly expects it to bring him back to youthful exuberance, or if it is done in dread that the doctor may be wrong. If he attempts to divorce his hope from vital and positive involvement in the present, he loses it; but if it has no dimension beyond the present, he loses it too. He trusts in a healing direction if he co-operates, but he does not deny or defy circumstance. His hope, then, requires statement in both present-oriented and future-oriented terms. It is not enough that the two be present, but also that they be joined in a certain way by a certain attitude. So far as we can see, this is a reasonably close analogy to the Christian hope in its broader sense.

Those sections of the Christian community that have been bowed by circumstance tend toward defining the Christian hope in future-oriented terms. Those, like the United States, where circumstance has been more propitious, tend to put their definition in present-oriented terms. If our reasoning is correct, each tends to overlook some aspect of the reality. Real sustaining emerges only when the direction is toward healing; but when circumstance stops healing real sustaining transcends the arrest. Unless one is true, the other cannot be true. If the direction toward healing is not actually present, then hope is compensatory and illusory. If the force of circumstance is denied and hope identified with the fact of healing, then it is bound to be frustrated and disappointed. Both these views are distortions.

We can see the nature of hope illuminated also through the examination of bereavement. The death of one who is close to us makes necessary the process of grieving. The healing intention and direction of grieving is to free us, eventually, from the bonds we have had to the deceased—so that we may be able to live at peace both with the image of the deceased person and with other real persons. But the specific processes of grief that we go through in moving in such a direction are painful, at first so acute that such a goal itself seems devoid of hope.

Especially through the studies of Erich Lindemann and his colleagues, we know that impediment to the grieving process may bring severe negative results even to one's body.[6] Such impediments may take many forms. One person may be unable to deal at all with the (at first) very painful image of the deceased. Another may clothe the image, so to speak, in robes of gold, as if he were still present in existence. Still another may seek diversion, as if the pain of living with the image could be bypassed. When hope is entirely futurized, there is an impediment against the necessary present work of grieving. But when hope is seen entirely in the present, then there is equally an impediment to grieving.

Summary

In this chapter I have examined the sustaining aspect of the ministry of shepherding. As in the chapter on healing, this has been done mainly by examination of one-to-one-relationship situations, not because sustaining is confined to these but because they are simpler to study. If the principles induced are valid, they extend to other relationships as well.

It was indicated that sustaining is that form of shepherding that stands by when healing is not possible or not possible now. Its relevance was indicated in two main types of situation: when there is shock or loss and when some irreversible process of impairing is at work. It was indicated that sustaining, like healing, may be available to those within or without the faith. We noted the similarity of our "sustaining" to the old "comfort" in its original meaning, but were warned that the timing was often wrong when such ministry was conceived as "encouragement." But sustaining, we were warned, was to be stripped of connotations that would imply a strong one giving to a weak.

I then asked how a ministry of sustaining is actually to be carried out and presented a contemporary instance of ministry to a sick patient. We saw the key to the "how" in the way in which negative feelings were dealt with. Recalling how much of the present problem in pastoral theology is lack of positive identification with our pastoral heritage, we then turned to examine several of Ichabod Spencer's sketches in which he was exercising dominantly a ministry of sustaining. We saw him sustaining an anxious inquirer whose anxiety resisted deliverance, one of the faithful who was dying at peace in the Lord, one who was deeply depressed, and one who felt hopeless in the face of both death and hell. Each of these sketches, it was contended, shed valuable light on Spencer's ministry of sustaining.

As in connection with healing, I dealt critically with Spencer's literalism, his compartmentalizations, and many of the specific ways in which he went about his task. He was also criticized for undervaluing the ministry of sustaining, of being unduly suspicious about its value even when circumstances permitted nothing else.

On the other hand, a basic principle was suggested to us by Spencer, namely, that the ministry of sustaining actually sustains only when its aim transcends sustaining in the direction of healing. Sustaining, we concluded, does not sustain if it settles too easily for supporting, for supporting turns readily into dependency. Yet sustaining, if it really sustains, is itself healing within the limits of circumstance. It is, therefore, not inferior or secondary to healing since, directionally speaking, it is part of healing. We noted the relevance of the main implications of this principle for the contemporary ministry.

Finally we turned to the light these studies shed upon the theological questions of dependency and of hope. We supported from our data the Protestant suspicion of human dependency in its intention but dealt critically with the forms this has often assumed. Data were presented suggesting that hope is self-defeating unless it has both a present and a future orientation, linked in a particular way; and it was contended that these data are relevant to the construction of a Christian doctrine of hope.

It can now be seen that our line of demarcation between the ministry of healing and the ministry of sustaining is not directional (for both aim at the restoration of functional wholeness) but circumstantial or situational. The distinction is important and has theoretical as well as practical value. But it is not directional in character. This is another indication why healing and sustaining are of the same basic perspective.

CHAPTER 8

Guiding

"GUIDING" IS A RISKY WORD. FAR MORE THAN "HEALING" OR "SUSTAIN-ing," it may carry unintended connotations that blur or distort. The term "guidance" in modern psychology and education sometimes suggests meanings that our position must reject. For reasons of this kind we shall take special pains to define what we mean by guiding as an aspect of shepherding.

A spiritual guide is more than a reflective mirror. But he is not in any sense a director in a way that implies coercion. To clarify these distinctions, let us resort to an analogy.

Assume that we contemplate a trip through the North Woods and want a guide. From this guide we shall expect certain things: familiarity with the terrain, with dangers peculiar to the region, with the kinds of animals that may be hunted and the conditions pertinent to each, and the like. On many matters we rightly expect him to know more than we do.

About other things, however, our knowledge is greater than that of the guide, and we rightly expect him to pay attention to us at these points. Even though one animal is plentiful and easy to find, we may have good reason for wishing to seek another that is more elusive. We may have an allergy to the material contained in the kind of sleeping bag the guide recommends, and we shall expect him as a result to take second choice. However superior may be the guide's general knowledge of trips like this through this general terrain with such people, there are crucial points to which the guide's general knowledge is not relevant unless it is supplemented by specific knowledge of us, our goals and our idiosyncrasies. In order to be a guide, he does not have to coerce us, or ignore us, or override us.

But just as we rightly are opposed to his coercing us, so he should be against our possible coercion of him. If we say we want to hunt tigers in the North Woods, and he knows that none exists there, it is proper for him to note this fact instead of nodding sagely and then going about his own conception of the business at hand.

The spiritual guide, too, is rightly expected to know the general terrain. He should also be familiar with the dangers peculiar to the spiritual territory to be traversed and have some good notion of the goals that are relevant to this kind of search.

On the other hand, there are many things about the trip to be undertaken concerning which the guide knows less than his parishioner. And he is the wrong kind of guide if he directs in a way that ignores or overrides these basic individualities. That is what is meant by coercion, and it must be wholly absent from spiritual guiding.

But the spiritual guide, while not coercing his parishioner, is not coerced by him either. The guide cannot conscientiously follow a method of which he disapproves toward a goal he regards as illusory. Whether such things are dealt with explicitly or implicitly, spiritual guiding demands that they be noted and dealt with.

Guiding as Shepherding

If guiding is to be regarded as one of the three aspects of the shepherding perspective, then it must first meet the general requirements of shepherding. I have previously defined this as having the following characteristics: the situation is such that the shepherd's solicitous concern for the welfare of the persons is dominant, there is some degree of recognition of need within the persons, and there is some degree of receptivity to help. The story of the good Samaritan was cited as indicating a situation in which the shepherding perspective is dominant. It was indicated that the shepherding perspective was not exhaustive. If the good Samaritan proved to be a political zealot, who used his hospital delivery of the injured Jew to sabotage the Jewish water supply, another perspective (that of organizing) would have to be brought into play to deal with him.

When we were dealing with the healing and sustaining aspects of shepherding, they met our criteria so obviously that the point required no argument. When we turn to guiding, however, the situation is different. We rejected discipline as an aspect of shepherding on two grounds: first, that its original meaning of training in discipleship had been almost irretrievably lost; and second, that it tended to merge in

146

actual existence the concern for the welfare of the person and the protection of the whole group, when in fact this merger occurs only under ideal conditions. As to the second, we admitted, indeed contended, that in the language of modern penology the best possible protection of society lies in the best possible rehabilitation of the offender. Under ideal conditions the two concerns are mutually supportive. But we felt it dangerous to assume this mutual support under all actual conditions, in which it has often been assumed that what is good for society or the church is automatically good for the person or smaller group, but in which it has occasionally been assumed that what is good for the individual or small group is bound to be the best for the whole society or church. Either assumption, we contend, is likely to be mistaken. We are in no sense arguing that these interests are always and everywhere implacable enemies. Wherever in fact they are mutually supportive, as they often are, this should be lifted up. But we are arguing against a notion of their automatic harmony, which shuts off inquiry and may easily do grave injustice to person or group.

We propose, therefore, that guiding as an aspect of the shepherding perspective be regarded as concentrating on the welfare of this person or this smaller group (short of the whole church or society) in terms of immediate need—temporarily setting aside the question of the welfare and protection of the larger group. That there is need to protect the latter, we hold to be without question; but we suggest that, where it is properly dominant, it is the organizing rather than the shepherding perspective that is being exercised dominantly.

The good Samaritan, binding up wounds, is healing. Giving a cup of water, he is sustaining. Taking the injured man to the hospital is guiding. All three aspects are dominantly of a shepherding character. If it should turn out that the Samaritan seized upon this opportunity to get inside the Jewish lines so as to poison the water supply or bribe the police department, a different perspective would have to become dominant. The fundamental attitude toward the Samaritan under the new hypothetical situation would not change. But at all other levels than the most basic, we should see something different in the acts and events of dealing with him.

Another way to see the distinction is in terms of timing. When the victim is lying injured by the side of the road, recognizes that he needs help, and has some receptivity to it, we set about giving that help *at that time*. That may include the guiding, as well as healing and sustaining, that gets him to the hospital and away from the place of danger (with his consent and even initiative). At that time we do not know whether anything else will be required in relation to him at a later time. He may indeed be a saboteur, waiting to get at the Samaritans. If he is, we cannot assume sentimentally that a few days of solicitous hospital care will cause him to throw away his poison. But at the time the situation calls for shepherding, it is given him including its guiding aspect. During World War II the best possible medical care was given, for instance, to German prisoners of war by the medical corps of the Allied military forces. The key conception is timing.

Pastoral Theology and Moral Theology

This discussion provides a clue to answering a very basic question about the nature of the body of divinity that has up to this point been postponed. This is the question of the nature of "moral theology." It has already been said that Christian ethics or moral theology is to be regarded as among the logic-centered bodies of knowledge about the faith (along with Bible, church history, and so on). In order to perform this function, the field of ethics (like any other) has an aspect that reaches over to apply itself to operations and is concerned for the welfare of all society and not only of Christians. That meaning of Christian ethics or of moral theology is not the issue; we take it for granted.

The issue is whether, starting from operations, there is something that can be called moral theology in a sense that would make it a discipline cognate with pastoral theology as it has been defined here. Something of this order has been true in the more Catholic aspects of the tradition. The alert reader, perhaps especially the Anglican, may have been asking almost from the beginning of the discussion why moral theology has not been considered. Our answer is that we do not regard it as a function-oriented discipline cognate with pastoral theology. The key to the reasoning involved in this conclusion has already been given in the discussion of the present chapter.

We shall not seek to identify "moral" with its original derivation from the Latin *mos* or *mores*, meaning custom or customs. In Christian thought it has always far transcended that. Indeed, the touchstone of Christian morality, from the apostle Paul onward, may be regarded as loving God in Christ and doing as you (the new you) please. In its thrust this was the very opposite of mere conformity. In Christ the law was not final (although not irrelevant), but it was transcended. As his-

148

torians have made clear to us, by the second century Paul's doctrine of Christian liberty was being watered down; and legalism mounted, as Protestants see it, until the Reformation. But any ideal statement of Christian morality contains freedom as well as law and demand, is about the "good for man," and is not just following the "obligation of conscience" as defined by the group.

It is our contention that the points that have been made about discipline in the tradition are also for the most part true about morality. Discipline had a reference to the welfare of the person and the protection of the community; so had morality. Under ideal conditions the two references were and are mutually supportive. And we do not advocate categorical separation. But we do argue against any assumption of automatic harmony in relation to morality just as we did in relation to discipline. Indeed, if our concern is to make what is potentially capable of mutual support an actual mutual support, the best way to move in this direction is to recognize differences or antagonisms wherever they exist. As in relation to discipline, it is in part the failure to do so that has sometimes caused such curious things to happen to Christian morality.

Christian morality is concerned with what is good for the Christian and also with what is good for the whole community or society. Ideally these are mutually supportive. But in actual existence there may be tremendous tensions between them. Such tensions cannot be resolved automatically, a priori, in favor of the supposed interest of the community without running the risk of making morality into nothing but duty and duty into doing what you wish you could avoid. Christian morality cannot be said to have escaped unscathed from this danger, although such a notion cannot possibly be equivalent to Christian morality in a normative sense. We must add that the tensions cannot be automatically resolved in favor of person or small group, as if no protection of the whole community were required.

Ideally the two functions of morality support each other. In actual existence they may not do so. To blur the latter fact, or to regard it as of no consequence in trying to maintain the former cannot possibly help the situation.

How, then, can we deal from a function-centered point of view with morality? Where the dominant perspective, as made necessary by the situation, is toward the protection or purity or general welfare of the community, morality is an aspect of the *organizing* perspective. And where the dominant perspective, as made necessary by the situation, is toward enhancing the welfare and the good of the person or of the group smaller than the whole community, morality is an aspect of the shepherding perspective. In the latter instance whenever there are actions of pastor and church, then we have guiding as an aspect of the shepherding perspective.

This position asserts that morality is not a perspective in itself, cognate with shepherding, communicating, and organizing. It is a combination of our perspectives, and we believe it valuable to preserve the distinctions. In morality there are times when the purity of the church is dominant. But in Christian morality the good of the person is not a concession. Shepherding is not inferior to organizing but cognate with it.

The question may be asked: If you consider one type of concern as shepherding in character and the other as organizing, are you not bifurcating morality? The reply is that we are recognizing a duality of concern that actually exists. To deny such a duality is to argue implicitly for an automatic harmony doctrine of one type or the other, either that the purity of the church automatically defines the good for the person or that the good of the person automatically defines the purity of the church. We deny that either one is automatically or necessarily true in actual existence.

A good deal of Protestantism rose up against what it regarded as casuistry, rightly or wrongly regarding the Catholic use of casuistry as idolatrous—retaining fixed and legalistic general principles, but manipulating within them for the arbitrary advantage of some individuals. For a long time Protestantism has been in danger of being under the illusion that it could dispense with any casuistry. Rightly understood, casuistry is the criticism of all general principles in the light of the person. There is at least one aspect of the way in which the Catholic branch of the tradition has used casuistry that is urgently needed by Protestants. This is that, whatever the general principles, the welfare of the person must be steadily sought in relation to them. That this can lead to abuse of the type Protestants felt they were rejecting is clear. That the study of instances can be dispensed with in favor of the mere enunciation of general principles is now widely recognized as an error in relation to morality at any level.

But if our point is accepted, that both the shepherding and the organizing perspectives involve aspects of morality (ideally united), then it follows that a relevant casuistry is never a one-way street from general principle to specific instance. It is always a two-way street, including the movement from specific instance to general principle. Christian moral principle is illuminated, and its understanding perhaps corrected by inquiry into operations from both the shepherding and the organizing perspectives.

It may then be asked: If there are differences and conflicts of the two concerns of morality in actual existence, how do you propose to arbitrate them? Under the old scheme at least it was believed that an arbitrator existed. Here there appears to be none. In an important sense the answer is that there *is* no final arbitrator in the sense of having an automatic answer to each instance. The most careful inquiry may appear to end in a deadlock of interests. What our point of view is concerned to avoid is the premature solution of such conflicts in either direction so that in effect genuine inquiry ceases. There is no arbitrator in the sense requested, nor is inquiry itself to be so regarded. But it is the method by which negotiation becomes possible. Negotiation, which forswears absolute certainty, is Protestantism's replacement for arbitration.

The guiding aspect of the shepherding perspective, then, includes that dimension of morality that is focused on the welfare of the person or of the group smaller than the whole community. When the situation calls for guiding of this sort, we are viewing it from the shepherding perspective. When the other legitimate concern of morality is dominant, another perspective takes the lead. When the prodigal son returned home, he was guided to the table with the fatted calf, his welfare being his father's overarching concern. Suppose that, replete with veal, he had proposed to return to the far country of dissolution, to bring his erstwhile friends for the express purpose of consuming all the livestock in a week-long jubilee. Beyond a certain point the guiding might have to shift from a shepherding to an organizing perspective. Again the timing is plainly important.

Criteria of Guiding as Shepherding

Let us now return to our main constructive task, of defining the content of guiding as an aspect of the shepherding perspective, having established the point that this includes moral guiding when the timing of the situation calls for a dominant concern for the good or welfare of the person or persons. We shall contend that such guiding, if it is part of shepherding, is eductive in character—that it "leads out" something that may be regarded as either within the person or potentially available to him (through resources other than ourselves).[1]

151

Such guiding cannot be coercive. If it seeks to coerce, it ceases to be shepherding. Even coercion, we may note, is at times necessary; but when it must be exercised, the dominant perspective is organizing rather than shepherding. In denying pastoral guiding any use of coercion, we are not rendering it powerless. But the power used is used with, not against. It is not power over but power to bring out or to educe.

By the same token guiding in the shepherding perspective cannot be "persuading" in its usual connotation. For persuading implies an external-istic appeal. If a person follows such and such a course, we tell him he will be glad later on, even if nothing in him (or working within him, such as the Holy Spirit) now feels any degree of kinship with the proposal. But the fact is that the course is not capable of being carried out by him unless there is some such feeling of kinship (however dim). In so far as this is what persuading implies, it cannot be the procedure of pastoral guiding.

If pastoral guiding is eductive, then it must also reject the conception of its function as the definition of alternative courses. In what is usually implied by defining alternative courses, there is also externalism. The pastor would say, "You have your choice of Course A, Course B, and Course C. If you follow Course A, this is likely to happen. If Course B, . . ." The same objections may be made as to persuasion. In rejecting this, we do not deny the pastor the right and obligation of helping a person to examine possible consequences of a certain course. But the externalism involved in a list of alternatives is excluded. So viewed, alternatives are projections into the future and are only as meaningful as the genuine assimilations of the past into the present.

As the defining of alternatives must be rejected from pastoral guiding because of the way it deals with the future, so interpreting in its usual connotation must be rejected for the way it deals with the past. It also implies an externalism, explaining connectives that would otherwise be unseen by the person. It is also likely to contain an unstated but future-oriented if clause: "*If* you feel such and such because of so and so past circumstances, then. . . ." The implication may be quite explicit for a future course. But this is building on the pastor's understanding of the past, not on that of the person. If there is a discrepancy, new problems arise.

We reject, then, coercion, persuasion, interpretation, and the defini-tion of alternatives as tools of guiding in the shepherding perspective. We concede that there may be pastoral situations in which each of these types of proceeding may be relevant and needed. But when that is the case, the shepherding perspective has ceased to be dominant. We regard this point in itself as of great importance. Some of its implications may be noted.

It has been argued that no one of the perspectives exhausts the meaning of any concrete operation. A contact between a pastor and a parishioner is not guaranteed in advance to involve nothing but the shepherding perspective. And in view of the nature of the pastoral function as a whole, there is nothing reprehensible if the situation requires a shift in dominant perspective. For instance, suppose that a parishioner under inner stress has poured out his negative feelings, has found more positive feelings emerging, has assimilated something of the past, and has been able to begin projecting plans for the future. There is no law saying he cannot ask the pastor to expound to him the meaning of sin or the relevance of atomic energy to the future of the race. To be sure, if such shifts are defenses against considering his own situation, they will be so treated. But they need not be. In that case the harm comes only when the shift is unacknowledged. The temporary movement from shepherding as dominant perspective will not hinder its effectiveness if the shift is explicitly acknowledged. If not recognized, then the situation tends to become clouded or what Harry Stack Sullivan calls "parataxic." [2]

In recommending an eductive approach in pastoral guiding, we are asserting that a certain kind of connection must exist between internals and externals if the guiding is to meet the requirements of shepherding by concentrating on the welfare of the person or group as the factor of immediate need, such as in the story of the good Samaritan. Externals must be there: words by the pastor, his feelings and convictions, his knowledge and information, his concern and his skill. But they are drawn upon only as they may evoke or educe from and within the parishioner that which he will regard as his. Now what is his, we know, is not an unchanging entity. He who becomes a new being in Jesus Christ changes the meaning of what is his and not his. When any healing of the whole psyche is under way, the meanings attached to "his" are constantly undergoing change. What may be evoked, therefore, that is his may be different today from what it was yesterday. But if what is evoked is not felt to be his, however dimly, then it is externals trying to break in instead of externals attempting to make contact with internals and consolidate and strengthen and guide them by bringing them to the light of human symbolic awareness.

Does this mean that pastoral guiding is nondirective and client-centered? In the sense of the purpose for which those terms were coined by Carl R. Rogers, the answer is Yes.[3] "Nondirective" was intended to show that the imposition of externals on internals, however subtle, would not finally be therapeutic in result. "Client-centered" was intended to show that one begins and proceeds from the best possible grasp of internals—that is, the inner frame of reference of the other person in so far as it can be grasped. With these intentions we are wholly in accord. Precisely how one acts in order to be nondirective or client-centered is, however, another question. Silence may be coercion in some situations. Refusing to acknowledge when one is puzzled may be far from client-centered. But the original intention of these terms is inescapable.

Eductive Guiding

The case of a young woman I shall call Mrs. Coe may help us to define what is meant by an eductive approach to pastoral guiding. It is used here with the permission of Mrs. Coe and the time-consuming and most gracious co-operation of Pastor Key. Mrs. Coe was an attractive young married woman, wife of a graduate student who planned to go into education. At the time she consulted Pastor Key, they had been married a little over three years and had one very small baby girl. Mr. Coe was earning a good part of his own way through school by factory work on shifts, which gave him odd hours, especially along with his classes, and meant that Mrs. Coe had to do excellent planning for the family budget to survive at all.

Mrs. Coe's first approach to Pastor Key was indirect. A mutual friend came to the pastor and asked if he would be willing to talk with Mrs. Coe. He assented, suspecting rightly that she found it very difficult to consider talking with anyone. After she had asked to see the pastor and the appointment was made, she arrived and was very apologetic.

MRS. COE: I really hate to take up your time with this. It isn't as if there was any one particular thing on which I could ask your advice. It's just . . . well, I don't quite . . . well, how would you . . . like me to begin?
PASTOR KEY: Actually it may not make much difference where you begin. If we could tell a story clearly from A to Z, it probably wouldn't be necessary to tell it at all. From what you say, I gather it isn't easy to get into. Why

154

don't you just start somewhere, and we'll both know the whole story is more than that?

MRS. COE: Well, all right. Well, it's about my husband—about me and my husband, that is. We met in college. (*Here she gives a rather detailed factual account of their meeting, becoming engaged, and finally getting married.*) Now I sometimes wonder whether I was ever actually in love with him—whatever that means.

PASTOR KEY: It looks different when you look back from now?

MRS. COE: Yes, but I guess I wasn't sure even then.

Mrs. Coe then told how her mother had urged the match, but her father had been skeptical about it although cautious in what he said. During the remainder of the first interview Mrs. Coe poured out the story with unusual coherence. She had had a very affectionate relationship with her father. Everyone in her home town, she said, had regarded her mother as a wonderful person, who was always doing things for other people. She agreed on this estimate of her mother but was often out of favor with her for not wanting to do good deeds her mother had thought up. When she was low in spirits, it was always her father who with a brief word could make her feel better. When he quietly failed to show enthusiasm for her marriage, she said, "I guess I felt this more inside than I realized at the time." But her mother began to sweep ahead with wedding plans, and "I guess after that I never really did stop to think it over."

The second interview was devoted mainly to a discussion of Mrs. Coe's husband and to the difficulties between them. At first it went like this:

MRS. COE: And another thing, he's just so self-righteous. Oh, I suppose I must look like that to him too. But he always thinks he's right, and then I hate to hurt his feelings, and—oh, I don't know!

PASTOR KEY: I wonder if there is some particular incident of the last day or two that you could tell to make this clearer. Sometimes an actual story brings out our feelings more clearly.

The incidents were far more damning to Mr. Coe than the general discussion had been. Unless the incidents were to be regarded as sheer fabrications, Mr. Coe emerged as boorish and self-righteous. Mrs. Coe, on the other hand, having told some incident which left its own stark impression, always qualified this, apologized for her husband, and made some deprecating remarks about her own place in the incident.

During the course of several rather widely spaced interviews, during which the pastor's function consisted entirely of helping to clarify her feelings as they were emerging with a slow increase in sharpness, some genuine though painful light was shed on many things that had previously been puzzling. Mrs. Coe saw that her feelings toward her husband were more negative than she had previously confessed to herself and that her constant self-scrutiny even in those incidents that most revealed the difficulties in her husband came from a depreciation of herself. She did some historical tracing of the latter. All this hurt very much, but she felt she was moving toward psychic honesty. During this period she began several interviews by saying, "Well, I saw some more this week. But I guess I'm as bad as ever."

Her lack of self-confidence first came to focus on the issue of how she should deal with her husband when his requests to her were unreasonable. She would decide to stand up for herself, do so once, then backslide, and then come to Pastor Key with the statement that she was as "bad as ever." After about fifteen interviews, however, the issue became more serious. "How in the world can I live with him? Or should I consider separating?" This was worked at in the same way. For the most part the pastor needed only to help her clarify her feelings. When the focus of consideration was a projected action (for example, "Should I leave him?"), the pastor, once her feelings had been expressed, had no hesitation in saying, "Why don't you go ahead and think through aloud what you believe would happen if you did that?" Her doing so helped to take certain vague fears out of the shadows. But the emerging overarching issue was: "How can I do anything when every little thing upsets my self-confidence?"

From the beginning of her talks with Pastor Key, Mrs. Coe had expressed the hope that her husband would talk with someone. Since he had refused point-blank to consider talking with Pastor Key, on the ground that the pastor must have sided with his wife if he was willing to see her several times, this was not an option. The services of an excellent counselor, not a pastor, were made available to him; and he had several interviews in which, the counselor later indicated, "there was an almost complete absence of insight, so obvious as to be frightening."

During this whole period of perhaps six months what was happening was that Mrs. Coe was becoming increasingly aware of the serious difficulty she was in, that no change in action or feeling on her part would eliminate or alleviate Mr. Coe's tremendously negative characteristics, and that there could be no solution in her merely knuckling down to his moods and tantrums. She felt that it might be better for all concerned, including the baby, if there was a separation; but she also felt that what she was gaining in psychic honesty and confidence might be enough to make the situation tolerable. She see-sawed between these positions.

At this point we may pause for comment. Let us assume that the pastor was right in deciding, as time went on, that 95 per cent of the difficulty came from Mr. Coe, which later events seemed to bear out. The fact remained that it was what I have been calling Mrs. Coe's lack of self-confidence that played right into this. If the pastor, considering only whose characteristics produced the unpleasantness of the situation, had decided this was overwhelmingly Mr. Coe and as a result indicated he would support separation, he would certainly have been wrong. For if Mrs. Coe's ego could not have stood this, in what sense could it have been right? If, on the other hand, he had taken the position that the marriage should be preserved at any price, he would have been just as wrong; for this would have guaranteed that no self-confidence would ever rise in Mrs. Coe. That is, his not attempting to direct at such a point by standing on this side or that was not a matter of restraining himself from telling something he knew quite well. *Granting all the circumstances, he literally did not know.* His virtue was not self-restraint but clear perception.

At this point the Coes' situation took a dramatic turn. Late one night Mr. Coe had a bad accident in his old jalopy. In the hospital he was found to be full of barbiturate drugs, which had caused him to black out. The hospital examination showed that he must have used these drugs heavily for a long time past in order for them to have produced such an effect. The attending psychiatrist concluded that he was probably not psychotic but was on the borderline and should not be permitted complete freedom for some time. He went to live with his overprotective widowed mother.

This incident greatly shocked his wife. When Pastor Key, hearing of it, went to see her, her first reaction was concern for her husband, then self-recrimination that she must have driven her husband to use drugs. At that time not all the data given above were available. She was at this time in a state of near shock. Pastor Key told her so, said he realized this battered her ego, pointed out that her husband was in the best possible hands, and indicated he would be ready to talk about it as soon as she was.

Especially because of Mrs. Coe's sense of guilt over her husband's secret and excessive use of barbiturates, the shock lasted for some days. During this period she saw the pastor twice. She was half-dazed ("I can't think") and half-frantic ("What should I do?"). The pastor listened but also said, "Look, Mrs. Coe, this isn't the time to make plans. We have to wait until feelings come down before that can be done." This was explicit verbal reminder of something originally arrived at by Mrs. Coe herself with Pastor Key's help. It seemed to him essential to keep the timing straight. One might call it an intermediate ministry of sustaining, defining the nature of that period in that way.

Within about two weeks the shock condition lessened, and Mrs. Coe said, "Maybe this will take the decision out of my hands. Maybe this is a substitute for the courage I didn't have." If that fact had begun to make a decision for her, the attempts soon made by her husband and his mother to take custody of the baby consolidated it. She was still much concerned for her husband and rejoiced when he was seeing a psychiatrist. But it became increasingly clear to her that a separation or divorce had to be secured. Every time she would begin to come clear on this feeling, however, she would also move the other way. With one exception decision see-sawed for some time—not a waste of time but a necessary part of the assimilating process. The exception was the work on her self-confidence. "Even if I make a decision," she kept asking herself, "how can I make it stick?" Even after she had firmly decided that a separation must be had, she continued to doubt that Pastor Key as a pastor could approve this, which always led to a consideration of her self-confidence. But every possible examination of the past showed her that, when she had acted in the light of her best impulses with however much fear and trembling, she had almost always been more right than if she had cowered somewhere. This in itself helped to give the needed confidence. Her chats with the pastor declined in frequency. Within a year, apart from the separation from her husband, she made a very important decision in her life without specifically consulting Pastor Key. After the decision was made, she came to him and said, "I wanted to talk with you about it, but here's the way it was, and I know you'll see how I worked at it anyhow. It may prove to be wrong, but the other decision would have been so much more wrong that I'm going right ahead."

In this rather complex situation there were periods in which healing was dominant, then sustaining, and then guiding. The whole, if the pastor's report is accurate and if this brief summary of his long report is adequate, was of a piece. If he and I have told it accurately, those periods in the relationship that required guiding were just as eductively approached as were those others in which healing or sustaining were in the forefront.

It would be a mistake to suggest that there was no guiding here because the pastor did not suggest what Mrs. Coe should do or feel, for example, after her husband's use of drugs had been exposed. The pastor's relationship to the rapidly changing situation was such that healing and sustaining do not describe all that was required. Again and again Mrs. Coe would move ahead and mobilize her resources. Then the new determination would be sniped at from the rear by her sense of guilt or lack of self-confidence. At such points there was guiding, a firm reminder to hang onto what had been achieved until the dizziness, so to speak, had passed. But that which was external always built on something internal that Mrs. Coe recognized as hers. It was, at least as reported to me, never merely external.

Even in the second interview the pastor did some guiding of Mrs. Coe. Reporting a concrete incident might be much more fruitful than talking abstractly about feelings. It would be poor indeed to make a rule of this, for it could often be wrong. A person ultrasensitive against any possible signs of direction would have resented this and perhaps discontinued the relationship. In this situation it helped to make Mrs. Coe's feelings concrete more rapidly than would otherwise have been the case. It turned out that she could tell a concrete story that would demonstrate and express her feelings very well, while she found it very difficult even to identify the feelings when using abstract terms without incidents and events. Perhaps the pastor was fortunate here. Had he proved wrong, he could have told her so. The eductive principle would have remained.

Very often the pastor finds himself in complex situations of this kind, which have their counterpart in group as well as in individual and family relationships. Even where it is clear that the dominant perspective must be shepherding, there may be bewildering shifts, as with Mrs. Coe, from healing to sustaining to guiding. He may not always be as right as Pastor Key seems to have been with Mrs. Coe. This may not matter greatly, however, if he is alert to the possible need for shifting gears.

In the discussion of sustaining we saw that it is genuine sustaining only when moving in a healing direction but slowed or stopped by circumstance. We now see that guiding in the eductive or evocative sense is also moving in a healing direction. Unlike sustaining, it is not stopped by circumstance, especially external circumstance, but by what

159

we might call "emotional backsliding." There has been movement toward wholeness; but the enemies of wholeness are powerful and, seeing the prospect of losing the war, they mobilize all their resources in one spot in a kind of kamikaze suicide flying. More than anywhere else here is where pastoral guiding is relevant. For the enemies are subtle and vicious. They will work directly on the weakest part of the person's line: his lack of self-confidence, his fear of his own ignorance, his anxiety at being made to appear a sucker, or whatever it is. Guiding is a reminder of resources that have been available before and will be available again.

The reader may object that there must be more to guiding than reminding. If it is to be guiding, there must be some novelty in it. Thinking back to the North Woods guide, he did have an expert general knowledge of the terrain that he did not mind sharing with others. But in making the connection with that which is internal, the novel is not relevant unless the remembered has some readiness for it. If both things are kept in mind, a more accurate picture of guiding will result.

The reader may also ask, especially in relation to Mrs. Coe, how it can be said that moral guiding was done since, finally, Mrs. Coe separated from her husband. There is no doubt that some branches of tradition would stand against this solution on the basis of the data given (no evidence of adultery), and some would be against a divorce under any conditions. But no branch of tradition stands against separation under every circumstance. A separation in itself, therefore, is not regarded as immoral always and necessarily by any part of tradition. So the morality of this separation cannot be ruled out in advance.

As we saw, there was a conflict within Mrs. Coe between her deep desire to make the marriage work despite circumstances that included her readiness to make a serious change in herself to that end, and her growing conviction that nothing she did could make the marriage even tolerable. If the latter was actually true, persisting in the marriage would run counter to genuine good for her, for her child, and no doubt for her husband. In that case the continuation of the marriage would be immoral from the point of view of the good of the persons involved. Whether the marriage, regardless of what Mrs. Coe did, would have been absolutely intolerable, no arbitrator can finally say. But the evidence pointed in that direction.

But even if continuation of the marriage was proved to be plainly intolerable for all concerned, there still would be a conflict between the good of the persons immediately involved and the good of the whole community. The moralist at this point may reason statistically: If there are too many separations, no couple will commit themselves finally to marriage, and then where shall we be? This is not irrelevant. Or he may reason ideally: Every couple becomes "one flesh" whether they acknowledge the union or not, and the breaking of the bond for any cause whatever is an offense to God. For our part we shall simply have to reject such reasoning as legalistic whenever it confuses the goal or ideal with actual existence. We agree that the breaking of the bond is a vastly deeper and more serious matter than many couples realize, but we cannot deny that the conditions suggesting separation may also be very deep and very serious to the point of intolerability.

At this point a crucial question along a different line may be asked: If this case is correctly reported, then is it not true that this couple should not have married at all? Was not the seed of immorality planted when there was inadequate guiding at the time of the marriage? In the light of subsequent events there is no doubt that this question is well asked. And if it leads, as it should, to more careful pastoral preparation of people for marriage, very good. But the question is not relevant to the situation of the Coes at this time. If the absence of a guard rail has permitted a car to fall off a cliff, it is an excellent idea to decide on building a guard rail to protect subsequent travelers. But such decision and action are not relevant to the need of the persons lying injured in the car at the foot of the cliff. The building of the guard rail and the preparation for marriage come dominantly within the organizing perspective on operations. But what is required now in relation to the Coes is shepherding.

From our point of view there is no final arbiter who can say that Mrs. Coe's decision for separation is plainly moral or immoral. But where the need is such that the shepherding perspective must be dominant, the weight is very much in favor of the morality of this decision especially where its opposite appears to be intolerable. A Protestant approach to such matters cannot be absolute or rigidly codified; that is, each situation requires inquiry from the point of view of the relation of internal to external factors without assuming the automatic priority of one over the other.

Spiritual Direction

In considering the whole range of pastoral guiding from the shepherding perspective, we may note that this is where in our scheme most of what has traditionally been called "spiritual direction" will fall. When a person seeks help in the life of prayer and meditation; when after the passing of some acute crisis he wants aid in bringing the threads together to form a new life pattern; when he wants a kind of general checkup, like seeing his dentist twice a year—situations of this kind have been called "spiritual direction" in the Catholic tradition.

Such direction need not be legalistic, authoritarian, coercive, or directive in the usual connotation. As T. W. Pym has said, the answer to the question of how to carry out spiritual direction is: Don't.[4] In our language no spiritual direction helps a person move in the direction that will in fact be best for him if it is not built on some internals that he recognizes as his. A life of prayer cannot be taught from a statistical rule. Unless the guiding helps the person make contact with something felt as his, it will not finally be effective. From the Protestant point of view the Catholic side of the tradition seems often coercive at such points; and to the extent that this is so, spiritual direction must be rejected. But in matters such as guidance of prayer and meditation Protestantism seems mostly to have fallen into a mediocre legalism of easy devotional booklets, far more devoid of relation to individual internalities than anything the Catholic side of the tradition has advocated. Once it is realized that guiding can and must be noncoercive if it is to be effective, perhaps a genuine but unfeverish recovery of devotional guidance may take place in Protestantism. Such inquiry would perform for Protestantism much of the function now performed by ascetical theology in the Catholic tradition. Perhaps our structure, which suggests the understandable but unfortunate conflict that has existed in Protestantism on this point, can have some releasing and motivating value to such inquiry.

Internals and Externals in Guiding

Recalling again that our peculiar historical situation in pastoral theology involves a lack of sense of identification with our own pastoral roots, we shall consider briefly some of Ichabod Spencer's pastoral work that involved guiding within the shepherding perspective.

One such experience is in some respects amusing to us and no doubt was not devoid of such an effect on Spencer, for he called this sketch "The Bird of Paradise."[5] Mrs. L. was a woman of middle age married to a man of seventy. When they had married, they had been both wealthy and prominent. But their circumstances had altered radically a few years before, and they were now poor. Spencer talked with both of them about religion. Neither had ever been Christians. Mr. L. from Spencer's point of view proved to be "as stupid as any sinner can be." But Mrs. L. was in earnest and wanted to become a Christian.

One day Mrs. L. came to Spencer, "to tell me of her hope in Christ, and how happy she was now, in the belief that God had forgiven and accepted her." Spencer questioned her "by way of examining her state of mind," which seemed "quite satisfactory." But then came the following:

SPENCER: How long have you had this hope and "this delightful happiness," which you mention?

MRS. L.: Since last Thursday night.

SPENCER: What then led you to believe that God had "heard your prayer, and sent you an answer of peace?"

MRS. L.: It was what I saw (*with hesitation, as if reluctant to answer*).

SPENCER: What did you see?

MRS. L.: It was (*hesitating*)—It was a great light (*solemnly, with evident sincerity but some excitement*).

SPENCER: Indeed! And where did you see it?

MRS. L.: In my room.

SPENCER: What was it?—what caused it?

MRS. L.: I don't know what it was, but it was *wonderful!* I shall never forget it.

SPENCER: Did it frighten you?

MRS. L.: Oh no, not at all.

SPENCER: Was it moonshine?

MRS. L.: No, not at all like it.

SPENCER: Did it shine in at the window? or through a crack?

MRS. L.: Neither; it was just in the room.

SPENCER: What did it look like?

MRS. L.: It was very wonderful, the sweetest light I ever saw. It was brighter than any sunshine; but it was so mild and soft that it did not dazzle the eyes. It was *perfectly* beautiful—most enchanting.

SPENCER: Well now, Mrs. L., just tell me all about it; I want to know how that was, the time, and all about it.

MRS. L.: I had been sitting up a long time after Mr. L. went to bed, reading my Bible and trying to pray, and I almost despaired of mercy, because my heart was so wicked and obstinate. I felt as if I *could not* go to bed that night, without some proof that God would have mercy upon me. . . . Finally I went to bed. I had been lying in bed about half an hour thinking of my condition, and all at once, the most beautiful light I ever saw shined all over the room. . . . It was mild and so soothing, it filled me with perfect peace, a kind of sweet ecstacy, like a delightful dream. Then, in an instant, as I was thinking how delightful it was, there appeared the most beautiful creature that I ever saw. . . . It was a bird. He had a rainbow in his bill, and a crown of glittering, soft-shining gold upon his head; he was resting on a globe of the softest blue, the most enchanting color that ever was. . . . I was amazed and perfectly happy. "What is it?" says I, "What is it?" "Why it is the bird of Paradise," says I. "My precious Father has sent it to me from heaven, I will not despair any longer. . . ."

SPENCER: What makes you so happy?

MRS. L.: Because, I think God has forgiven me, and because now I love Him and trust Him.

SPENCER: How do you feel about sin?

MRS. L.: Oh, I hate it. It displeases God, and separates me from Him.

After this type of interrogation had proceeded for a time, there came the following:

SPENCER: Do you think the appearance which you saw on Thursday night, was something sent by God?

MRS. L.: Yes, I suppose it was.

SPENCER: How do you know but the devil sent it?

MRS. L.: I never thought it could come from anything but God.

SPENCER: For what purpose do you think He sent it?

MRS. L.: To give me peace.

After a time Spencer asked where Mr. L. was at the time of the bird's appearance.

MRS. L.: He was asleep.

SPENCER: If he had been awake, do you think his eyes would have seen them?

MRS. L.: Certainly, I suppose so.

SPENCER: Why didn't you wake him?—is not he fond of birds?

MRS. L.: I don't know but he is fond of birds. . . .

SPENCER: Have you got a canary-bird?

MRS. L.: No, sir.

SPENCER: Did you ever see a bird of Paradise?

MRS. L.: No, sir, not alive. I have seen stuffed ones.

SPENCER: Which are the prettiest,—the stuffed ones or the one you saw that night?

At this point Mrs. L. "cast her eyes down, with a look of mingled sadness and confusion, evidently thinking by this time that I meant to ridicule her vision."

MRS. L.: Nothing on earth can be compared with what I saw that night.
SPENCER: Did the bird sing any?
MRS. L.: No, sir.
SPENCER: That is a pity. If he had only sung, then you would have had a song of Paradise. What became of the bird?
MRS. L.: It went away.
SPENCER: Why didn't you catch it and cage it? It would have brought a good price in Boston. Did it fly out of the window?

After a time Spencer said:

SPENCER: It is a great pity you did not catch that bird. If the sight of him is so effectual, we could carry him around here among impenitent sinners; and, as soon as they saw him, one after another, they would become happy, excellent Christians, and your bird would be worth more to convert sinners than forty ministers like me.

Spencer asked her if on reflection she did not think this had been a dream.

MRS. L.: It was no dream. I was awake. Don't you think I saw that light, sir?
SPENCER: No, madam; I don't believe you saw any such thing. I believe you think you saw it; but I believe it was all in your own imagination, and nowhere else.

Spencer then explained in detail to Mrs. L. what he believed had happened. Before going to bed, he indicated, she had very much wanted happiness in Christ and had wanted something to lead her to that happiness. "Then, in a state betwixt sleeping and waking, . . . your imagination just wrought out the expected wonder. . . . This accounts for all you thought you beheld. . . ." He then analyzed impressions made by dreams as against those made in a waking state and asked Mrs. L. if her impression was not more like a dream than like the waking condition.

MRS. L.: Indeed, sir, I am at a loss. That does seem more like a dream than like a real thing. But I was awake. My eyes were open. I don't remember waking up.

SPENCER: I don't wish you to reason, or argue, or decide anything about it, whether you were asleep or awake. I only wish you to tell me as you remember that night, whether your impression resembles most the impression of a dream, or an impression made when you were awake.

MRS. L.: (*Slowly and thoughtfully*) It is just like a dream; but I was awake, for my eyes were open.

SPENCER: Very well, madam, I will not trouble you any more. If you want to know what *religion* is, ask your Bible, don't ask night birds, or night rainbows.

The interview closed. Later on, when Mrs. L. was sick, she had "some other strange sights which I know were fancies," and this finally convinced her that the bird of paradise had also been a fancy. When these new appearances had come, Mrs. L. had got out of bed to examine them and found them gone. She was then able to concentrate on becoming a Christian without the evidence of signs and wonders, and her final statement to Spencer was:

MRS. L.: I wish you would not say anything about that bird of Paradise, and the blue globe I told you about at first. I was deceived. I know they had nothing to do with religion, and I do not rely upon them at all as any witness that God has given me a new heart.

Spencer concluded this report with this comment, "The religious treatment of persons of strong imagination and weak nerves, is one of the most delicate and difficult duties." Spencer felt that "it is not likely that all I said to her would entirely have corrected her erroneous idea, had not her subsequent experience lent its aid."

Once the story of the bird had emerged, Spencer saw but two alternatives: either to agree or to disagree that it was real, to agree that it had been there or to demonstrate that it had been imagination or like a dream. If we were called upon to deal with Mrs. L., no doubt we should proceed from a wider choice of alternatives. We might accept the psychic reality of the bird, its reality to Mrs. L., and aid her to express and clarify what its appearance symbolized for her.

But a moment's recollection will show that Spencer tried to do just that. He did not begin by saying the bird was unreal; he said that only in later reply to a direct question by Mrs. L. He attempted to analyze for her the psychic condition that had produced the vision. That is, he attempted to demonstrate to her that he understood her feeling of the reality of the vision. For a time he used satire, or what he called "ridicule," thinking this might shake her belief in the vision's reality; but when this did not work, he abandoned it.

So at first glance Spencer seems to us all wrong, and we could not follow his specific words and techniques. Yet with the exception of the satire what he was attempting to do was not basically different from what we should try. He communicated the understandability of the vision and thus his acceptance of Mrs. L. as a person, including her vision; but he tried to guide her to evaluate the vision differently from what she had done at first. Yet with the possible exception of the satire this guiding was through attempting to make contact with internal experience she felt as hers. This is most evident in the discussion of dreams.

We are more impressed than Spencer that, if Mrs. L. had been aided to grasp the symbolic meaning of the dream to her on her own, this would itself have begun to lead to re-evaluation. At such a point Spencer was more externalistic than we should try to be. Yet with all our acceptance of "psychic reality" the most we might achieve might be little more than Spencer, namely, guiding Mrs. L. to get out of bed and try to grab it the next time a bird appeared.

Single-minded as Spencer was, he feared that Mrs. L.'s retention of the vision as a sign of God's mercy would lead her to try to live the Christian life by lying in bed watching for birds. If this was the result, then she could hardly put much trust in the Bible and the way of salvation it made plain. Birds, even imaginary birds, might be all right in their place; but if it was to be birds versus the Bible, out with the birds.

It is true that we would work harder than Spencer to attempt to educe from Mrs. L. the symbolic meaning of her vision, the dynamic function it performed in her psychic economy. Yet finally we, like him, should be concerned if persistent and continued attention to the vision would not release her to consider what was fundamentally important to her life. We could pay attention to the vision in such a way as to make us forget our ultimate concern. Against this Spencer is a warning.

With Mrs. L., Spencer is guiding. He is guiding for her welfare. His specific methods are not congenial to us. And yet the real guiding takes place, as he himself finally stated only in so far as he could link externals with what Mrs. L. felt to be internal to her. Guiding, even in Spencer, was not imposition. What did the genuine guiding was that which made contact. Anything that did not make such contact might as well have been left unsaid, so long as it remained clear that Spencer did not necessarily agree with Mrs. L.'s interpretation.

A very brief story shows another side of Spencer's guiding.[6] A young woman member of Spencer's church urged him to see her sister. He was reluctant because the sister belonged to another denomination, and he did not want to "appear of a proselyting spirit." But on the sister's insistence he went. Spencer found Miss A. "very much agitated, trembling and sighing."

SPENCER: You seem to be very much troubled. What is it that distresses you?
MISS A.: I have been converted three times, and I feel as if I needed it again!
SPENCER: Take care that you do not get converted again *in the same way.* All that has done you no good. Has it?
MISS A.: No; not at all!
SPENCER: Then, do not get converted *so,* again. You want a religion that shall last,—a religion to die with; and I advise you to get an entirely new kind.

Spencer talked with her for some time, "aiming to teach her the nature of religion, and to quell the excitement of her mind, which appeared to me to arise more from an agitation of her sensibilities, than from real conviction of sin." All this, it turned out, did no good. At an "exciting assemblage" one evening she was converted again in the same old way, "was as joyful and happy as she had been before, and her religion lasted this time about six months." Spencer concluded his report, "Fanaticism is not faith."

Since Spencer failed here, even he cannot contend that what he did was necessarily best. We can see that serious attention on our part to what had happened to Miss A. might have prepared the soil for an "entirely new kind" of religion, and we may be justly critical of Spencer for attempting to plant seed without prior soil cultivation. In the absence of this he was not able to make a vital contact with anything felt as internal by Miss A., whereas the "exciting assemblage" did just that, illusory as its results may have been. Because Spencer did not take Miss A. with the same seriousness as he took Mrs. L., the guiding was far less effective.

A final brief story of Spencer's is necessary to show his ministry of guiding.[7] A young man (we shall call him Mr. T.) was clerk in a dry-goods store. He came to Spencer with a problem of "conscience in trade."

His employer expected him, he said, to do some things which he knew were not quite right. As an illustration,

he must learn to judge by the appearance of any woman who entered the store, by her dress, her manner, her look, the tone of her voice, whether she had much knowledge of the commodity she wished to purchase; and if she had not, he must put the price higher, as high as he thought she could be induced to pay. If there was any objection to the price of an article he must say, "we have never sold it any cheaper," or, "we paid that for it, madam, at wholesale," or, "you cannot buy that quality of goods any lower in the city."

Mr. T.'s boss had told him everybody did this, that one could not run a store in any other way, that all was fair in trade, and that he was green. Indicating that his old mother back home would not think it right for him to do such things, Mr. T. paused.

SPENCER: And do you think it right?

MR. T.: No,—I don't know,—perhaps it may be. [My employer] says there is no *sin* in it, and he is a member of the church; but I believe it would make my old mother feel very bad, if she knew I was doing such things every day.

SPENCER: I venture to say, that your mother has got not only more religion, but more common sense than a thousand *like him*. He may be a member of the church, the church always has some unworthy members in it, I suppose; but he is not a man fit to direct you. Take your mother's way and refuse his.

MR. T.: I shall lose my place.

SPENCER: Then lose your place, don't hesitate a moment.

MR. T.: I engaged for a year, and my year is not out.

SPENCER: No matter; you are ready to fulfil your engagement. But what was your engagement? Did you engage to deceive, to cheat and lie?

MR. T. Oh, not at all.

The conversation continued in this manner. Spencer finally predicted, "I *do* believe, *that man will fail!* Mark him well; and remember what I say, if you live to notice him ten or twenty years hence."

The young man returned to the store determined to be honest and was soon fired. But he found "another place," then went into business for himself and "prospered." In contrast "his employer became bankrupt about seven years after he left him. . . . He still lives, . . . but in poverty." In this instance the sun apparently decided to shine only on the just.

On first examination Spencer's guiding seems to be entirely external-istic. From nearly the first word, he tells Mr. T. what to do. He brushes aside objections and even appeals to prudence to support what is right and punish what is wrong. Such an impression is not wholly mistaken. And yet it is not the whole story. Why did the young man come to Spencer, a minister? Why did he speak of the dissatisfaction his old mother back home would have if she knew? Spencer was right in assum-ing that the coming of the young man to him and in this way indicated that he was already leaning toward risking his job in order to be honest. Spencer met this expectation, pushed away the considerations on the other side, and thus strengthened the conscious resolve of Mr. T. to stop cheating.

What we cannot approve of in this dealing is the brushing away of the other side of the conflict (the negative feelings in this case, the fear of having no job, and so on) instead of bringing it up for examination; so that, once examined, it could be clear that the young man would probably not have come to Spencer at all unless he had been leaning in the one direction. Spencer did not understand this kind of process. Hence he rode one side of the conflict, while the other was pushed away. In this instance apparently miraculous results were achieved. But if Mr. T. had found himself unable to get another job and told himself that he had followed Spencer's advice, then Spencer would have contributed, how-ever unwittingly, to the decrease of Mr. T.'s responsible management of his own life.

Here, more than in the sketches cited previously, we can see that Spencer's ministry of guiding was handicapped by his lack of knowledge of the dynamics of negative feelings, which is now available to us if we wish to use it. Spencer perceived his guiding function in a far more externalistic way than we need to do. If Mr. T. is ready to talk with us at all, then there is some kind of leaning in a direction he associates, rightly or wrongly, with us. This makes it all the more important that we help him to express and assimilate feelings on the other side of the conflict. Here Spencer took great risks that we see were partly un-necessary.

Even in the ministry of guiding we find ourselves with some con-siderable kinship with Spencer, more so in his dealings with Mrs. L. than in those with Miss A. and Mr. T. Even he saw that the guiding that was successful proceeded by making contact with what the parishioner felt to be internal. But in the absence of psychological knowledge of the meaning of actual procedures, Spencer tended to foreshorten the guiding and to fail to make significant internal contact.

Summary

We began this chapter with the analogy of a guide to the North Woods. This was to show that the guiding aspect of the shepherding perspective is not a coercive, persuasive, interpretative, or defining-alternatives type of function when those terms are used in their ordinary connotations, but that guiding is eductive. The guide is to be expert but is never externalistically expert about that which this person requires guidance about. Like healing and sustaining, guiding, I contend, proceeds through evoking or leading out, through making contact with that which is internal and is (however dimly) so felt. This does not eliminate novelty from guiding, and such novelty may be needed and relevant when it builds on that which is felt as internal.

We recognize that guiding may proceed initially from concern to protect the community or church rather than the individual or small group; but guiding in such situations, I contend, belongs under the organizing rather than the shepherding perspective. Discipline and morality belong sometimes in one dominant perspective and sometimes in another. While in ideal form they are mutually supportive, the unity in actual existence should not be taken for granted. For reasons of this order we should reject moral theology as being cognate with pastoral theology, however important it may be to have an inquiry called moral theology.

We noted a contemporary pastoral situation in which shepherding was dominant and in which periods of healing, sustaining, and guiding were all involved. The attempt was made to show that the guiding aspect is, when done rightly, as eductive as those of healing and sustaining. Whereas sustaining is to be understood as a thrust toward healing but slowed or stopped by circumstance, it was argued that guiding should be conceived as a thrust toward healing mainly through reminder of resources that have been present, are now absent or weak, but that will return. This does not exclude the possible need for instruction and information; but it is my contention that the shifting of perspectives, when not done for defensive purposes, is not harmful when the shift is understood and acknowledged.

It was suggested that spiritual direction and ascetical theology have been unduly neglected in Protestantism and that reconsideration of the

171

purposes of these under the guiding aspect of the shepherding perspective might help their recovery in a truly Protestant form.

We turned, finally, to three of Ichabod Spencer's sketches to examine his ministry of guiding. Where his guiding was successful from our point of view, we saw that it made contact with and built on something recognized as internal by the persons with whom he was dealing. When it was merely externalistic, we found ourselves compelled to reject its pattern.

The implications of what I have said about guiding for a pastoral theology are less obvious than was true in the discussion of healing and sustaining. I have suggested important implications about the relation of morality. And I have indicated that the kind and quality of courses of action that will be taken are directly dependent, but not entirely dependent, upon the approach taken by the pastoral guide; thus the nature and definition of that approach is itself a point in pastoral theology.

A great deal of guiding that belongs under the shepherding perspective falls under the theological rubric of sanctification. Healing, salvation, or redemption have in some significant sense taken place. But new thorns arise along the path or new spiritual aches within the Christian. Guiding of a shepherding kind helps clear away the underbrush or relieve the ache, or perhaps helps hang on until the ache vanishes later on. The point that has principally been argued is concerning the how of such guiding, that its building on internals is itself a point of theological significance.

PART IV

Cognates

CHAPTER 9

Communicating

WE HOLD THAT THERE ARE TWO PERSPECTIVES COGNATE WITH SHEPHERD-ing, communicating and organizing. We now consider communicating.

It is important that the reader be clear about the purpose of the subsequent discussion and about its limitations. This book is about pastoral theology. It has not committed itself to an exposition of branches of theology arising out of inquiry from the perspectives of communicating and organizing. Strictly speaking, a discussion of communicating and of organizing as perspectives upon the functions of minister and church do not belong *within* a volume on pastoral theology as I have defined it. If the meaning and structure and content of pastoral theology from the Protestant Christian point of view were well established, and if our discussion was merely the presentation of a novel idea here and there within well-charted terrain, we could relegate communicating and organizing to those professing expertness about them.

But that is not the actual situation. The conception, meaning, method, and structure of pastoral theology in Protestantism are all amorphous. Our attempt to set forth a constructive preface to pastoral theology, therefore, has required us to bring some order to the whole field of which according to our view pastoral theology is a part. It has even been necessary to give some attention to the whole body of divinity, and still more necessary to consider those branches of theology that are operation-centered or function-centered rather than logic-centered. It has been at this point that we have had to discard many aspects of previous theories in order to find out with what branches of theology our own subject, pastoral theology, is cognate.

This in itself creates a peculiar situation. Setting out with no intention of constructing any theological theory other than pastoral theology,

I have nevertheless found it necessary to propose two cognate branches of theology, neither of which is generally recognized in the form in which I have proposed it. If I had alleged my expertness in those areas, perhaps the anomaly might be less. I do not in fact claim such expertness. Yet the meaning and method and content of pastoral theology will lack clarity unless we can in some degree support these conceptions by reference to cognate branches of theology.

Anomalous as it may be, therefore, we must examine communicating and organizing as perspectives upon all the operations of pastor and church, cognate with that of shepherding. We must, at least in a general way, indicate why we believe the study of operations from each of these perspectives will lead to a branch of theology. But the purpose for us is illumination of the shepherding perspective and the pastoral theology that results from its inquiry.

We noted previously that communicating deals with the Word or the Christian message, that the focus of this is saving truth and not merely any truth, but that the relationship this message bears to other knowledge or to knowledge in general cannot be stated accurately without the use of some model like that of the field theory. Even the most elementary form of the latter, it was contended, was useful in a theoretical statement of the relation of the gospel's focus and center to other knowledge and to culture. We agreed with the intention of Tillich's terms "ultimate concern" and "preliminary concern," but we felt this metaphor to be a chronological or linear interpretation, and required supplementation. We rejected the question of whether just this or that is the gospel and just something else bears no relationship of any kind to the gospel. We asked, instead, the question: What is the focus of the gospel, and what place in the field is occupied by this or that area of knowledge or culture? What is in the field, if we know its vector (force, position, and direction, so to speak), that points toward the focus, positively or negatively?

It was suggested that the study of communicating the gospel would be aided by a model such as the field theory. For when the focus is forgotten, idolatry should show up. When it is kept in mind directionally, then many things from the field may help point toward it. It was argued that such modes of thought could help to keep inviolate that which is unique about the gospel and yet would force inquiry about every area or vector of the field that may lead toward communicating and receiving of the gospel. We push on now to deeper dimensions of communicating.

Communicating as Relational

Behind all our specific ideas on communicating the gospel, there is the assumption that, if it is communicated (received and assimilated), something happens. Just because the gospel deals with saving truth about that which is most deeply important, the receiver of it can never remain unaffected by it. He is not like a warehouse that may elect to put the goods in dead storage. If the goods are not in evidence, we assume they have not actually been received.

Communicating the gospel finds a better analogy in the organic nervous system, however, than it does in warehouses or telephone systems. Even though the complexity and intricacy of telephoning has become very great, the analogy fails to suggest the immediate and total alerting that occurs when the organic nervous system is touched. Pathologies are of course possible in that system; but in their absence stimulus brings immediate, automatic, and in some respects total effect. We assume that the gospel, in the absence of "pathology" about reception, does the same.

If we continue to adhere to this assumption after due deliberation, as we must, then it follows that the study of communicating the gospel is always a study in relationship.[1] It is indeed necessary to study the nature of the gospel that is to be communicated and the nature of the human being who is to receive that gospel; but from the point of view of communicating the gospel, each of those studies is an abstraction from the total relational process. Suppose that we studied only the gospel itself. In that case, however pure our understanding of it should become, we should not be studying communication; for we should be paying no attention to the "pathologies" preventing its reception. If, on the other hand, we studied only the actual reception of the gospel, or the pathologies preventing such reception, we should be avoiding a critical consideration of our understanding of the gospel. Study of communicating the gospel must, therefore, be relational. If it is somewhere near being the true gospel and if not wholly impeded by pathologies in the receiver, then something happens. Where it does not, study of the whole relational process is required.

When we were examining shepherding, we saw that one of the dangers lay in such a close identification with one-to-one relationships that the shepherding perspective on all pastoral relations and operations might be lost sight of. When we turn to communicating, the danger lies in the opposite direction, that we shall make so close an identification with one-to-many relationships that the relevance of the communicating perspective to *all* pastoral operations may be obscured. Our own use of material involving mainly one-to-one relationships has been for the practical reason that they lend themselves more simply to analysis.[2]

It is natural that, when we think of communicating the gospel, our first word association is "preaching." But when are we studying preaching? If our assumptions are correct, even the most accurate and detailed study of a sermon on paper would succeed only in illuminating one factor in preaching as communicating the gospel. If the sermon was studied as delivered by the preacher, that factor would be delineated still more accurately. But no amount of study of the sermon and its delivery by the preacher can be regarded as in itself an adequate examination of communicating the gospel through preaching. To that end study of the congregation and of the relationship between preacher and congregation is also necessary. If the study of the discourse is careful and minute, and carried out in terms of basic principles, and the study of congregation and relationship is "by guess and by gosh," then there is a disproportion that will distort understanding of the communicative relationship.

A sermon and a preacher are, relatively speaking, very easy to study. A congregation and the relationship between preacher and congregation are, relatively speaking, very difficult to examine. It is in part for this reason that all the study that has been done through the Christian ages about preaching has still left us today without a thoroughgoing theory of communicating the gospel. Our understanding of congregation and relationship is still for the most part lacking in basic principles. We sometimes conceal this ignorance by calling preaching an "art," and it is true that any great preacher has an intuitive grasp of many basic principles as has any great artist. But an art that is not steadily inquiring about its basic principles, analytically as well as intuitively, may not advance and certainly cannot be practiced satisfactorily by those not great enough to grasp the principles by intuition.[3] Difficult as it may be to carry out and slow and halting as progress may come, there will be little advance in our understanding of preaching as the relational process of communicating the gospel until inquiry is directed to the whole complex relationship and not alone to the sermon and its delivery.

As in the discussion of shepherding, we shall examine communicating by way of one-to-one relationships, mainly because they are simpler to study. The choice is for this practical reason and represents no lack of belief in one-to-many or each-to-all modes of communicating the gospel. But let the reader be warned that the discussion will not succeed in touching all the complexities of communicating that are to be found in the latter types of relationship.

We call communicating a perspective upon all the acts and operations of pastor and church because there can be no such act or operation in which communication does not occur, even though in many situations communicating may not be the leading or dominating perspective. When shepherding was discussed, we saw that even the "purest" acts of shepherding could never have their meaning exhausted when examined only from the shepherding perspective. Perhaps the good Samaritan, pouring oil on the wounds and binding them up, never uttered a word that could be regarded as communicating by verbal means. Nevertheless his very act might do much to communicate his gospel in showing that it produced men like him who could perform acts of mercy like his.

Now that we are studying communicating, we shall find the reverse to be equally true. There is no act or operation so purely communicative in nature that shepherding is not involved. When we are considering specific operations, therefore, we bear in mind that our lifting out of their dominant communicating aspects does not exhaust their meaning.

As with shepherding, the nature of the communicating perspective may become clearer if we examine its aspects, by analogy like the bands of light after a beam has gone through a prism. We may first look at the way in which the tradition saw these.

Aspects of Communicating

To begin with, the tradition made a rather sharp distinction between communicating the gospel to those inside the faith and those outside. For those not in the faith communicating was "evangelism," "apostolics," halieutics," or "apologetics." For those inside the faith a single term other than "preaching" was not ordinarily used; but when it was, it was "edifying." For those inside the faith communicating was more regularly seen in three aspects: instructing or "catechetics"; celebrating or worshiping or "liturgics"; and "edifying" as deepening in the faith, usually identified with congregational preaching.

The first issue is, then, whether a sharp distinction is to be made between communicating the gospel to those inside as against those outside the faith. Some distinction there certainly is, or there would be no reality to salvation, redemption, and the new being in Jesus Christ. In persons the distinction is decisive. But does the Christian, after he has been made into a new creature, absorb and assimilate and learn new depths, aspects, and implications of the gospel by communicative processes that are essentially different from those by which he was brought to redemption? If so, then there would be a categorical distinction between "evangelizing" and "edifying." If not, then the distinction concerns quality and value and perhaps specific subject matter, *but not basic processes of communicating.* It is the contention here that the distinction, while decisively important *for persons,* is minor when viewed in the light of the processes of communicating.

The Christian is still a sinner. In principle (which Tillich notes means "in power and beginning") the sin that has alienated him from God has been forgiven, set aside. He has been made a new creature. But if he believes that his new creatureliness guarantees the disappearance of actual sin, that nothing in him is alienated from God, then he is professing angelic stature not human redeemed creatureliness. He may indeed have received the gospel "in power and beginning," but he cannot coast on that fact. Unless there is cultivation, the flower will be choked by the weeds. Unless the gospel is received more deeply, unless previously unexamined aspects or implications of it are attended, unless there is a continuing process by which the Word ("what drives Christ") is assimilated, that which was "in power and beginning" stops there and more likely regresses. Edifying communication is needed.

The fact that a beginning has been made indicates that a course has been set. The fact that this beginning was made in power means that one knows, so to speak, where to get gas for the entire trip; it does not mean that he has already loaded his car with all the gasoline the whole trip will require.

Every newly realized implication or depth of the gospel emerges out of the same kind of ambiguity that preceded the initial reception. The great mystics and the great prophets testify equally to this truth. The mystic has his "dark night of the soul" and the prophet his days in the wilderness. And in a lower pitch the same thing is true of every Christian. Where the new depth or implication is not recognized to be emerging through ambiguity, evil consequences result. Either the implication is rejected (for example, about race relations, the economic life, or sex) with ensuing bigotry; or it is embraced without humility, and the consequence is zealotry.

To be sure, there is a decisive difference to him who is saved "in power and beginning." [4] But the processes by which this salvation was first communicated to him are the same processes that can guide him to move within it toward sanctification. His old Adam is dead in principle but not in continuing fact and motive.

Without in any way attempting to minimize the decisive importance of being a Christian as against not being a Christian, however this be defined, therefore, we deny that there is a categorical distinction between Christians and non-Christians in terms of the processes by which the gospel is communicated. An adequate theory of communicating the gospel will devote attention to each of these as special cases, but a general or comprehensive theory is something we hold to be possible. A theory of communicating the gospel to non-Christians would not in our view be a general theory unless it also revealed at the same time the processes involved in communicating new depths and implications of the gospel to those who are already Christians. We must, therefore, reject the sharp and categorical distinction that has sometimes been made by the tradition, recognizing that the intention of the distinction was good, to show the decisive difference made by the gospel once received, but that this does not lead to a different process by which communicating is effected.

For those inside the faith the tradition noted instruction, edifying (deepening), and celebrating. For them instruction clarified, edifying deepened or made more real, and celebration reminded. If we make the terms more general, we can see that learning and deepening (or realizing, or absorbing, or assimilating) apply to those both outside as well as inside the faith in terms of process, if they will attend at all. Celebrating as re-minding can apply only to those who have been somewhere first. But participation with those who are being re-minded may be a means of communicating even to those not in the faith. In this sense, therefore, even celebrating may be said to have a communicative function to both those outside and those inside the faith.

As interrelated aspects of the function of communicating the gospel, therefore, we can accept: (1) learning, understanding, or instructing; (2) realizing, deepening, or edifying; and (3) celebrating, reminding, or commemorating.[5] The communicating perspective, then, can be used to examine all operations of pastor and church, perhaps best through the three related aspects of learning, realizing, and celebrating.

When we considered healing, sustaining, and guiding as the three

181

aspects of the shepherding perspective, we saw that healing was the process leading to restoration of a whole, sustaining was movement in a healing direction but stopped by circumstance, and guiding was the reminder that healing would begin again since it had been in process before. We can now say something similar for the aspects of communicating. Learning then becomes the realizing or assimilating of what we had not known or possessed previously. Realizing or deepening becomes the recognition of new, deeper, or broader meaning to that which has been known or possessed before. And celebrating is realizing or assimilating that becomes deeper not through new ideas or the perception of new connections, but through corporate acknowledging.

To suggest that communicating may be discussed in much the same way as we have considered shepherding is the main purpose of this part of our inquiry. Without attempting to argue in detail for the three aspects of communicating, as was done with shepherding, we shall let these rest on their own oars. We have established the connection of our proposed aspects with those of tradition; but at one important point, the sharp distinction between communicating to those inside and to those outside the faith, we have rejected the conclusion sometimes drawn by the tradition. In terms of the way in which the basic processes of communicating the gospel work, we see no categorical distinction between those within and those without the faith.

There is one thing more that I need to describe and in summary fashion attempt to demonstrate—that the study of all the operations of pastor and church from the perspective of communicating will result in a branch of theology cognate with pastoral theology. If such study is to result in theology, it must be that what is learned from the study of operations, when approached with theological questions in mind and followed by the drawing of theological conclusions, brings light or knowledge that is theological in character. The movement from operations to conclusions must be regarded as theological. The proper study of communicating the gospel is, then, both an application of theology and a contribution to theology. If it does not contribute to theology, it is not a branch of theology. If it does so contribute, in its own function-oriented way, then it is a branch of theology cognate with pastoral theology. This is our contention. As with pastoral theology, the movement is two-way rather than one.

If one asks whether such a "theology of communicating" exists neatly organized, clearly stated, and bound in leather, the answer is No.

182

Students of preaching have become timid when dealing with the in-escapable conclusion of their study, that this leads to theological contri-butions and does not merely apply theology discovered elsewhere. Students of religious education have of late been even more timid, although some of their predecessors recognized our point even if they sometimes confused the contribution of a theology of communicating with that of a systematic doctrinal theology. But a theology of com-municating cannot be a replacement for a doctrinal theology. It is not a competitor. If there prove to be points where it casts light correcting some doctrinal understandings, that does not make it a competitor but a cleansing helper.

If communicating is understood as clarifying, making real, and re-minding people of the Christian gospel, then it is communicating that was constantly in the mind of Ichabod Spencer. He viewed the way of salvation as beginning in religious instruction, leading through experi-mental religion to anxious inquiry in which the deepening realization of one's sinfulness (law) drove one to the mercy of Christ (gospel), after which one celebrated his rescue in joy and peace but always mind-ful lest reliance on good works, doctrine, the natural man, or even faith as one's possession should lead by backsliding into the old state.

As we saw in previous chapters, shepherding in its various aspects appeared often in Spencer's ministry. But it was to him less important than communicating. We noted that this was a good reason for studying shepherding through Spencer, since the absence of bias in favor of shepherding might teach us things difficult to learn where a pastoral leaning was obvious. A rough and no doubt subjective examination of the dominant perspective in each of Spencer's seventy-seven sketches shows that perhaps two thirds of them are most occupied with communi-cating. We shall have, therefore, no problem in finding material in Spencer.

One of the sketches indicates very well how Spencer attempted to communicate the gospel when the other person was openly resistive to embracing it as the level of depth Spencer regarded as necessary.[6]

Prior to his first call on Miss S., Spencer wrote as follows:

About to call upon a young woman, to whom I had sometimes spoken on the subject of religion, but who uniformly appeared very indifferent; I began to consider what I should say to her. I recollected, that, although she had always been polite to me, yet she evidently did not like me; and therefore I deemed it my duty, if possible, not to allow her dislike to me, to influence her mind against religion. I recollected also, that I had heard of her inclination towards another denomination, whose religious sentiments were very different from my own; and I thought therefore, that I must take care not to awaken prejudices, but aim to reach her conscience and her heart. The most of her relatives and friends were members of my church, she had been religiously educated, was a very regular attendant upon divine worship; and I knew, therefore, that she must have considerable intellectual knowledge, on the subject of religion. But she was a gay young woman, loved amusements and thoughtless society; and I supposed she would be very reluctant to yield any personal attention to her salvation, lest it should interfere with her pleasures. And beyond all this, I had heard, that she possessed a great share of independence, and the more her friends had urged her to attend to her salvation, the more she seemed resolved to neglect it.

Spencer rang the bell at Miss S.'s house, and she soon met him in the parlor. Spencer told her at once he had come to talk with her about religion, if she would, and asked whether she was ready to do so.

MISS S.: I am willing to talk with you; but I don't think as you do, about religion.

SPENCER: I do not ask you to think as I do. I may be wrong; but the word of God is right. I have not come here to intrude my opinions upon you, but to induce you to act agreeably to your own.

MISS S.: (*With a toss of the head*) Yes, you all say so. But if anybody ventures to differ from you, then they are "heretics," and "reprobates."

SPENCER: I beg pardon, Miss S. I really do not think you can say that of me.

MISS S.: Well—I mean—mother, and the rest of them; and I suppose you are just like them. If I do differ from you, I think I might be let alone, and left to my own way.

SPENCER: Most certainly, if your own way is right.

MISS S.: Well—I am a Unitarian.

SPENCER: I am very glad to hear it; I did not know as you were anything.

MISS S.: I mean that I think more like the Unitarians, than like you.

SPENCER: I doubt it; but, no matter. Never mind what *I* think. *I* am no rule for you. I do not ask you to think as *I* do. Let all that go. You may call me fool, or bigot, or—

MISS S.: (*Interrupting*) You are no *fool*; but I thing you are a *bigot*.

SPENCER: Very well, I am happy to find you so frank. And you—

MISS S.: (*Interrupting and blushing*) Oh, I did not mean to say that; indeed I did not. That is too impudent.

SPENCER: Not a bit. It is just right.

MISS S.: Well, it is true that I *think* so; but it was not polite to *say* it.

SPENCER: I thank you for saying it. But no matter what *I* am. I wish to ask you about yourself first; and then you may say anything to me that you please to say—Do you believe the Bible?

MISS S.: (*Tartly*) Yes—to be sure I do!

SPENCER: Are you aiming to live according to it? For example are you daily praying to God to pardon and save you?

MISS S.: (*With an impudent accent*) No!

SPENCER: Does not the Bible command you to pray? . . .

MISS S.: Yes, I know that; but I don't believe in total depravity.

SPENCER: No matter. I do not ask you to believe in it. But I suppose you believe you are a *sinner?*

MISS S.: Why, yes (*impatiently*).

SPENCER: And need God's forgiveness?

MISS S.: Yes.

SPENCER: Are you seeking for it?

MISS S.: No.

SPENCER: Ought you not to be seeking for it?

MISS S.: Yes; I suppose so.

SPENCER: Well, then, will you begin, without any more delay? and act as you know you ought, in order to be saved?

MISS S.: You and I don't agree.

SPENCER: No matter for that. But we agree in one thing: I think exactly as you do, that you ought to seek the Lord. But you don't agree with yourself. Your course disagrees with your conscience. You are not against me, but against your own reason and good sense—against your known duty, while you lead a prayerless life. I am surprised that a girl of your good mind will do so. You are just yielding to the desires of a wicked and deceitful heart. I do not ask you to think as I think, or feel as I feel; I only ask you to *act* according to the Bible and your own good sense—Is there anything unreasonable, or unkind, any bigotry in asking this?

MISS S.: Oh, no, sir. But I am sorry I called you a bigot.

SPENCER: I am glad of it. I respect you for it. You spoke as you felt—But let that pass. I just want you to attend to religion in your own way, and according to God's word. I did not come here to abuse you, or domineer over you, but to reason with you. And now, suffer me to ask you, if you think it right and safe to neglect salvation, as you are doing? I know you will answer me frankly.

MISS S.: No; I do not think it is.

SPENCER: Have you long thought so?

MISS S.: Yes; to tell you the truth, I *have*, a good while.

SPENCER: Indeed! and how came you still to neglect?

185

MISS S.: I *don't know!* But they keep talking to me—a kind of *scolding* I call it; and they talk in such a way, that I am provoked, and my mind turns against religion. If they would talk to me as you do, and reason with me, and not be *dinging* at me, and treating me as if I were a *fool,* I should not feel so.

SPENCER: They may be unwise perhaps, but they mean well; and you ought to remember, that religion is not to be blamed for *their* folly.—And now, my dear girl, let me ask you seriously;—will you attend to this matter of your salvation as well as you can, according to the word of God and with prayer, and endeavor to be saved? Will you do it, without any farther delay? If you are not disposed to do so; if you think it best, and right, and reasonable to neglect it; if you do not wish me to say anything more to you about it; then, say so, and I will urge you no more: I shall be sorry, but I will be still. I am not going to annoy you, or treat you impolitely.—What do you say? shall I leave you and say no more?

MISS S.: I don't wish you to leave me.

SPENCER: Well, do you wish, to seek the Lord?

MISS S.: I wish to be saved. But I never can believe in total depravity. The doctrine disgusts me. It sounds so much like *cant.* I *never will* believe it. I abhor it. And I *won't* believe it.

SPENCER: Perhaps not. I do not ask you to believe it. But I ask you to repent of sin *now*—to improve your day of grace, and get ready for death and heaven. I ask you to love the world supremely no longer—to deny yourself and follow Christ, as you know you ought to do. When you sincerely try to do these things; you will begin to find out something about your heart, that you do not know now.

MISS S.: But I don't like *doctrines!* I want a practical religion!

SPENCER: That practical religion is the very thing I am urging upon you; the practice of prayer—the practice of repentance—the practice of self-denial —the practice of loving and serving God in faith. I care no more about doctrines than you do, for their own sake. I only want *truth,* which shall guide you rightly and safely, and want you to follow it.

MISS S.: Well, if I attempt to be religious, I shall be a Unitarian.

SPENCER: Be a Unitarian then, if the Bible and the Holy Spirit will make you one. Do not be afraid to be a Unitarian. But get at the truth, and follow it, according to your own sober judgment. Study your Bible, for your own heart. Get right. Pray God to direct you. And never rest, till you feel, that God is your friend and you are his. I beseech you to this; because I love you and wish you to be right and happy.—And now, my dear girl, tell me, will you try to do it?

MISS S.: Yes, sir, *I will.*

SPENCER: I thank you for that promise. And I do trust God will bless you.

In a few days Miss S. sent for Spencer. She said her heart still rebelled and her mind would wander. Spencer "said but little to her, except to direct her to God's promises." After about ten days she sent again for Spencer. She had never before imagined, she said, how wicked she was. By this time she had reached the stage of genuinely anxious inquiring, as Spencer saw it. Although several more weeks and interviews were required, Miss S. finally "found peace and joy in believing in Christ." During the intervening period Spencer, "without letting her know it," asked Miss S.'s "officious exhorters" to keep quiet and stop dinging at her. The final statement by Miss S. as reported by Spencer was as follows:

Miss S.: I never should have believed it, if I had not found it out by my own experience. It was just as you told me. When I really tried to be a Christian, such as is described in the Bible; I found my heart was all sin and enmity to God. And I am sure, I never should have turned to Christ, if God had not shown me mercy. It was all grace. Now I believe in total depravity. But I learnt it alone. You did not convince me of it.

To which Spencer replied with a truth that followed the letter of the law, "I never tried."

In evaluating this attempt by Ichabod Spencer to communicate the gospel, there are some obvious counts against him from our point of view. There were occasions when he distorted what Miss S. was trying to convey, as when he assured her that he too was in favor of a "practical religion," while the meaning of "practical" was quite altered. He failed to admit honestly that in his judgment the tenets of Unitarianism were unchristian. Through much of the contact he seems to be pushing Miss S. in a direction in which she was not inwardly prepared to move. And he makes a categorical distinction between religion and everything else (including Miss S.'s feelings on everything but sin and salvation) that we have previously argued against. Perhaps most important, he seems to listen and attempt to understand—only as a preliminary to what he may say. Expression by Miss S. of her negative feelings about religion is encouraged by Spencer, so that he can tell her verbally that she has also other feelings.

A close look at this relationship, however, suggests some weighty virtues. At the beginning of the first contact Spencer explicitly defines the situation. He has come to discuss religion if Miss S. wishes to do so. If she does not, that is that. We may reject Spencer's compartmentalized view of the nature of religion. But we must acknowledge that there is an interpersonal honesty in this procedure that we must admire. Without such honesty, however achieved or brought into the open, communication is always in danger of becoming "propaganda" in the invidious sense. Perhaps Spencer was blunt where subtlety would have been better. But there was no deceptiveness about stating the purpose of his visit. If thereafter Miss S. permitted him to stay, it was by *mutual* agreement that the subject of their discourse would be religion.

There are some psychotherapists who believe that structuring the situation or defining the situation tends to be ineffective to the extent that it must be made explicit by the counselor. We should agree that the grasping of the situation by the person himself, when the whole context makes this possible, may be better; for this would indicate that he is further along toward the point where the therapy can aid him. But we believe that, where someone holds a view of the situation radically different from our own, and we sense this, we may be communicating psychic dishonesty if we do not say so. Suppose a person says to us that he is in trouble, that he wants to tell us his story and ask our advice, and all we reply is, "Go ahead." Having told his story, he will (with justice, since we seemed to accept *his* definition of the situation) request our advice. If we, then, indicate that we do not proceed by offering advice, he will be understandably indignant. If we had made a brief but explicitly corrective statement of the situation from our point of view at the beginning, counseling might proceed after the story was told.

Perhaps the best demonstration of the fundamental principle involved has come from Kurt Lewin's studies of group processes.[7] He and his colleagues made several studies of groups in which different kinds of leadership were exercised. Lewin called these "authoritarian," in which the leader completely dominated the group; "*laissez faire*," in which the leader was simply passive in relation to the group; and "democratic," in which the leader defined the situation so far as seemed necessary and then strove to transfer responsibility and decision to the group. The authoritarian leadership brought either passive conformity or antagonism. The *laissez faire* leadership proved ineffective not only from the point of view of the task to be performed but also from the standpoint of internal group relationships. The so-called democratic leadership proved more efficient as to task and more satisfactory as to communication within the group and between leader and group. At every point it had more honesty.

Although we may indeed regard Spencer's definition to Miss S. of the purpose of his call as blunt, and although we may reject his compartmentalized view of religion, we must agree that he did set a context of interpersonal honesty without which communicating might not have taken place at all. In *Heaven's My Destination*, Thornton Wilder pictured an obnoxious young man who went about asking people, "Are you saved?" [8] Rightly do we rebel against such crudity which, as Spencer noted, is likely to arouse only antagonism and resistance, and thus make communication negative. But if our ultimate interest is in helping people to be saved, and we regard this as taking place through the communicating and receiving of the gospel, then we cannot swing to a *laissez-faire* point in which for the old "Are you saved?" we substitute, "Do you mind if I just say hello?"

If we are serving as ministers of Christ and his church, then our interest is never merely and finally one of saying hello. To say hello may be fine. To say nothing but hello on a certain occasion may be excellent. But if we do not see and at the right time acknowledge the connection between what hello symbolizes and the reception of the gospel, then we are being dishonest. Crudity is bad, but failure in honest acknowledgment of ultimate goals may be just as effective in preventing communication of the gospel.

Spencer, however bluntly, defined the situation. In indicating her readiness to talk with him, then, Miss S. was agreeing to discuss what Spencer felt was crucial. Another thing Spencer does in his attempt to communicate to Miss S. is to reach for her "internals," for what she recognizes as hers. After the opening scene, in which Miss S. has declared herself more like the Unitarians, Spencer asks her if she believes in the Bible—rightly anticipating that even one with Unitarian leanings will have to say Yes to that. In the way in which it is done, this strikes us as coercive. But Spencer's intent was plainly to reach some ground that Miss S. would say was hers. This had to be, so to speak, common ground, in which Miss S. and Spencer shared, if communication was to result. We have already indicated our disapproval of Spencer's dealing with communication from Miss S. to him as only preliminary. Nevertheless, if he wants to communicate to Miss S., he must find some ground internal to her that is also related to what he wants to communicate. Taken alone, this principle can lead to exploitation and hence cannot stand alone. But however it is achieved and whatever other principles must be used as a safeguard, it is true that communicating does not communicate if it does not touch internals, or something one feels (however dimly) to be his.

In the third place, Spencer shows us that he believed there was a basic and reliable process by which the gospel was communicated, and that this process, especially because of the variety of forms in which it might appear, should be a subject of constant inquiry by the minister. "Sometimes one doctrine, or class of truths, and sometimes another, will take the lead in the reflections of an anxious mind, and so varied will these reflections become, that (it is believed), no wise man will ever attempt to describe religious experiences, which shall embrace all possible varieties." [9] The aim of all the conversations reported in the sketches was, Spencer wrote, "simply to cause the truth to be understood, felt, and received, as the sole and sure guide." [10] Although he warns in the first quotation against believing we have the whole truth about communicating and in the second defends the unity only of aim, the whole testimony of his study, as indicated in the very writing of the sketches, is for inquiry into the forms by which something felt to be unitary is to be achieved. Spencer saw the unity in the truth of the gospel, not in process terms, when he thought abstractly. But in concrete situations, as with Miss S., he assumed that A must occur before B will take place. Whether or not we agree with his understanding of what is basic in the process of communicating, we admire his perception of such a basic process and his recognition that it may assume a variety of forms.

There is a fourth virtue to be noted in Spencer's attempt to communicate to Miss S. From her point of view Spencer accepted her in a way that her mother and others did not. They kept "dinging" at her, she said, and treated her as if she were a fool, while Spencer's approach was to reason with her. They did not accept her but kept after her with a "kind of scolding." Whatever Spencer's approach looks like to us, to Miss S. it was acceptance in a way that her relatives and friends had not supplied. We do well to keep in mind that what does or does not convey acceptance is culture-bound, that the specific behavior that would convey acceptance to Miss S. in 1850 would probably fail in 1950.

Assuming that Miss S. did feel acceptance from Spencer, what basic factor produced it? The answer, as given by Miss S. herself, is that he accepted her right to state and hold her views and ideas without dinging at her. He did not accept these by agreeing with them except where he believed there was common ground; but he did accept her, we might say, as a person who had a right to hold these ideas, good or bad, true or false. The dinging by implication was of the order, "Oh, my dear, you mustn't believe that! If you do, why, it will be awful." To Miss S. such failure to consider her right to hold the ideas was felt as non-acceptance. So far as ideas and views are concerned, therefore, acceptance lies not in agreement but in communicating respect for the ideas because of respect for the person holding them. We should regard this as a general principle.

Finally, despite what seems to us like his much speaking, Spencer did believe profoundly that the ultimate agent of communicating the gospel is the Holy Spirit. That this doctrine may have been used by him at times, as it has been used by many others, as an excuse for obscurantism, we cannot flatly deny. But even when he was wrestling most vigorously with an anxious inquirer, it was never out of his mind that his activity alone could not be sufficient. This gave him often a surprising humility about the small place his own explicit attempts to communicate had had in a situation. Spencer dealt with one quiet and unemotional young woman who seemed to have the right ideas about religion who, although she was "still without peace," demonstrated "no additional anxiety" over this fact.[11] Finally, at an evening worship service Watts's hymn was sung that included these lines:

A guilty, weak, and helpless worm,
On thy kind arms I fall.

Later the young woman reported, "I sat all the evening, just looking at that hymn. I did not hear your prayer. I did not hear a word of your sermon. I do not know your text." To Spencer it was the Holy Spirit working through the hymn, rather than through his prayer or sermon or text, that communicated Christ and his gospel to the young woman.

Great teachers seem to have a quality of this kind. When attempting to convey something by explanation, they may put their whole mind and heart into it, and may have some gratification if they discover that the explanation itself produces enlightenment in some students. If no such results are achieved, they may re-examine their explanation. But if a student comes to say he has seen the point through work in the laboratory not through the teacher's explanation, the teacher will be delighted. He did the watering, and he must study watering; but the land gave the increase. Evidence of successful watering is to be found indirectly as well

PREFACE TO PASTORAL THEOLOGY

as directly and is never an excuse for euphoria. Perhaps such a teacher never thinks of the Holy Spirit, but he is respecting the function of something like the Holy Spirit in the communicating process.

As we have already noted of Spencer as a shepherd, Spencer as a communicator was more sensitive to varieties and complexities than he permitted his own theory to acknowledge. For instance, having got Miss S. to express some of both her positive and negative feelings about religion, he was inclined to attribute what resulted to his demonstration of the contradictions. We believe that this occurred only because of the context that had been established, that what was dynamic was the emergence of the two kinds of feelings, not Spencer's logical pointing to their contradiction. Spencer's theory did not acknowledge this, and yet he did not so state the contradiction as to negate the feeling of acceptance Miss S. felt from him. Here, as at many other points, a more adequate theorizing from his actual experience would have made him reinterpret aspects of his practice.

Some General Principles of Communicating

There have been in recent years many new approaches to the study of communication. Social psychology, group dynamics, psychoanalysis, industrial psychology, semantics—these are only some of the many fields that have turned to examining the processes of communication. As yet, there are few synthesizing studies that pick up the contributions from various areas. But the near future will undoubtedly see the advancement of understanding in specific areas and more adequate synthesis of what is now known from various perspectives.

In so far as these studies reveal general and comprehensive principles about the processes of communicating, they are of great interest to those concerned with communicating the gospel. The following brief remarks will suggest that we can profit from an understanding of these principles, although it is necessary for us to see them in the context of the operations of pastor and church.

The first principle that has emerged is that real communication takes place only in a certain kind of context or atmosphere.[12] For instance, group dynamics points out that the basic atmosphere must be accepting, initially by the leader and later by members one of another. As experience proves this acceptance to be genuine (not necessarily resting on agreement), each member will find it possible to communicate more of his deeper and more negative feelings. When these are in turn accepted, other members will be able to move in the same direction. The basic atmosphere, acceptance, helps each person to move toward the communication of new depths by absorbing wider and deeper areas of content that would at first have been divisive. The emergence of negatives that bend the group but do not break it is, therefore, a mark of the right atmosphere, not an indication that the group has failed. The point is that there is movement from one level of acceptance through the expression of negative feeling to a deeper level of acceptance.

Psychiatry and psychoanalysis have also made contributions to our understanding of context and atmosphere as the first requirement for communication.[13] In the study of psychotic sufferers, for example, we see a paranoid patient (who handles his difficulties by centering the blame for them on some person or thing) comprehend every word we tell him yet twist the total meaning, inevitably and compulsively, to fit within his delusional system. His rigid defense system provides a context in which there is no real communication. Yet we see also the mute catatonic patient, who may spend months in a stupor without saying a word or indicating that he hears one, emerging some day to recall everything he had heard during the period of stupor.

From various sources we have learned that anxiety consciously felt and experienced (which is painful) does not destroy capacity to communicate, but that anxiety denied to awareness is bound to impede or distort any communication at all. This suggests the second principle, that distortion of communication arises not alone from the absence of something (especially context and atmosphere) but also from the presence of something else. If communication is distorted, the people involved have somewhere, somehow, learned this distortion. This is good; for if distortion has been learned, it may yet be unlearned.[14]

Private meanings attached to something may distort communication. Experts on semantics are impressed with the difference between the public and private meanings that something may have to a person.[15] If you refer to a chair but manifest anxiety in doing so, I may feel baffled since we both attach the same public meaning to a chair. But I may not know, and you may have forgotten consciously, that you were once struck by a chair in the hands of someone with a beard like mine.

A third general principle of communication is that it must touch the frame of reference of the person or group to whom it is addressed. If it makes significant contact with this internal point of view, then attention can be paid by the person to those aspects of it that may be novel from the internal frame of reference. If such contact is not made, it will be not only rejected but also misunderstood.

The fourth and last general principle we shall note (there may well be others) is that communication becomes, finally, a two-way rather than a one-way process, or else it ceases to exist. Something may go on (the whipping up of prejudice, the adding of details), but communicating as assimilation and reception of what was not previously possessed ceases.

We regard these principles as both general and important, which means that they will be involved whenever there is successful communicating of the gospel. For the most part they are, however, merely descriptive. It is possible to follow all of them and thus to achieve a kind of communication—but to use this for exploitative purposes. This simply underscores the importance of having Christian principles of communicating that include and do not negate general knowledge but which are normative in regard to the functions of communicating.[16] Put in general terms, what must be added to the four principles above is the integrity of him who would communicate and his genuine receptivity to return-communication, which he accepts but without necessarily agreeing with it.

If we do not keep these last two points in mind, we may be misled into believing that the pattern for effective communication is what is sometimes seen in the media of mass communications. They do follow carefully at least the letter of the law of the first four principles. Atmosphere may be made folksy or elegant if those qualities have wide appeal. Appeal to private as well as public meanings may be seen not only in the pin-up girl advertising dog food but also in drawings of exotic food or remote fashions. Why must the average fashion model be about four inches taller than the average woman? The answer lies not in the positive valuation of female height, but in the proportion of length to breadth, appealing to the private ideal of many women. The frame of reference of those addressed may indeed be touched. And there may even be an invitation to two-way communication: "Write in care of this station."

But in some forms of mass communication we see many other principles at work: Don't hesitate to make the claims extreme as long as they keep the knob on; make it "corn" but don't say so; make the spine tickle through showing good fortune or bad; and repeat, repeat, repeat. It may be asserted that the purpose of these practices is to sell goods, that most fraudulent claims are not able to be advertised, that the buyer does not lose because most goods are of high quality and advertising calls attention to one trademark as against another. All this may be true. But if true, then what goes on in these forms of mass communication is not really communication in our sense at all. A free society may well tolerate it. The harm will come if we equate statistically successful mass communication with the communicative process in general and unconsciously use it as a pattern for communicating the gospel. There is an inevitable cynicism in contending that laboratory tests, or scientists, or a group of well-known physicians, or sources close to the White House, or men of distinction, all contend that Soap A works better on their washboards than Soaps B through X and Detergents 1 through 42, especially when we know that a major preoccupation of these gentlemen from the cradle up has been to keep as far as possible from a washboard. But there is no necessary harm in this if it does not become a pattern for real communication between real human beings.

If he who wishes to communicate actually has a treasure that he wants to share, then he does not need to soup up his claims. If the other reaches out to touch the treasure, to test it, or to knock it down, he feels no need to be defensive; the treasure can take care of itself, and even an attempted blow may turn into a bow. Communicating cannot, then, be a one-way process in which our sole job is to find the proper technical means to "put it across." It is a two-way process, or else we are not dealing with a process that is capable of transmitting the gospel.

If we are dealing with a person who is bereaved, attempting to offer him a ministry of sustaining and to communicate to him the sustaining aspects of the gospel, our ministry becomes ultimately comforting and sustaining to him only as we are first open to his communicating to us in full depth and intensity whatever it is that he feels, whether it be positive or negative and whether at first blush it seems to have anything to do with religion or not. This can be no mere gimmick or technique. Either we mean it deeply or it is nothing. But if we do mean it deeply (and granted the inevitable imperfection in its execution), some new depth of the gospel will be communicated to us and not alone to the other or others. When we restate it, this new depth may appear quite simple. Before, we might have said, "I know how deep suffering goes." Now we might say, "I know how deep suffering goes." Such a difference can conceivably mean a world of increase in theological understanding.

And what is increased when of this order is *theological* understanding.

Solely for the practical reason that one-to-one relationship situations are less complex than one-to-many or each-to-all, they have been used in this discussion of communicating. But it would seem that the basic principles that have been enunciated are equally relevant in more complex relationships. Unlike the one-to-one relationship situation the member of the worshiping congregation may not be able to question the preacher point by point nor to tell the preacher his ideas then and there. Translation of the principle of two-way communicating must, therefore, be other than literal. But if the preacher in preaching gives no evidence that he has ever listened to those who are having difficulty receiving the gospel and does not suggest that he will be prepared to do so again, then he is rendering the two-way principle null and void. We may indeed have convictions that we wish to convey to others. But our act and attitude of listening (past, present, or future), of understanding the private world of the other, carries with it our respect for it, our acceptance of it as a fact of human life. We understand its understandability; we do not listen merely as a prelude to putting our views across.

Human communicating has several modes and innumerable degrees. It may be casual, neutral, or intimate. It may proceed through gesture, through touch, through tone, or through words. Sex in its most basic aspect is a language of intimate communication. The most distinctive thing about most human communication, however, is its use of language, a language that always has private as well as public meaning. We whose calling is to proclaim the Word of God and to attempt to bring it to men for needed salvation shall be greatly in error if we think of words (or of intellect) as mere passive accompaniments to the vitalities of life that are presumed to lie elsewhere. As the principal tools of communicating, words (and intellect) may and should have vitality.

Summary

We have directed a brief inquiry to communicating the gospel as a perspective upon all the operations of pastor and church, cognate with the perspective of shepherding. This has been for the purpose not of presenting a systematic and rounded theory of communicating, for which there is neither space nor skill, but of attempting to demonstrate the meaning, structure, and content of pastoral theology in part through showing that with which it is cognate. If it had been possible to find a discussion of communicating elsewhere that met our requirements, it could have been referred to and this discussion omitted from our inquiry. But with due respect to the wisdom contained in many writings on preaching, on Christian education, and on principles of communication, none considers all the factors I felt it essential to mention even in so brief a space.

The branch of *theology* that, we have noted, will arise out of a study of operations entered on with theological questions in mind has only been implied or hinted at here. More time has been given to method than to content, in the belief that the potentialities in studying communicating may be better shown thereby. We noted communicating as a two-way process, as a process that can be understood only in relational terms. We posited a single basic process of communicating, relevant equally to him who has not become a Christian and to him who has. It was suggested that study leading to better understanding of this process and the variety of forms in which it appears would itself result in knowledge of a theological order.

It was suggested that communicating might be studied through three aspects: learning, understanding, or instructing; realizing, deepening, or edifying; and celebrating, reminding, or commemorating.

We analyzed in some detail an attempt by Ichabod Spencer to communicate the gospel to a young woman who had considerable resistance to receiving and assimilating it. We criticized Spencer in several respects but were impressed by the truths about communicating to which he called our attention. We liked his courage in an honest declaration of his communicative purpose. We liked his intention of making contact with the "internals" of him with whom he would communicate. We agreed with his conviction that there is a basic and reliable process by which the gospel is communicated, however much our ignorance about it should counsel our humility. And we felt that his communicating succeeded to the degree that he accepted the person to whom he was communicating. Finally, we were recalled by Spencer's communicating to reconsider the doctrine of the Holy Spirit.

Last we turned to a sketchy summary of basic principles of human communication that have emerged from modern inquiries. In so far as these principles are general, we argued their relevance to communicating the gospel. But it was asserted that these descriptive principles are not in themselves adequate for a theory of communicating the gospel, so some normative principles were suggested to go with them. A full theory of communicating the gospel, we hold, must include both kinds.

CHAPTER 10

Organizing

AS IN THE PREVIOUS CHAPTEP ON COMMUNICATING, THE CONTENT OF THE present discussion on organizing is not strictly speaking a part of pastoral theology according to our definition. Like the consideration of communication, it is included to show what is cognate with pastoral theology and in that indirect way to illuminate the content of pastoral theology.

The central idea with which we shall be dealing is fellowship, the processes by which an association becomes a body and then acts like a body. The English language does not have a word clearly connoting this notion. "Incorporate" has lost such power. Even the "incorporation" of a church suggests its legal status rather than the concrete processes by which it becomes the body of Christ or a part thereof.[1]

"Organizing" also has misleading connotations. It ought to mean, as we shall here use it to mean, "making into an organ," the processes by which the organs (interconnected parts) are formed, maintained, and act, and therefore the processes by which a body is formed, maintained, and acts. But we have to fight the language for this meaning. A "good organizer" is one who lays everything in neat rows or who does everything on schedule, even if the rows and the schedule are not worth the effort. A "good organization" operates efficiently; never mind what it is about. That is, these words have not lost their reference to an organ or a body, but the organ or body have become a kind of lump. What is suggested is not the mutually supportive intricacy of concrete internal functioning, but the compact entity of mass seen from outside. All these connotations are misleading for our purposes. But in the absence of a better term, we shall have to refer to "organizing."

In this discussion we have seen the first object of shepherding to be persons; of communicating, the gospel. Co-ordinately the first object of organizing is the fellowship, the "body of Christ." The organizing perspective examines all the operations of pastor and church to see how they produce a body or an organ within the total body. In Chapter 4 it was indicated that this involves two phases: first, the making or emerging of the body or organ; and second, the interrelationships of the functioning body or organ as such. Organizing was called "the perspective of social embodiment."

The Biological Metaphor of the Church

Organizing in our use does imply ordering and structuring, but of a kind that produces an organ or a body (intricate functioning of interconnected parts) and in which any organ so functions that it is a mutually supportive part of the body of which Christ is head. In the intricacies of ecclesiastical negotiation some churchmen regret that the great leading metaphor of the church as the "body of Christ" was taken from biology. In contrast we should assert that this is its strength. Every fundamental advance in biological understanding provides potential new tools for grasping the deeper meanings of a body or an organ. There may indeed be occasions when the metaphor of organic functioning is inadequate as a framework for discussing the church, although these become less as the nature of organic functioning becomes better understood. Even so, we should hardly want to think of the church as a suborganic or inorganic lump. No theory of the church has viewed men as monads connected with the top (God or Christ) but wholly unrelated to one another. To be members one of another in a body having the same head is, however, the basic meaning of the organic metaphor.

It is tempting to pursue the organic metaphor itself in the light of new learning in biology, and the neglect of this by churchmen is unfortunate.[2] We shall, however, make only a few points especially pertinent to our concern. For one, an organ never grows by mere accretion, but according to a pattern determined by its function within the total body. Growth by accretion alone would be a cancer. Even if such pathological growth was in straight rows or lovely curves, it would be harmful because straightness or curvedness would not be the pattern facilitating the organ's function within the total body. To prevent such a connotation, we now say that an organ "develops," thus suggesting patterned movement according to function. Organic development proceeds from an original diffuse unity toward finer and finer differentiations, all of which, however, are to result in a new and more intricate order of functional unity. If there was no differentiation, there would be no flexibility, complexity, and specificity of function. If the differentiations were not brought to new levels of unity, however, the organ would cease to be an organ.[3]

Another point about organic functioning is that it is mutually supportive and in tension at the same time. The parts aid one another, and yet they do so in tension. A tensionless organ would be dead, but an organ with non-co-operative parts would disintegrate. A false picture of organic functioning is given if either tension or mutual support is mentioned without the other.

A third point about organic functioning is that an organ has functional autonomy, but that this autonomy is meaningful only in relation to the whole body. The organ performs certain functions; the same functions are not assigned indiscriminately to every organ. But each function, finally, would be without meaning if not within the context of the whole body.

The final point I shall make is that the processes of restoring equilibrium to organic functioning (homeostasis) and of mobilizing the organism for threat or challenge (emotion) are the same but operate in reverse directions according to the nature of the context.[4] These and other principles of organic functioning offer promise for deepening the meaning of organizing the fellowship or the church.

If the organic metaphor is relevant at all, then, we may say the following things about the organizing of the fellowship. First, such organizing is not to be viewed as mere accretion, as growing bigger. If the pattern is not appropriate to function within the total body, no amount of growth will be helpful or relevant. Second, there can be no fellowship without the concurrent presence of mutual support and tension. To stress unity as if tension and diversity were evil in themselves is a misunderstanding. To stand on tension and diversity as if they could exist outside a context of mutual support is also an error.

Third, each unit of the fellowship is responsible for directing itself, and this directing does not exclude novelty. But the autonomy is itself real only in relation to the whole church of Christ. Finally, those processes that will lead to the "peace and unity of the church" are the same as those used to protect it, the directions simply being reversed according to the context. The processes are not wholly different in nature.

It is not my desire to dwell unduly on the organic metaphor. What has been said is simply to suggest the potentialities it has as preliminary to our consideration of organizing as a perspective upon the operations of the church and pastor.

Aspects of Organizing

Organizing the fellowship of the church may be seen in three aspects: (1) nourishing, feeding, or aiding its development; (2) protecting or purifying from threats within or without it; (3) relating it, positively or negatively, to other bodies such as institutions, cultures, or states. All of these aim at the organic wholeness, integrity, and welfare of the fellowship; but each is dominantly relevant in a different kind of situation. Nourishing is to aid organic development in its subjective or autonomous aspect, when threat is minimal. Protecting is dominant in the face of threat. Relating is dominant when threat or potentiality from other bodies demands attention.

As was indicated in the discussion of shepherding and communicating, there is no concrete event or operation from which organizing, as used here, is absent; but in some situations this will be dominant. The same is true of each of the aspects of organizing. Nourishing tends to be dominant in corporate worship, but it is not absent from pastoral counseling or religious education. Protection tends to be dominant when discipline and moral questions are at issue and when the perspective is mainly for protection of the fellowship, but it is not absent from other events. Relating tends to be dominant when social ethics or ecclesiastical foreign affairs are the operations, but it is not absent from preaching or evangelizing.

On the question of how the fellowship is organized in each of its aspects, how nourishing, protecting, and relating are to be carried out, there have been deep differences of conviction. Ernst Troeltsch drew the distinction between the "church type" of church and the "sect type" of church.[5] Especially when these are regarded as ideal types, so that no actual church is ever entirely of one type or the other, they are useful even for our present purpose.

To the (ideal) church type of church, nourishing is carried out primarily through the rites and sacraments. To the (ideal) sect type of church, nourishing is done principally by the Word, which is also brought home to persons in the sacraments. In both instances development of an organic kind is desired, but each has a different emphasis as to what is most basically important to produce that result.

To the church type, protection of the church is achieved mainly

201

through guaranteeing something about its priesthood, for example its apostolic succession. To the sect type, protection of the church is handled mainly through entrance requirements for members, including the clergy.

To the church type, relating tends to move in the direction of control of other institutions and culture. To the sect type, relating tends to move toward withdrawing to the extent possible.

When these implications of the ideal church and sect types are put so sharply, the immediate reaction is toward both/and. And there is something to this, since even the newest and most enthusiastic sect-type church is not without church-type features; and even the most monolithic church type has some sect elements. But the fact remains that every church tends dominantly toward one type or the other. The ecumenical movement does not deny this, nor should it. Its task is to find and declare the common context within which those differences that are enriching may be shared and those that are divisive may at least be discussed.

Types of Organizing

Before going further with our theory of the organizing perspective, we shall consider what Ichabod Spencer did with this. It is already clear that what Spencer mainly thought of was communicating the gospel. At first glance it would appear that organizing was far from his mind. Yet the fact is that his view represents a certain theory, mostly of the sect type, of organizing.

The situation I am about to describe was called by Spencer "The Persecuted Wife." [6] Since he does not give her a name or initial, we shall call her Mrs. W. Spencer wrote that he had seen Mrs. W. several times and had suspected that she wished to join the church. When he called upon her one day and broached the subject, Mrs. W. replied that she did want to take such a step, and she felt that the "Holy Spirit had renewed her heart, and Christ had accepted her." But there was, she continued, an obstacle in her path. She feared that her husband would oppose this move. He was, she went on, a somewhat intemperate man; and she implied that he, when properly soaked with the means of intemperance, was likely to be "tyrannical." As she had thought all this over, it had occurred to her that her husband never said or asked anything about religion or the church. Since she wanted to join the church and felt that Christ had accepted her, and since her husband was unlikely to say anything about church, she had concluded that the thing to do was to go right ahead and join—but to say nothing to her husband about it.

At this point in Spencer's account, one can see the hackles rising. He wrote, "To this proposal, I could not consent." Spencer gave Mrs. W. his reasons. For one thing, Mr. W. was Mrs. W.'s husband; and as such she was obligated to honor him. Besides, whatever his faults, she ought to be kind to him, and secrecy would not be kindness. If he should find out that she had joined the church secretly, he might be less kind to her than otherwise; and in any event he would be more against religion and the church than ever. Spencer summed up his rejection of her secretly joining the church in these words:

She must not be ashamed of Christ, or fear to do her duty in the face of all opposition. . . . And if she had so little faith, that she could not confess Christ for fear of any wicked man's displeasure . . . ; I could not have confidence enough in her piety, to consent to her reception into the church.

After Spencer had given his reasons for opposing this move, the following took place.

MRS. W.: Then I can never come to the Saviour's table!

SPENCER: I think you can, Madam. In my opinion, your husband will not be so much opposed to you, as you think. If he should be, you can pray for him; and He who hears prayer can remove his opposition.

MRS. W.: (*Much agitated*) What shall I do? I do think it my *duty*, to come out from the world and own Christ, as my Saviour and Lord; and I long to do so. But I am afraid of my husband. I know he would never consent to it; and would abuse me, if I should name such a thing in his hearing!

SPENCER: You have not tried it, Madam. You have nothing to fear. God loves his children; and for their sakes often restrains wicked men. Besides, your husband is not so bad a man as you think, probably.

MRS. W.: Oh! sir, you don't know him. He sometimes talks to me in a dreadful manner, if he finds me reading the Bible, or crying.

SPENCER: Well, it is nothing but talk. He has just manliness and courage enough, to bluster and abuse a poor woman like you, with his tongue, but he will go no further. If you do your duty, he will not dare to injure you. And quite likely, when he sees you are firm, your example will be the means of leading him to repentance.

MRS. W.: What *shall* I do? I wish you would tell me.

SPENCER: I will tell you, Madam. When your husband comes home, take some favorable opportunity, when you are alone with him, and when he appears calm, sober, and good-natured; and just tell him seriously and kindly, how you feel, what you think of your past life, what you believe God has done for you, and that you have come to the conclusion, it is your duty to unite with the church. If he is angry, or speaks unkindly to you; have no disputes, not a word of argument, hear all he has to say, in silence. You may tell him, if you think best, that you have done all your duty to him, as well as you could, while you had no religion; and now you mean to do it better. But you think you owe duties to your God also, which ought not to be neglected. But do not say one word, unless your feelings are kind, and mild, and calm. You must feel rightly, or you will not speak rightly.—You can at least tell him this; and see what he will say.

Mrs. W.: Well, I will do it, if you think it best.

Three days later Spencer returned and found Mrs. W. in a "deep depression." She had followed Spencer's advice to the letter. After she had spoken her piece, her husband had at first been silent. But then he had begun to work himself "into a dreadful passion." He had sworn that he would not live another day with his wife if she joined the church, that he would turn her out of the house. All church people, he had said, were "hypocrites" and the minister was a "*villain.*" If the minister ever came to his house, he had said, he would "put him out of the house quick."

Nothing daunted, Spencer asked when Mr. W. was likely to be home. Mrs. W. replied that he would be there in about an hour but begged Spencer not to return at that time.

Mrs. W.: Oh! no, sir, no! I hope not! He will abuse you. I don't know what he would not do!

Spencer: Never fear. He will not trouble me. You need not tell him I have been here, this morning. And if I meet him here at noon, do not leave me alone with him; stay and hear what he will say to me.

Mrs. W. implored Spencer not to return, but in an hour he was back. Here is Spencer's account of his interview with Mr. W.:

I spoke to him, gave him my hand, and conversed with him for some minutes. He was rather taciturn, appeared a little sullen, but he did not treat me with any special rudeness. I mentioned to him the altered feelings of his wife; and expressed my hope, that he would himself give immediate and prayerful attention to his salvation. I solemnly assured him, that without being born again he could not see the kingdom of God; and that though he had neglected it so long, salvation was still within his reach. But that he would soon be on the down-hill of life, even if God should spare him, of which he had not an item of security. To die as he was, would be dreadful. And if he would seek God, like his wife, they would live together more happily for themselves, and would set an example for their numerous children, which certainly would be beneficial to them, and be fondly remembered by them, when he and his wife were gone to the grave.

Mr. W. apparently listened to this discourse in silence, sighed occasionally, but "did not seem to be much affected by it." When Spencer rose to leave, Mr. W. said farewell "coldly."

Some time later, Mrs. W. not having come to church, Spencer made another call. He found her more "determined than ever, to yield to her husband's wishes." With even more vigor than before, Spencer argued against this. Mrs. W. was more specific about the consequences she feared.

Mrs. W.: I do know it is my duty. I feel it. The Testament makes it plain in Jesus Christ's own words. But we are poor people. I am a poor woman, without friends, dependent upon the daily labor of my husband, for myself and my children. He says he will not live with me a single day, after I join the church; and I don't know what will become of me and the children. The most of them are very young. I have eight of them, and the oldest is not sixteen. And what would become of this baby, if I had no house or home?

As she cried, she held the baby in her arms; and the scene was too much for Spencer, who "turned away, and wept." However, his conviction was not changed; and in a few minutes he continued to urge her joining the church. He assured her that her husband would not turn her out of the house. She had the solemn duty of following Christ, as Christ's own words made plain, he said, and added, "I cannot alter them." When Spencer left, Mrs. W. was distressed.

As some months passed, Mrs. W. came occasionally to church; and Spencer exchanged a brief word with her on these occasions. At this stage Spencer wrote, "It appeared to me to be no part of my duty to urge her to unite with the church. I never had done so. I believed God would teach her her duty, as she prayed for the Holy Spirit."

After a year Mrs. W. sent for Spencer. She said she had decided to go ahead and join the church, and that although she feared she might lose courage as the day approached, she was determined to proceed.

Spencer approved and made suggestions as to how the news should be broached to her husband. When Mrs. W. told her husband, he repeated his threats. Spencer called again and urged her to remain unaffected by the threats.

On his own Spencer then engaged a woman to take care of the W. children on the great Sunday and a carriage to take Mrs. W. to church since it was too far to walk. But as it turned out, these arrangements were not needed. When Mrs. W. awoke on the Sunday morning when she was to join the church, she found that her husband was gone. This was contrary to schedule, and she was alarmed. To her amazement, however, Mr. W. soon returned and said:

MR. W.: (*With a sort of careless accent*) Wife, I suppose you want to go to church to-day; and it is too far for you to go afoot. You know I am too poor to keep any horse; and I have been down to Mr. B.'s to get a ride for you in his wagon. He says you can ride with him, as well as not, if you want to go. And I will stay at home and take care of the children.

Glory hallelujah, and baby-sitting besides! Mrs. W. "was so astonished, that she could scarcely believe her ears." But then, recovering, she threw her arms around her husband and "wept like a child." Mr. W. wept too, although "he aimed to conceal it." The day was triumphant, and nobody threw anybody out.

Thereafter Mrs. W. found it no problem to go to church. We are left with the impression that Mr. W. became Sunday cook and baby sitter. When later on the day came for the children to be baptized in the church, even Mr. W. joined the party. "For a time," wrote Spencer ominously, "he was more temperate," but "I never knew of any decided change in his habits," and he never joined the church.

Spencer concluded his account, "What it was, that produced the sudden change in his feelings on that Saturday night, I never could ascertain." Whatever it was, Spencer felt it was the work of the Holy Spirit.

This story of Spencer's dealings with the W. family brings out some things about him that have not been obvious before. Perhaps most important, it shows how far Spencer leaned toward the sect conception of the church in Troeltsch's ideal sense.

To Spencer the first issue was whether Mrs. W. had accepted Christ's promises, been convicted of her sinfulness, and then made an inner decision to become a Christian. This had already been accomplished at the time the story opens. Spencer was satisfied that the gospel had been communicated to Mrs. W. and that she had received it. In most instances when that decision had been made, it followed with no difficulty that the person would "unite with the church." But with Mrs. W. a whole new issue arose more terrible than the first. She wanted to make public profession of her faith but wavered between her fear that either Christ or her husband would reject her depending upon which course she took. Ordinarily Spencer would have been little concerned about a person's joining the church, not because this was regarded as unimportant, but because it would happen automatically. Here, where the crucial issue was about joining the church, he took the same stand that he would have taken on the question of receiving Christ through "experimental religion."

Just as there could be no substitute for being convicted of sin and receiving peace in Christ, so there could be no substitute for public declaration of this decision. It was this public declaration, when based on genuineness of inner experience, that really made one a member of the church in Spencer's view. Baptism was not insignificant, and in the case of an unbaptized adult it was a necessary part of the procedure of uniting with the church; but if seen alone, without the inner decision, Spencer would have felt it had no efficacy.

To Spencer, then, the local church was first that place where people who had found experimental religion testified of this fact to one another. He would of course have added that it was the place where the gospel was preached so as to lead to experimental religion. But the impetus to the inner experience might come directly through church or through Bible reading and prayer. Certainly the visible local church was not the sole agent of the Holy Spirit at this point.

This view of the church leans toward the sect type. One has inner experience, perhaps induced directly by the visible church but not necessarily. This experience calls him out from his previous way of life and his lostness, and brings him peace and joy. To this he testifies by uniting with the fellowship of others who have had similar experiences, and in that fellowship he is edified and nourished so that the experience continues. There is no substitute for the inner experience. No external act, whatever its nature (baptism, confirmation, or anything else), is a substitute for it. If one unites with the church without this experience and becomes a communicant at the Lord's Supper, he eats and drinks unworthily. No halfway covenant is possible. Uniting with the church is a public declaration of something that has occurred privately and inwardly.

When we consider the three aspects of the organizing perspective, it becomes even clearer how much Spencer's view leans toward the sect conception of the church. To him nourishing is carried out primarily through the Word. The Word is received in ways which, finally, are controlled by the Holy Spirit not by men, including the pastor and the visible church. The sacraments are not insignificant, but they are signs and seals, that is, they follow something inward that has already occurred. Even with Mrs. W. the important thing about joining the church was not her baptism but the public profession of her faith, of something already received.

Protecting the church to Spencer was carried out by attention to the entrance requirements. No one who had not already received Christ inwardly could unite with the church worthily. But if there was evidence of experimental religion, then all other requirements took care of themselves. Those who had already had the experience and had testified to it by joining the church had only one real task in protecting the church, namely, to discourage any would-be joiners who did not give evidence of the inward experience. If there was such evidence, there was no problem.

The third aspect of organizing, which was called "relating," does not come into open view in Spencer's story of the W. family. The local church is the local fellowship of those who have had a certain inner experience, which may come in many varieties but has some things in common. Its real task is to bring other men to this state and to nourish those who are in it. Corporately it is to have relationships with other bodies and institutions, but all this is consequent and rather secondary to the main task of the church. So Spencer saw it, although he wrote little about it. He did not advocate literal withdrawing from the world in the way practiced by some pietistic groups. But his view could be regarded as pietistic withdrawing from entanglements of the world—through becoming clear about one's Christian experience and then following its implications, especially ethical, regardless of consequences. We saw this in Spencer's dealing with the young clerk whose employer wanted him to misrepresent goods.[7]

But Spencer's view of the church, however far it leaned toward Troeltsch's sect conception, was not wholly of that type. For instance, he believed in infant baptism of children whose parents had had the inner experience and pledged themselves to bring up their children looking to the same. Thus baptism to Spencer had a different meaning for a baby from what it had for an adult, a position that the Baptists, whose view of the church leaned more to the sect conception than Spencer's, rejected. Baptism of an infant did not testify to an experience he had had, but to the intention of his parents based on their experience. Baptism of an adult was not possible except following prior inner individual experience. In Spencer there was, then, a mixture of the sect and the church conceptions. In the pure or ideal church conception an act such as baptism would be more important, would place the child under the oversight of the church; and the intention, experience, and oversight of the child by the parents would be relatively secondary.

Spencer's theory of the ministry, too, was not so "low" as would be found in the ideal sect-type church. There the responsibility for bringing others to experimental religion would be shared by all, with a strong suspicion of anyone set aside in any way with special responsibility to that end. Spencer believed lay members had obligations to testify to others, but that a pastor was needed; and as we have seen, he believed the pastor had a professional obligation to become competent through study of actual instances of his ministry.

Finally, Spencer's cannot be regarded as a pure sect-type notion of the church because he regarded it as operating in the world. What he meant by this is suggested precisely in his instructions to Mrs. W. about how to talk with her husband. She was to be kind but firm, unemotional but definite. If she did not feel so, she should not speak. Having felt so, she should speak and let the consequences of the "world's" action (in this instance Mr. W. is the world) take care of themselves. Positively, she should let her Christian decision help her perform her duties to her husband even better than before—so long only as they did not interfere with her duties to God. By such actions the "world" might be turned to Christ, individual by individual. Such a view leans strongly toward the sect conception but is mixed with elements of the church conception.

Organizing the church to Spencer, then, was centered in the action of the Word upon persons who united with the church genuinely (that is, organically) after they had had such experience through the Word. Uniting (becoming integrated) with the church is a term that could not be used by those having dominantly a church conception of the church. The organic unity of the church was protected finally by the

Holy Spirit, man's part being to see that only those who have had inner experience of Christ be permitted or encouraged to unite.

Viewed in the light of his dealings with the W. family, there are some extraordinary strengths in Spencer's conception of the church. Consider these in terms of their result upon the persons involved. Mrs. W., who was too much frightened of her husband to be an autonomous person, became the self she had wanted to be and was not thrown out of her house. We may indeed think Spencer took unneeded risks in assuring her that her husband would not carry out his threats; but the fact remains that, when she stood up to him in the name of her faith, he capitulated. If Spencer had permitted Mrs. W. to join the church without telling her husband about it, the result would have been different. In this case the insistence upon inner and personal decision at every point contributed to personal autonomy. This would not have happened had it not rested upon a view of the church as made up of persons who had found their selfhood in Christ, in such a way that irate husbands could not break the unity brought to the church by common inner experience.

In addition what happened affected the whole W. family. At the mention of possible family breakup Spencer did not shy away as if nothing could be more reprehensible. To him the solidarity of the family was desirable; but if it had had to be sacrificed for the sake of salvation, so be it, however regrettable. This is a stern view. The church as the company of those who have had experience of redemption can have no human or institutional competitors, not even in the form of the family. There is no talk about what will happen to society if the church, however regretfully, puts salvation above family peace at any price. Stern as this may be, it is certainly a virtue in its rejection of merely romantic notions of the family that not infrequently clothe a peace-at-any-price view. If the family believes nothing to be higher than its own existence, a strain is put upon family relationships that they cannot sustain. After the crisis in the W. family Mrs. W. will be tempted no more with family idolatry. From what we know today, the effect of Mrs. W.'s increased autonomy and of the new family atmosphere should be favorable for the development of the eight children.

But what of Spencer's dealing with Mr. W.? Here we must be much more critical. Had the latter shown the slightest move toward becoming an anxious inquirer, we know that Spencer's solicitude would have been indefatigable. As it was, Mr. W. was impervious to the type of experience that would have made him eligible for church membership. Whatever his reasons (Spencer guessed that they were Saturday-night rum), he never became a Christian. We saw that Spencer gave him an awesome picture of how hell would swallow him if he made no change, but the most he would do was attend church on the Sunday his children were baptized.

Spencer did not report any attempt to find out what specifically in Mr. W.'s life was behind his negativism to his wife's joining the church. It was something to be fought or ignored, not to be understood. This might, we now know, have stemmed from various sources. Merely as one hypothesis, Mr. W. may have been a dependent type of person, who wanted to lean on his wife and felt that dependency threatened if she had any other loyalties. He may have used rum courage to castigate her when alone with her but may have been too intimidated in the face of Spencer's strength to repeat his anger. Today we should be interested in trying to get Mr. W.'s point of view—not just his view of his becoming a Christian, but also his inner feelings about his wife's desire to do so. Such negative feeling accepted as a fact, we believe something constructive might then have occurred in Mr. W.

We can now see that it was in part Spencer's view of the church that made him uninterested in trying to understand Mr. W. The church is made up of those who have had an inner experience. Anxious inquiring leads to this experience. One who is neither inquiring nor anxious can only be warned and challenged. If he does not respond, then one might be keeping him away from anxious inquiring if one tried to accept and understand how he felt.

We believe there is a psychological error behind such a view. The child who will respond best to discipline as it may be needed is the child who feels he is loved, not the child from whom we are careful to keep any marks of acceptance. To accept is not, of course, to approve anything that may exist. But a suspicion lest we be too accepting fails to provide the context needed for change to occur. Thus Spencer's view of the church, as we see it, made him withhold love unless there was evidence that judgment was being accepted—even though he asserted that love rather than judgment was the means by which souls are won to Christ. This in turn was based upon his compartmentalized view of the faith.

By using again our field theory analogy, we can see schematically the strengths and weaknesses in Spencer's view of organizing the fellowship. The church to Spencer was by analogy all the iron filings that had felt the pull of Christ's magnet and had come to rest directly upon its pole.

Any filing anywhere out in the field that looked yearningly or anxiously to the pole would be sure of Spencer's attention. Those filings looking in another direction or unable to see the Christ pole could be warned and urged; but until they moved in the direction of the pole and reached it, they would not be in the church.

The church conception of the church would see the organic nature of the church differently. Some iron filings would be seen as farther from the pole than others; but so long as they were within the field of force, they would be in some degree within the church. To come within the field of force would rest not upon some internal happening, but upon some given or received type of action (probably baptism). The crucial question would not be a subjective decision to join the church, but coming within the field of the church's influence. To protect that influence, care must be taken about the loyalty and correctness of the organizers; and hence the church is finally protected by the priesthood.

The modified sect view of the church, like Spencer's, becomes strong in its encouragement of personal religious experience that can withstand assault and that makes for responsible lay action within the church. But it is unrealistic, finally, because it does not recognize degrees of becoming a Christian. It is always in danger of deserting the Protestant principle when it believes it knows just what are the evidences and what are not. And if it simply relaxes its application of the principle, then the virtues of the sect type are lost without taking on those of the church type.

The church-type conception of the church, on the other hand, has the virtue of realism in its recognition of the many degrees of Christian faith that persons may hold and attempting to have the church as that organic body that tries to influence them all by first including them within itself. Its obvious fault is that, by including all, it may cease to move those who are ready in the direction of experience with that which is ultimate.

How would the church conception of the church have approached the W. family? A pastor with this view might simply have baptized Mrs. W. and urged her to come to church (and confession, and so on). But any of these acts would have been regarded as so many steps in a long series, and with the possible exception of baptism Mr. W. could not point anywhere and accuse his wife of having united with the church. Possible result: Mrs. W. would carry water on both shoulders and fail to move toward personal autonomy. As to the possible breakup of the W. family, this pastor might have stood more openly for the solidarity of the institution. This could have resulted in compromise or family idolatry. Thus, in dealing with Mrs. W. and with the family as family, Spencer and the sect view seem to have from our point of view some advantage.

In dealing with Mr. W., the situation might be otherwise. There is nothing in the church view itself that would make the pastor sit down and try to understand what was bothering Mr. W. any more than there is in the sect view. But since the church would be regarded as embracing both Mr. W. and his wife, although in varying degrees, he might be encouraged to come to church as a way of moving toward entrance (for example, baptism); and this attitude might in turn strike him as partial acceptance, to which he might respond. Eventually, if he felt accepted, he might tell the pastor what was gnawing at him, whether religious or otherwise. Of course we must acknowledge that the sect view, faced with this argument, would say that Mr. W. might remain a half-Christian all his life; and a half-Christian is worse than none at all.

Church, Sect, and Body

Perhaps the reader should be reminded that the discussion of Spencer, of the W. family, and of the sect-type and church-type views of the church has been to shed light on the organizing of the fellowship—upon what does in fact make the nourishing, protecting, and relating of this a body and a body of which Christ is head. Unless I am greatly mistaken, the sect view and the church view have each noted correctly certain requirements to organize a body, but have neglected others.

The first point made about organic functioning was that it never develops merely by accretion but according to a pattern of its meaning within the whole body. This development is from an original diffuse unity through differentiation toward a more complex unity. The church view always remembers that the pattern of the organ's development is finally directed by the whole church. The sect view always remembers that without the development of differentiation unity, even within the context of the whole body, is deceptive.

The second point was that organic functioning is mutually supportive and in tension at the same time. The sect view tries to resolve the tension by having all who are genuinely in the church become mutually supportive through a basic identity of prior experience. The church view tries to achieve mutual support by taking all the tensions into itself. Neither accepts the continuing necessity of both tension and support.

The third point was that each organ has a kind of functional autonomy, but that this autonomy is meaningful only in relation to the whole. The church type tends either to discourage the functional autonomy or to permit it only cautiously. The sect view is inclined to have all the organs performing the same function, which is not enriching. Both are sensitive to the whole, but one polices and the other impoverishes.

The fourth point made about organic functioning was that the processes of mobilizing and of restoring equilibrium are approximately the same, but that they operate in reverse directions. The sect type, we might say, is always mobilizing, while the church type is always restoring equilibrium. If each realized that analogically homeostasis and emotion are the same process, they could then see that the crucial factor is not the process but the timing.

I am not suggesting for a moment that all the problems of understanding the church can be solved by pursuit of the organic analogy. But if I have gone far enough to show that each of the major types of views about the church, sect type and church type, have stressed some aspects of the metaphor and neglected others, some promise in further exploration of this kind shall have been indicated.

In any event, a study of the acts and operations of pastor and church from the organizing perspective can hardly be worth while if it does not shed at least some light on what makes the church an organ or a body. If such data do emerge, then it is plain that this study from the organizing perspective would lead to a branch of theology; and it is my contention that this would be cognate with pastoral theology.

Group Dynamics

There is much potential material for understanding the organizing of the fellowship in the modern study of small groups. Probably the most seminal mind in this inquiry was that of Kurt Lewin, but many others are now making important contributions. There has been only a beginning in studying the principles from the point of view of the church. So far there has been little basic research or publication.

One of the first things that became evident when small groups were studied seriously was that two factors must always be considered and that the relation between the two provides a basis by which the group's success may be evaluated. These two factors may be called the "task" and the "group process," or the "function" and the "fellowship." The task is whatever it is the group is to perform: raising money, getting altar flowers, selecting hymns or pew cushions. The group process is what produces the quality of interaction among members and between members and leader. A group cannot be evaluated without attention to both.

What does a good group do? At the beginning with the special help of its leader it defines its task as that can be then understood and defines the way in which it will proceed with respect for the views of every member, no evasion of negative feelings, how and when a certain degree of agreement will or must be reached. As the group proceeds, all available knowledge and brains are thrown upon the task; but there is not preoccupation with the task at the expense of mutually participative relationship, negative feelings are brought into the open when they exist, and discussion is held of the actual processes going on within the group. There is a good deal of evidence that such group movement is superior from the standpoint of both group task and group process.

In a preceding chapter we noted Lewin's distinction among the authoritarian, *laissez-faire*, and democratic types of groups.[8] As to task, the authoritarian is preoccupied with it, the *laissez faire* neglects it, and the democratic gives it due attention. As to process, the terms explain themselves. As used by Lewin, they indicate a kind of relationship that tends to exist in groups between task and process. If the group becomes so "groupy" that it forgets it has a task, even if the task is mutual therapy, then a *laissez-faire* pattern is likely to result, sometimes under a democratic label. If the group becomes so task-centered that it pushes aside its members, then it is authoritarian and cannot long enlist the energy of its members for the task. The democratic view in Lewin's term implies a mutually supportive relationship between process and task, fellowship and function.

However it is defined, the task of the church must be about that which is finally and ultimately important. But if there is preoccupation with that task in a way that does violence to the process by which the task should be performed, then something is wrong and there are backfires. The modern discoveries are about group process. And put in simplest terms, they show that group coherence ("organizing" in our sense) is directly dependent upon establishing a group context in which negative feeling can be expressed, accepted, and rendered nondominant. It is this above all else that can be the new gold nugget in our theory of organizing the Christian fellowship. In the church as nowhere else organizing must show an integrity between task and process, function and fellowship. The working out of a theology of organizing can help us to that end.

Notes

Chapter 1. Task

1. Huldreich Zwingli, *Der Hirt*, 1524.
2. Poimenics, homiletics, and the other studies that developed from the offices are considered at greater length in Chapter 3. See also Note 7 below.
3. *The Reformed Pastor*, ed. John T. Wilkinson (London: Epworth Press, 1939), p. 83.
4. *Ibid.*
5. *The Pastor: Pastoral Theology* (Philadelphia: J. B. Lippincott & Co., 1880), p. 9.
6. Matt. 22:37, 39 (R.S.V.).
7. Virtually all lists of the offices include homiletics, liturgics, catechetics, and poimenics. Homiletics and liturgics have at times been viewed as a single office and at other times as two offices. Beyond this brief list we find variation. Some nineteenth-century writers, for instance, added apostolics or halieutics, attempting to deal with what we would now call evangelism and missions. There was no nineteenth-century term for what we now call church administration, which we find today in all lists of the offices. Social action or outreach has an even more curious position in this list. Recognized from the beginning as a type of function of the church, it had nevertheless no ancient title. In the more Catholic traditions it was considered under moral theology; in the more Protestant, under Christian ethics, which was in turn usually regarded as a branch of doctrinal theology. The modern work in social ethics has been in part an attempt to demonstrate the functional office side of Christian ethics, but its specialists have usually protested being lined up with the offices. Of course both Catholic and Protestant traditions have been concerned with personal and social relations and obligations to the whole of society and not only to those within the fellowship.
8. In spite of the statement here and elsewhere that the offices will continue to have usefulness, we are aware that the advocating of an alternate and, I believe, superior way of organizing the functions of church and minister will strike some readers like doubting the usefulness of the categories of space and time—so deeply have these offices become a part of our inner intellectual frame of reference. Like the categories of space and time in physics, they may indeed have utility for certain purposes. But they are conveniences not compartments, abstract types not exhaustive descriptions of concrete operations, useful tools but not categorical masters. Indeed, it is my contention that the continuing usefulness of the offices for certain purposes will be enhanced by a recognition of their abstract character. At any time special students have examined seriously any single office, they have emerged with the conclusion that their study was more than an office. In our century, for instance, this happened with religious education. Religious educators saw rightly that their work and study were relevant to everything the church did and that a purely compartmentalized description of it was a distortion. Some of them, using a valid insight but an inadequate structure, then created a kind of religious education imperialism, in which religious education and counseling, or religious education and worship, became studies paralleling the study according to the offices. The intent of this, I contend, was correct. The structure was wrong because the protest against the abstract and compartmentalized types of the offices was not followed by the construction of a better structure in which the educative functions or perspective could be seen.
9. The problem involved in the relation of shepherding to pastoral care is made more difficult by the fact that the recent knowledge about both has emerged primarily from concentrated study of pastoral dealing with individual persons and families. Indeed, pastoral care has come to be thought of as almost synonymous with pastoral help to the individual person. Such a view forgets that pastoral care has always had a general as well as a special aspect, that is it related to a group and a congregation as well as to an individual and a family. But most of our recent knowledge of pastoral care has

come in the past generation through the study of ministry to individuals and families; and the assumption that pastoral care is simply a matter of individual persons is, while inadequate, nevertheless understandable. We believe the new studies of group work, group dynamics, and group leadership in the church are on the threshold of making significant progress that will restore to pastoral care a group or congregational as well as an individual dimension.

But pastoral care, even though its definition is made more adequate through including the group as well as the individual dimension, is still not equivalent to shepherding, because, as we use the terms, they emerge from different structural frames of reference. From the structure of the offices, pastoral care looks at types of functions that can be so designated and set against other types of functions, in the same way one would distinguish riding in an automobile or in a boat or on a bicycle. Shepherding emerges from a different kind of thinking about structure. It is dominant, the principal thing, in some situations and events; but it is never wholly absent from any. Any analogy like that of riding different vehicles would fail to represent its meaning.

The primary new data, and indeed the stimulus and motivation, in relation to both pastoral care and shepherding have come out of the same kinds of modern study, focused on helping individuals and families. That has certainly been the primary experience of this author and of many others. Because these are the concrete data with which we are most familiar, it is primarily to these that we tend to go when asking the basic questions involved in this book. But my use of concrete data involving mostly one-to-one relationships should not mislead the reader into believing that either pastoral care or shepherding is confined to such relationships.

The important thing to remember, however difficult it may be, about the relation of shepherding to pastoral care is that, as used in this book, they involve two different ways of structuring what is frequently the same data. But ideally, the data are more diverse than our discussion, if read uncritically, might suggest.

10. This means that theology, or any of its branches, is to be understood as an attempt to articulate the faith more or less systematically, in one or more of its aspects, from one or more perspectives. So viewed, theology is human and fallible; but its intent and concern are always to move toward articulation and clarification of the faith in all its dimensions. Theology has inescapably an intellectual dimension. We have to think about it by using the same tools with which we think about anything else. But the intellectual activity is never to be seen as divorced from faith and experience, as if it were only a passive ordering of things after their occurrence. It bears creatively upon our assimilation of the faith itself and therefore of anything that may be called experience. Any branch of theology, in order to qualify, must, therefore, emerge from the faith, examine with all possible intellectual tools some basic aspect or dimension of the faith, and return to the faith with a creative and systematic account of its fallible but illuminating findings.

11. The word "autonomy" runs some risks of being misunderstood, even when we qualify it at every point by indicating the interrelationship of the several branches of theology. By analogy what I want to say is what Paul Tillich says in using the terms autonomy, heteronomy, and theonomy in a different connection. If the branches of theology were heteronomous, they would be related but in the pattern of a power structure such that some would engulf others. If they were merely autonomous without genuine relationship, they would be anarchic. In the other context Tillich uses the term "theonomy" to indicate the fulfillment of man, man's law, through God, God's law. Autonomy not seen in this context is not true autonomy but anarchy. See Tillich, *Systematic Theology*, University of Chicago Press, 1951, I, 147 ff.

Any branch of theology that regarded itself as the whole of theology would be either anarchic or imperialistic. While it cultivates rightly the subject matter peculiar to its nature, it also pays attention to the subject matter that is common currency for every branch. It aims at precision in what is unique about it, but it also brings its offerings to the common table. If pastoral theology exists and is important, as this volume contends, then it is necessary for its autonomy to be recognized in order that it may not

217

prematurely be the victim of an intellectual or theological heteronomy that would, for example, regard it as merely practical without the ability to make genuinely theological contributions.

12. What I am calling the "logic-centered" fields of theological inquiry are sometimes referred to as the "theological sciences." This term is unsatisfactory, not only because of the specialized way in which the term "sciences" is now used, but also because it implies that no real knowledge is involved unless it is organized in a certain way. We call these fields "logic-centered" to suggest that the key to their distinctive nature lies in a "logical" organization of subject matter. The logical organization of the subject matter in each field leads, then, to certain consequences which, potentially, enrich the whole.

For instance, biblical scholars now use linguistic analysis, archaeology, paleography, oriental history, and other special methods and disciplines in the pursuit of their inquiry that has the Bible as its logical center. A good deal of their work on these special methods has little immediate transmissive value to the ordinary church member. But the pursuit of the special investigations that follow from the logical focus is in the long run important even for that church member.

The point here is not of course to argue the case for the biblical scholar's need to pursue archaeology or oriental history, for he can do that far better himself. It is, rather, by clarifying the nature of the distinctive way in which he organizes his inquiry, to indicate that another way of organizing a branch of theological study may also be both possible and necessary. This point must be made in order to lay claim to the right of pastoral theology to be a theological discipline, even though its principle of organization is function-centered rather than logic-centered. Proper study of functions with resulting systematization of knowledge leads to a body of knowledge and not merely to skill or technique.

13. From the latter part of the nineteenth century until today the principal scheme of organizing theological knowledge that was used in the theological seminaries was fourfold, involving biblical, systematic, historical, and practical theology. The over-all error in this plan was the attempt to deal with practical theology, so-called, as if it were co-ordinate with each of the other items. If by practical theology we mean those branches of theology whose organizing center is functional rather than logical, then they are to be seen as structurally co-ordinate with all the logic-centered branches of theology viewed collectively, not as co-ordinate with each of them viewed separately. Whatever is felt to be the appropriate number of fields, logic-centered or function-centered, the whole number in each group is structurally co-ordinate with the whole number in the other group. To regard practical theology or any branch of operation-focused theology as one of a list of branches that are otherwise logic-centered is to force on a branch like pastoral theology organizational and structural criteria that prevent its making its inherent contribution to the whole body of divinity.

14. Table I attempts to represent the shape of the body of divinity according to the principles already indicated. On one side are the logic-centered fields and on the other the operation-centered areas. Each is shown connected with the other, as interpenetrating, as engaging in two-way communication. The primary point is not to argue for a specific number of fields and areas, but to demonstrate the proper mode of relationship among the fields and areas. If it is objected that this outline lacks unity because it insists on two different ways of organizing theological inquiry, two answers can be given. The first is that all attempts to deal with theological inquiry without making this distinction result either in an antipractical bias or in detheologizing the operational studies. In other words, I did not make the distinction but only discovered it. Second, the kind of unity that is needed for the richest theological inquiry is that which emerges from two-way communication at all points. No single field or area has the responsibility for integration in such a way that any other field can dispense with its integrative obligation. It is simply a fact that this linkage function must be shared or it cannot be performed at all. But that cannot be done by the equivalent of back-

slapping, acting as if there were no distinction in the organizing principles of the two types of theological inquiry. And it certainly cannot be done if the fields treat the areas like illegitimate theological children fit only to apply what has been learned elsewhere and incapable of creative theological contribution.

15. Against a common misconception, we need to protest that system does not refer to something imposed or superadded as a kind of intellectual Procrustean bed in which data are made to lie whether they fit or not. The best system is that which demonstrates the reality of relationship among the items so far as real knowledge goes, and then declares honestly its ignorance where the relationships are unclear or unknown. The fact that systems can and sometimes do become chains and walls is not the fault of system as such as I have defined it, but comes from an uncurbed desire to round things off whether the rounding stage has been reached or not.

It is my contention that pastoral theology, like any branch of theology, must become systematic in the sense defined above. In theology the question of system has been complicated because doctrinal theology has often used the term "systematic theology" for itself. Indeed, it is necessary for doctrinal theology to be systematic in order to be intelligible and coherent. But this use, although unintentionally, has sometimes obscured the fact that every theological discipline must be systematic, that is, must bring together into a statement the representation of the relationships actually seen among items of the data, including statement of that about which there is ignorance or unclarity. In other words, any good system is open, even though struggling to represent adequately all the relationships it sees among its data.

If every branch of theology has the obligation to be systematic, the question then arises: Systematic about what or around what? The principal answer is that it systematizes its data around the content of its unique organizing center. The biblical scholar is systematic about the Bible, not only in the sense that he overlooks none of its books, but also in the sense that all his data—whether they come from textual, historical, exegetical, archaeological, or other forms of inquiry—are systematically organized around the Bible. The historical theologian organizes his data systematically around a historical center, which he usually interprets as chronological sequence but which may assume other developmental forms. The system of the doctrinal theologian is focused around his logical organizing center of doctrinal relationship and coherence.

What has been said so far is adequate as a statement of what the system is centered about so long as we are considering that which is distinctive or unique within each branch of theology. But this is not all that needs to be said about the center of the system. Every branch of theology uses the common currencies of the faith—God, man, sin, and so on—without which it would not be a part of theology at all. In so far as each branch of theology has the obligation not only to pursue its unique task, but also to bring its contribution to the village green of theological integration, it has also, as a secondary focus for systematizing its knowledge, the common currency.

While dealing with its sister branches, any theological discipline rightly systematizes its knowledge around that organizing center that is different from that of other branches. This is the system of what might be called its domestic policy. In its foreign policy, however, each branch of theology must take more care to systematize both around the common currency and around the special focus.

Our special concern is of course the system that is proper to pastoral theology. Around what shall its data be systematized? The answer is that the primary center for its system is its organizing principle, which I have defined as shepherding when shepherding is understood as a perspective present in all pastoral events and dominantly important in some. Like any other branch, pastoral theology must use the common theological currency for a basic part of its content. But in domestic policy, while using the common currency in communication with its sister disciplines, it nevertheless organizes and systematizes itself around that which is distinctive, namely, shepherding. The organizing principle is also the focus of system.

This volume divides the shepherding perspective into three aspects: healing, sustaining, and guiding. As an inquiry what pastoral theology is systematic about is the actual process by which shepherding—healing, sustaining, or guiding—is brought about. When this knowledge is put together into a system, although an open one, clarifying the common currency of the faith, we have a systematic pastoral theology. Any demand to pastoral theology that its primary focus of system be something else, such as systematic doctrine or Bible or morals, would be denying its claim to be a branch of theology. While this book itself is only an introduction to such a statement of systematic pastoral theology, it does later on attempt to illustrate the meaning of system in pastoral theology in the sense described.

But pastoral theology has a foreign as well as a domestic policy. It is not the sole discipline that studies shepherding in the generic sense. So, each in its own way, do psychiatry, clinical psychology, social work, and other disciplines. In relation to these disciplines around what does pastoral theology organize itself? The answer is, around the common currency of the faith, although with special reference still to its shepherding perspective on that faith.

It is so obvious that the pastoral theologian can learn from contact with these other shepherding disciplines that the case need not be argued here. But the question may then be asked: How does his system center differ from theirs? The answer is not that he is a Christian and they are not, for many of them are. It is, rather, that the activity of beginning with theological questions, bringing them to the shepherding material, and returning either with theological answers or with new theological questions is the focal thing about his pastoral theological discipline. These workers, as persons or as Christians, may indeed do the same thing, as many of them now do so helpfully for all concerned. But doing this is not necessarily inherent in their discipline as such.

Pastoral theology, then, in summary, needs to be as systematic as any other branch of theology. That which distinguishes the center of its system within the body of divinity is its inquiry after and drawing conclusions from the exercise of the shepherding perspective. In relation to the shepherding disciplines which as disciplines are not theologically oriented, its system is focused around the common currency of the Christian faith. Thus the system of pastoral theology may be called bifocal, depending on whether it is speaking within the body of divinity or in relation to human knowledge in general.

Pastoral theology must have full commerce with every discipline that is studying shepherding. And every bit of relevant insight it discovers about shepherding, regardless of source, must be considered in the light of its theological significance. If the commerce is not open and free, the system finally becomes rigid and irrelevant. But if the inquiry is not theological, then new truth has no apparent theological root or implication; and vitality comes to be associated with nontheological orientations. If both tasks are carried out, then pastoral theology becomes an open and inquiring and theologically focused system, enriching the whole body of divinity and having an impact on nontheological disciplines as well as learning from them.

16. The principle around which data are organized, data in which one has some emotional investment, is often closer to one's personal center than he realizes. There tend to be resistances to the other fellow who appears to be using one's data but is organizing them in a different, and of course inferior, way. When the data involve the many similar elements that botany and pharmacology have in common, although organized in different ways, the resistance may not be strong. But when we deal with the kind of material found in the social and psychological sciences and in the humanities, resistances are greater.

The disciplines such as psychiatry or social work that are most closely co-ordinate with the function-centered theological disciplines tend to be in their present form of relatively recent development. They do not have the masses of data in their short history that other disciplines with longer study and self-conscious inquiry lay claim to. To the older disciplines these parvenus never appear to be quite autonomous or respectable. Social work, for instance, has been particularly beset on these grounds.

Not only is it accused by sociology, psychiatry, and clinical psychology of borrowing most of its data; it is often alleged to be destroying their meaning by the way it organizes them and the uses to which they are put. Needless to say, this is not a good picture of the facts. It is the parvenus who, whatever their claim to autonomy, are generally more sinned against than sinning. But when a newcomer becomes big enough, he may act exactly as does the sophomore conscious only that he is no longer a freshman. For illustration see some aspects of education in our century.

For pastoral theology the implications of this discussion are obvious. To be sure, it deals with something as old as the church itself. But the study of it in the form we advocate, leading to a branch of theology in the full sense, is recent. It is, therefore, a parvenu. So long as it kept its place as practical, deluding itself that it merely applied what had been found out elsewhere, its existence was safe but dull, uncreative, and intellectually dishonest. Now that, at least in the person of this author, it alleges its theological character and an autonomy similar to that of other disciplines, something other than a passive parallelism will have to take place. Perhaps other theologians are so uniformly enlightened that they will rejoice unambiguously at the emergence of this talking sibling. It is more likely that the pastoral theologian will meet some new resistances from within and without the theological fold. This is good; for it means, at last, genuine encounter. An adult may spank a baby, but he does not fight it. Pastoral theology wants to be encountered—accepted as a sibling if possible—but better fight and even lose than to be mentally clothed with diapers.

17. The relative lack of attention to theological method by any except professional theologians suggests that this matter should be discusssed, however briefly, if we are to demonstrate that pastoral theology conforms to the essential canons of any critical theological method. This may be done most briefly and sharply by speaking to three basic questions. First, how can theology be open and inquiring when it spends so much time looking backward, even asserting that in Jesus Christ there is already a final revelation? Second, how can theology be relevant to man's needs when it seems concerned only with *Heilsgeschichte* rather than with history or culture in general? Third, if theology articulates faith, how can it possibly do justice to doubt and despair?

As to the question about the backward look, we may note first that every science or discipline has some touchstone or basic principle on which it proceeds until or unless this is qualified or corrected. The history of any science is partly about the disentangling of what is truly basic from the particular and limited forms in which that has been seen. In physics such a principle would be that energy can be neither created nor destroyed. When atomic energy was discovered, this principle seemed to be threatened because it contradicted the form in which the general principle had previously been seen. What then occurred was a restatement of the principle on the basis of a wider understanding of the forms it could assume.

What Christian thought has been agreed on is that the nature and character of God have been revealed in the character and acts and existence of Jesus Christ, that this revelation has involved actual events and is therefore historical and not merely symbolical, and that the nature of God as revealed is about his dealings with men and about their response to him for good or for ill in some kind of personal rather than Olympian or "first-cause" sense. When a statement is made about God apart from God's dealings with man, an abstraction is being made from the total revelation. It may be necessary to do this, but the mischief comes if one forgets he is abstracting. The revelation in Jesus Christ is final in that no further basic clue needs to be given or new type of work needs to be done by God for the salvation of man. But the assimilation and understanding of the revelation by man is never final, nor is that work of God ever done that attempts to help man receive the revelation.

In terms of methodological principle the relation of the backward look (or the consolidation of principles) to inquiry (future-oriented instability) is now more similar in the sciences and in theology than for many centuries. As the sciences emerged in Western history, their movement has been from a study of the remote toward that of the near. They began with astronomy, moved to physics, and on to chemistry and biology. Only in recent years have psychology, sociology, and scientific anthropology been explored. The serious efforts of the "near sciences" have compelled a wrestling with the observer in a way that was not necessary for many years in the "remote sciences." The latter too are now examining the observer. In the sciences the backward look is both a resting upon a hard-won touchstone and a questioning of every possible premise. It includes examination not only of what is out there but also of what is in here.

Christian thought sees a vital and organic connection between its belief in the final revelation of God in Jesus Christ and the need for future-oriented theological inquiry. At best man's understanding and reception of the revelation is incomplete; most theologians regard it as distorted. Inquiry is necessary to correct our understanding of the revelation, which is not merely about God out there but about his relation to us. And inquiry is relevant about the vital details of life, for these are not made explicit in the revelation itself. Without the touchstone inquiry could not proceed. But every belief and presupposition about our understanding of the revelation is open to future-oriented inquiry.

The second question asked how theology could be relevant to man's needs when it seemed concerned only with the knowledge of salvation rather than with knowledge and culture in general. Of course it is true that theology is focused on the knowledge of salvation, but any authoritarianism or pietism that defines this in purely compartmentalized terms does injustice to the witness of the Bible that man is saved either as a whole or not at all. Theologians have of course taken different stands about the relation of theology to culture. Methodologically speaking, however, all great theologians have taken culture, or human knowledge in general, quite seriously. In his day Thomas Aquinas was a daring innovationist by insisting on relating Aristotelian thought to theology. Even those theologians of past and present, such as Karl Barth, who believe that theology is kerygmatic exposition and who are wary that any culture-related apologetic is letting the camel's nose in the tent, make use of and take for granted many of the results of culture-related inquiry such as historical criticism of the Bible. The biblical theologian does not wait cringing lest some new scrolls be discovered that force him to rethink something. Instead he regards the archaeological search as a positive instrument of his own methodology. To be sure, it may raise new questions, and there is always potential tension. But this is sought, not evaded, as a part of the task of theological inquiry itself.

The third question asked how it is that, if the task of theology is to articulate faith, it can possibly do justice to doubt and despair. If it claims to have the answers, how can it possibly take seriously the questions? The basic reply to this is that, while Christianity or theology may have the answer, no theologian or other man ever has the answer untinctured by the doubt, struggle, and despair to which the question refers. Theological method must be rigorous in avoiding the equation of our understanding of the faith from the faith itself as it must be in God's eyes. The more usual way to state this is in terms of the Protestant principle of God's judgment upon us lest we think we are God, on our ways, our thoughts, and even our church.

This point has unusual importance for method in pastoral theology. The would-be shepherd who believes that he possesses faith unmixed with doubt cannot help the doubting and deceives himself. If he knows anything basic about himself, he recognizes that doubt in some form has been a part of his past and is within his present. He is, therefore, able to accept both the doubt and the implicit faith in those he would help, not simply identifying himself with the one and rejecting the other. In the process of helping and the never-ending self-reflection that is a vital part of the helping and the inquiry the shepherd is aware that the theology—as the reception and assimilation of faith—is always in the making and never finished.

18. *Nature, Man and God* (New York: The Macmillan Co., 1934), p. 315.
19. This is the way Paul Tillich puts it in discussing his theological method as one of "correlation." He writes, "The method of correlation explains the contents of the

Christian faith through existential questions and theological answers in mutual inter-dependence." *Op. cit.*, p. 60. Not everything is yet clear about Tillich's use of the key term "correlation" to describe his theological method. Plainly he intends by it to establish theological relevance; theology does not talk in a corner by itself but speaks to the vital questions men ask. Thus he says to the theologian that culture and life cannot be neglected, and to the ordinary man that faith has a message for him. But to what extent is correlation a two-way method? Tillich apparently solves this problem by indicating that theology deals with matters of ultimate concern and other disciplines with preliminary concerns. But this does not solve the problem. No one can say in advance when the emerging knowledge or insight is going to be ultimate or only pre-liminary. Nor does it seem sufficient to say that the sacred may erupt from the profane.

Knowledge or insight of the utmost importance to theology may emerge at any time from a discipline that seems far removed from theology, and it hardly seems fair to say that that discipline has no claim to what it has discovered.

We believe that a full two-way street is necessary in order to describe theological method. If we hold that theology is always assimilation of the faith, not just the abstract idea of the faith apart from its reception, then it becomes necessary to say that culture may find answers to questions raised by faith as well as to assert that faith has answers to questions raised by culture. Tillich apparently hesitates to put the matter this way, and there is obvious risk to the ultimate meaning of faith in so putting it. But if psychiatry, for example, enables us to help someone to turn a corner and thence move on into the faith, how can we avoid saying that culture has given the answer to a problem posed by faith—provided we believe that our understanding of faith is never known apart from such actual concrete processes?

In the hands of Tillich there are great virtues in the word "correlation" as a key to theological method. In lesser hands we may wonder about the term, perhaps especially concerning methodology in the function-oriented branches such as pastoral theology. Much of the history of these disciplines shows them either remaining linked in purely reproductive and uncreative fashion with practice while failing to move on to articulated theory, or else devising some systematic theory without explicit recognition of how theory is evolved from practice. It would be desirable if a key methodological concept could be found that would guard against these prevalent distortions.

"Dialectic," especially if used along with "correlation," has something to be said for it. For it can suggest the recognition of tension or opposition within what never-theless remains a real relationship. But its tension connotation may exaggerate differ-ences that are only verbal or perspectival in character, even if it avoids a Hegelianism. A word has been sought, so far in vain, that would connote movement back and forth, acknowledging agreement or contribution when real, retaining tension when real. Explorations thus far may be briefly reported.

"Interconnect" in mechanics means that movement of any one part that moves each and every part. An interconnected theological method could mean that movement, inquiry, or discovery would imply and necessitate study of the way in which all theo-logical disciplines are thereby affected, as well as the search for that movement in all other disciplines that interconnectedly moves one's own.

"Interpenetrating" implies that anything moving toward depth in one discipline may do so for others also. "Interrelated" is like "correlated" but connotes, rather, one that finds its unity than two discovering what they have in common. "Intervolve," mean-ing to involve one with another, would be more promising if it did not look like a misprint. "Nexus" means precisely "interconnection" but in practice tends to suggest merely a point of juncture. We even toyed with "amphidetic," which means to be bound all around. Certainly that has been the conclusion of this verbal search.

20. We use the term "method" to mean more than "practice," however skilled, and more than "technical means." Every discipline, including theology, uses technical means. But technical means govern inquiry only after assumptions have been made, history and context have been reviewed, and a specific subject of inquiry set. After technical means have been employed, much yet remains to be done. Data must be organized,

their significance and relationships must be assessed, and implications need to be drawn from them. Method in any discipline is that which engages critically in all these procedures and not solely in those which use the technical means peculiar to the discipline.

21. See my "Bibliography and Reading Guide in Pastoral Psychology," *Pastoral Psychology*, Vol. V, No. 50, January, 1955.

22. See my "Psychotherapy and Counseling in Professions Other than the Ministry," *Pastoral Psychology*, Vol. VII, No. 62, March, 1956.

23. Although I must reject certain aspects of the book's content, Albert C. Outler's *Psychotherapy and the Christian Message* (New York: Harper & Bros., 1954) is nevertheless an important call to a consideration of these presuppositions. So is an earlier but in some respects a more deep-reaching book, *Psychotherapy and a Christian View of Man* by David E. Roberts (New York: Charles Scribner's Sons, 1950). William E. Hulme in *Counseling and Theology* (Philadelphia: Muhlenberg Press, 1956), also attacks this question but with a tendency to find an answer too quickly in parallelism of psychology and theology.

24. *The Mature Mind* (New York: W. W. Norton & Co., 1949), p. 1.

25. See especially Rom. 3:19-25, 27-28; 4:16-17; 5:1-5; 7:1-6; 8:1-11; 10:5-13.

Chapter 2. Person

1. *Op. cit.*, pp. 135-41.

2. *The Pastoral Office: Its Duties, Difficulties, Privileges, and Prospects* (New York: Protestant Episcopal Society for the Promotion of Evangelical Knowledge, 1859), pp. 53 ff.

3. *Op. cit.*, pp. 82-83.

4. *Pastoral Theology: or, The Theory of the Evangelical Ministry* (2nd ed.; New York: Harper & Bros., 1866), p. 238.

5. *Op. cit.*, p. 113.

6. H. Richard Niebuhr, Daniel D. Williams, and James M. Gustafson, *The Advancement of Theological Education* (New York: Harper & Bros., 1957).

7. *Ibid.*, p. 122.

8. *Ibid.*, p. 127.

9. The clearest general statement of this, of which the theological application is a specific case, is to be found in Alfred North Whitehead, *The Aims of Education* (New York: Mentor Books, 1949), pp. 27 ff.

Chapter 3. History

1. John T. McNeill, *A History of the Cure of Souls* (New York: Harper & Bros., 1951), p. 163.

2. From *Luther: Letters of Spiritual Counsel*, edited by Theodore G. Tappert, 1955, The Westminster Press. Used by permission.

3. Wilhelm Pauck, *The Heritage of the Reformation* (Glencoe, Ill.: The Free Press, 1950), p. 115. Used by permission of the publisher.

4. *Ibid.*, pp. 114-15.

5. *Ibid.*, p. 115.

6. *Ibid.*, p. 142.

7. The first volume I have been able to find trace of that used "pastoral theology" in its title was by C. T. Seidel, *Pastoral-Theologie*, 1749. My authority for this is the Netherlands scholar J. J. Van Oosterzee in *Practical Theology*, first translated and published in English by Charles Scribner's Sons in 1878. Van Oosterzee's bibliography of systematic works in this area up to his time is the most useful one available.

8. *Pastoral-Theologie*. Until after this time, apparently all the systematic works were in German. Van Oosterzee notes the following in the eighteenth century: S. J. Baum-

garten, *Kurzgefasste Casuistische Pastoral-Theologie*, 1752; J. F. von Mosheim, *Pastoral-Theologie*, 1754; V. D. Spörl, *Vollständige Pastoral-Theologie*, 1764; J. J. Plitt, *Pastoral-Theologie*, 1766; J. F. Jacobi, *Beiträge zur Pastoral-Theologie*, 1766; and J. G. Töllner, *Grundriss der Erwiesenen Pastoral-Theologie*, 1767. Prior to Harms's book in 1830, the following German works are noted as appearing during the nineteenth century: J. F. C. Gräffe, *Pastoral-Theologie in ihrem ganzen Umfange*, 1803; G. F. C. Kaiser, *Entwurf eines Systems der Pastoral-Theologie*, 1816; L. S. Jaspis, *Hodogetik*, 1821; J. Boroth, *Synopsis Theologie Pastoralis*, 1823; J. T. L. Danz, *Die Wissenschaften des Geistlichen Berufs im Grundriss*, 1824; and F. B. Köster, *Lehrbuch der Pastoral-Wissenschaft*, 1827.

I have seen very few of these books but have been aided by August Hardeland's history, *Geschichte der Speciellen Seelsorge in der Vorreformatorischen Kirche und der Kirche der Reformation* (Berlin, 1898).

9. Enoch Pond, *Lectures on Pastoral Theology* (Boston: Draper & Halliday, 1847).
10. See McNeill, *op. cit.* This is the great history of *Seelsorge*.
11. Zwingli, *op. cit.* This is summarized in *ibid.*, pp. 192-93. Bucer, *On the True Cure of Souls*, 1538. It is summarized in *ibid.*, pp. 177-81.
12. Quoted by McNeill, *op. cit.*, p. 178.
13. Most recently by Tappert, *op. cit.* See Note 2 above.
14. *Ibid.*, pp. 310, 311.
15. The most recent edition of Baxter in English was edited by John T. Wilkinson and published in London by Epworth Press, second edition revised, in 1950. Baxter's original title for the work was *Gildas Salvianus: The Reformed Pastor*. The meaningless character of the first two words now ordinarily results in their being omitted from the title.
16. *A Priest to the Temple: or, The Country Parson*, 1632; and Burnet, *A Discourse of the Pastoral Care*, 1692.
17. James Hastings Nichols—*History of Christianity, 1650-1950—Secularization of the West.* Copyright 1956 The Ronald Press Company.
18. John Smith, *Lectures on the Nature and End of the Sacred Office, and on the Dignity, Duty, Qualifications and Character of the Sacred Order.* Original publication date 1798; republished in Philadelphia in 1843.
19. *Ibid.*, p. 214.
20. John Mason, *The Student and Pastor: or, Directions How to Attain to Eminence and Usefulness in Those Respective Characters*, 1755.
21. The first volume with "practical theology" in the title appears to have been by Philipp Marheinecke, *Entwurf der Praktischen Theologie*, 1837.
22. *Die Praktische Theologie nach den Grundsäzen der Evangelischen Kirche*, 1850, p. 25. This book was published after Schleiermacher's death. His general definition of practical theology was as the "method of maintaining and perfecting the church." He took the position that practical theology is the larger discipline of which pastoral theology is a part.
23. This is also the understanding of Schleiermacher's position given me in oral communication by Jaroslav Pelikan. To the extent that this is true, Schleiermacher is the one premodern writer who in methodological principle foreshadowed the thesis of the present book.
24. *Op. cit.* See Note 7 above. The other works in practical theology were published in German. In addition to those by Marheinecke and Schleiermacher the following are noted by Van Oosterzee: K. F. Grupp, *Praktische Theologie*, 1848; J. H. A. Ebrard, *Vorlesungen Uber Praktische Theologie*, 1852; C. B. Moll, *Das System der Praktischen Theologie im Grundriss Dargestellt*, 1853; K. Kuzmany, *Praktische Theologie der Evangelischen Kirche*, 1856; F. Ehrenfeuchter, *Die Praktische Theologie*, 1859; and W. Otto, *Grundzüge der Evangelischen Praktischen Theologie*, 1866, and *Praktische Theologie*, 1869.
25. *Lehrbuch der Pastoral-Wissenschaft*, 1827.

26. *Homiletics and Pastoral Theology* (New York: Charles Scribner's Sons, 1867). Shedd viewed theological science as the "strictly theoretic branches" such as "philology, philosophy, and theology," while "all that part which relates to the public application of this theoretic culture, is practical theology." Pp. 319-20. Homiletics is seen as a part of practical theology but not of pastoral theology. The latter has to do with the "clergyman's parochial life" and the "care of individual souls." P. 320. In other words, to Shedd, the first comprehensive and systematic American thinker about practical theology, pastoral theology included the personality, study, and prayer of the minister, plus his visiting and catechizing; while practical theology included these plus homiletics and liturgics.

27. *The Office and Work of the Christian Ministry* (New York: Sheldon & Co., 1869). Like Shedd, Hoppin saw pastoral theology as a branch of practical theology. On structure the positions of Shedd and Hoppin were nearly identical.

28. *Ibid.*, p. 341.

29. *Op. cit.*

30. *Ibid.*, pp. 510-11.

31. *Op. cit.* Quotations are made from the second edition, 1866.

32. *Ibid.*, pp. 20-21.

33. *Ibid.*, p. 21.

34. *Op. cit.*

35. *Ibid.*, p. 3.

36. Shedd and Hoppin have already been discussed in the notes above. James S. Cannon's book was *Lectures on Pastoral Theology* (New York: Charles Scribner's Sons, 1853). Cannon was professor at New Brunswick. Regrettably the dramatic story of Cannon's early life—a sea-captain father who was killed while on a voyage with the poet Philip Freneau—did not reflect itself in his dry writing. C. F. W. Walther, founder of what is now the Lutheran Church Missouri Synod, published *Amerikanisch-Lutherische Pastoral-Theologie* (St. Louis: Concordia Publishing Co., 1872). This work strongly commended rather systematic private confession. Even McNeill is forced to call this a "laborious work." *Op. cit.*, p. 188. Thomas Murphy, *Pastoral Theology: The Pastor in the Various Duties of His Office* (Philadelphia: Presbyterian Board of Publication, 1877), attempted to be more practical than the systematic works, but he did not dispense with theory. He felt that many changes had taken place in the life of the local church, involving church schools, church financing, and more groups, and that these should be taken into account explicitly. His definition of pastoral theology was "that department of study whose object is to assist the Christian minister in applying the truths of the gospel to the hearts and lives of men. It is 'theology' because it has chiefly to do with the things of God and his word. It is 'pastoral' because it treats of these divine things in that aspect of them which pertains to the pastor." P. 13. This is one of the clearest statements available of a definition of pastoral theology that we must reject because of the way in which it regards theology as going only one way and pastoral as everything done by someone called a pastor.

37. (New York: Harper & Bros., 1874). The "hints and helps" school, which was to grow larger from this point on, was simply the extreme form of a tendency Van Oosterzee regretted in much pastoral theology. It was often "treated as a sort of instruction in the wisdom and prudence of the preacher . . . which now and then even degenerated into a frivolous casuistry; a pastoral medicine chest for all conceivable and inconceivable ailments." Van Oosterzee, *op. cit.*, p. 2.

38. Bedell, *op. cit.*, and Gladden, *The Christian Pastor and the Working Church* (New York: Charles Scribner's Sons, 1898).

39. Bedell took the position that pastoral theology "is the science of applying a knowledge of Divine things to the relationships and duties of a Pastor." *Op. cit.*, p. 45. To him pastoral theology was the large comprehensive discipline because it involved whatever was done by the pastor. He had much shrewd wisdom, for instance, about volunteer choirs. "A Minister's task in conducting the services with a volunteer choir sometimes becomes very difficult; always delicate; sometimes impossible. Even Solomon

226

committed part of such a responsibility to Asaph, Jeduthen, and their brethren." *Op. cit.*, p. 545.

40. *Op. cit.*, p. 5.
41. *Ibid.*, p. v. Gladden was very familiar with the older authors, but he felt that they paid no more than lip service to the idea of extensive and general work in church activity by the whole congregation. His is certainly the first serious modern work on group life in the church, and no previous book dealt seriously and comprehensively with this as did Gladden.
42. G. H. Gerberding, *The Lutheran Pastor* (Philadelphia: Lutheran Publication Society, 1902); and T. Harwood Pattison, *For the Work of the Ministry: For the Classroom, the Study and the Street* (Philadelphia: American Baptist Publication Society, 1907).
43. Gerberding's book contains a good deal of *Pastoralklugheit*, or pastoral prudence, derogated by Van Oosterzee and similar to the "hints and helps" work. Pattison was not interested in theoretical principles at all. "Of course pastoral theology cannot be taught, but we can catch the helpful spirit of the teacher, and gather practical suggestions and principles that each of us only really learns in the school of actual experience." *Op. cit.*, p. ix.
   There seem to have been very few systematic works on pastoral theology or practical theology written in Britain during the nineteenth century, although I have not explored the British literature thoroughly as I have the American. One exception to this was Patrick Fairbairn, *Pastoral Theology: A Treatise on the Office and Duties of The Christian Pastor*, 1875. This apparently had some influence on America. Fairbairn was a Church of Scotland minister who later joined with the Free Church of Scotland. From this vantage point the book seems inferior to some of the American works of the same period such as Shedd and Hoppin, and certainly inferior to Van Oosterzee.
44. New York: Baker & Taylor Co., 1890.
45. *Ibid.*, p. 137. Cuyler wrote that "while only one man in ten may have the talent to become a very great preacher, the other nine, if they love Christ and love human souls, can become great pastors." *Ibid.*, p. 9.
46. Also published under the title *The Minister as Shepherd* (New York, 1912). This is a plea for more pastoral work. "Shepherding work is the work for which humanity is crying. The twentieth century is the century of the shepherd." P. 82.
47. New York, 1896.
48. Only one such work is known to have been published in the United States in this century. This is John H. C. Fritz, *Pastoral Theology* (St. Louis: Concordia Publishing House, 1933). Pastoral theology is seen as the "doctrine of the knowledge of God and of divine things, applied by the pastor, the spiritual shepherd, to the spiritual needs of his flock." It is theology because it "has its source in the Word of God." The larger operational discipline is regarded as practical theology, which is in turn made up by homiletics, liturgics, catechetics, and pastoral theology. This is essentially a recapitulation of nineteenth-century structure.
49. See especially *An Introduction to Pastoral Theology* by Henry Balmforth, Lindsay Dewar, Cyril E. Hudson, and Edmund W. Sara (New York: The Macmillan Co., 1937). Although this book is now dated in certain respects, it was in the mid-thirties a careful attempt to relate the new psychology to Anglican pastoral theology with Catholic leanings. It is surprising and distressing that it has not been followed by other similar works.
50. For a more extended account of these recent forces see my chapter "Pastoral Theology and Psychology" in *Protestant Thought in the Twentieth Century*, ed. Arnold S. Nash (New York: The Macmillan Co., 1951).
51. See my *Clinical Pastoral Training* (New York: Federal Council of Churches, 1945); see also Niebuhr, Williams, and Gustafson, *op. cit.*
52. See F. Ernest Johnson, *The Social Gospel Re-Examined* (New York: Harper & Bros., 1940).
53. *The Exploration of the Inner World* (New York: Harper & Bros., new ed., 1952; 1st ed., 1936); and *Religion in Crisis and Custom* (New York: Harper & Bros., 1955).

Chapter 4. Perspectives

1. Halford E. Luccock has a book entitled Communicating the Gospel (New York: Harper & Bros., 1954), which, like all his writings, is stimulating and helpful. But perhaps owing to the point he puts whimsically when he writes, "In the field of theology, my amateur standing has never been questioned" (p. 56), his book is not concerned with a systematic theory in the same sense as the present discussion.

2. An attempt has been made to locate a discussion of field theory for the pastoral reader who has neither the time nor the background for the technical discussions. Perhaps such a work exists, but if so it proves elusive. There are good but not simple discussions in Andras Angyal's Foundations for a Science of Personality (New York: The Commonwealth Fund, 1941) and in Gardner Murphy's Personality: A Biosocial Approach to Origins and Structure (New York: Harper & Bros., 1947).

3. Op. cit., pp. 11 ff.

4. Among the competent but not technical discussions of general semantics, we may note especially S. I. Hayakawa's Language in Thought and Action (New York: Harcourt, Brace & Co., 1949), and Wendell Johnson's People in Quandaries: The Semantics of Personal Adjustment (New York: Harper & Bros., 1946). In psychology and psychiatry an important book is that by Jurgen Ruesch and Gregory Bateson, Communication: The Social Matrix of Psychiatry (New York: W. W. Norton & Co., 1951). New work in the field of speech is dealing with communication in the wider sense, for example, in the book by R. T. Oliver, et al., Essentials of Communicative Speech (New York: The Dryden Press, 1949). Some far-reaching technical study of communication is being done by persons like Bernard Berelson, Content Analysis in Communications Research (Chicago: Free Press, 1952). Larger social implications are explored by Lyman Bryson, ed., The Communication of Ideas (New York: Harper & Bros., 1948). An overall look at thoughtful work being done in the means of communication made possible by modern technology may be had through Wilbur Schramm, ed., Mass Communications: A Book of Readings (Urbana: University of Illinois Press, 1949).

5. Samuel W. Blizzard recently made a preliminary report on a study he made financed by the Russell Sage Foundation ("The Minister's Dilemma," The Christian Century, Vol. LXXIII, No. 17, April 25, 1956), of which the complete report is not yet available. Of the ministers co-operating in the study, he found that an average of two fifths of their time was devoted to work as "administrators" and another one tenth to work as "organizers," these two terms being defined in special senses. On such activity, Blizzard comments, the clock cannot be turned back; but he advocates more help and guidance to ministers on these aspects of their function. H. Richard Niebuhr in the first volume of the significant study of theological education that he headed under the auspices of the American Association of Theological Schools, The Purpose of the Church and Its Ministry (New York: Harper & Bros., 1956), is impressed with the same type of fact as Blizzard has noted, also believes it impossible to return to a day in which administration was of less significance in the pastor's schedule, but is concerned to draw a conclusion at a different level from Blizzard's. Noting that every major age of the church has had a leading or central image of its ministry (the priest in the middle ages, the preacher in early Protestantism), he asks whether that central image for our day ought not to be the "pastor director." In this image we understand him to be attempting to come to terms with the demands made upon ministers in our time, but to keep the message and judgment of the gospel upon the pastor's directing or leading of people. So far as he has stated, and we have understood, this thesis, it is wholly in line with our own intention. But there is a corollary in the Niebuhr discussion to which we must take exception. Niebuhr holds rightly that all the basic functions of the ministry must be performed by all ministers in all ages, although perhaps in different proportions. But since each past age seems to have had a single leading image of the dominant function of the ministry, around which the other functions were clustered, the conclusion is drawn that a single central image is needed for our own day. We cannot follow the logic of this argument. Why must every minister or church

have the same central image? What seems to us to be essential to the unity of the ministry is not lifting up one image of or perspective upon the functions of the ministry and ranging the others subordinately about it, but rather the recognition by all ministers that the image or perspective that has made the ministry live most deeply for them may be different from that making the ministry come alive for others, but that every minister must at the same time pursue what is the central perspective for him and not neglect the other major perspectives. I venture to suggest that our threefold perspectival approach to the functions of the ministry supports this point more weightily than if the sole tools available for analysis were the offices of the ministry. We cannot believe that Niebuhr has given as much thought to this vulnerable corollary as he has to the admirable main thesis.

6. Luke 10:29-37.

Chapter 5. Cases

1. *A Pastor's Sketches: or, Conversations with Anxious Inquirers, Respecting the Way of Salvation* (New York: M. W. Dodd, 1851). The second volume, with entirely different content but the same title, was issued by the same publisher in 1853. Subsequent notes all refer to the 1853 edition, "I" referring to the First Series of this edition, "II" referring to the Second Series. Nearly a half century later the Spencer works were reprinted by the Presbyterian Board of Publication. Inquiry there has indicated that even in this reprinted edition the books have long since been out of print.
2. *Ibid.*, II, p. 314.
3. *Ibid.*, I, p. 216.
4. *Ibid.*, I, p. 217.
5. *Ibid.*, I, p. 110.
6. *Ibid.*
7. *Ibid.*, I, p. 111.
8. *Ibid.*, I, p. 326.
9. *Ibid.*, I, p. 327.
10. *Ibid.*, II, p. 227.
11. *Ibid.*, II, pp. 227-28.
12. *Ibid.*, I, p. 252.
13. *Ibid.*, I, p. 255.
14. *Ibid.*, I, p. 262.
15. *Ibid.*, I, p. 267.
16. *Ibid.*, I, p. 272.
17. *Ibid.*, I, p. 273.
18. *Ibid.*, I, p. 159.
19. *Ibid.*, I, p. 294.
20. *Ibid.*, I, p. 306.
21. *Ibid.*, II, p. 76.
22. *Ibid.*, II, p. 83.
23. *Ibid.*, II, p. 141.
24. *Ibid.*, II, p. 409.
25. *Ibid.*, II, p. 177.
26. *Ibid.*, II, p. 65.
27. *Ibid.*, II, p. 67.
28. *Ibid.*, I, p. 197.
29. *Ibid.*, I, p. 319.
30. *Ibid.*, I, p. 256.
31. *Ibid.*, I, p. 376.
32. *Ibid.*, I, p. 51.

33. *Ibid.*, I, pp. 1-64.
34. *Ibid.*, I, p. 152.
35. *Ibid.*
36. *Ibid.*, I, p. 366.
37. *Ibid.*, I, p. 292.
38. *Ibid.*, II, p. 138.
39. *Ibid.*, I, p. 225.
40. *Ibid.*, I, p. 294.
41. *Ibid.*, I, p. 263.
42. *Ibid.*, II, p. 196.
43. *Ibid.*, II, p. 416.
44. *Ibid.*, II, p. 60.
45. *Ibid.*, II, p. 120.
46. *Ibid.*, I, p. ix.
47. *Ibid.*, I, p. 172.

Chapter 6. Healing

1. John 9:25 (R.S.V.). The entire story is John 9:1-41. The over-all point of the story is to show the special power of Jesus and the blindness of the Pharisees who would see this without believing.
2. Harold G. Wolff, coauthor with S. G. Wolf of *Human Gastric Function: An Experimental Study of a Man and His Stomach* (New York: Oxford University Press, 1943), in oral communication.
3. Two other discussions of this question, each differing from mine but both competent and well worth examination, are by Pedro Lain Entralgo, Spanish medical historian, writing on "An Approach to a Theology of Illness" in *Faith, Reason and Modern Psychiatry*, ed. Francis J. Braceland (New York: P. J. Kenedy & Sons, 1955); and *Faith Healing and the Christian Faith*, by Wade H. Boggs, Jr. (Richmond: John Knox Press, 1956).
4. In this entire chapter I am indebted greatly to Paul Tillich, especially through his article "The Relation of Religion and Health," *The Review of Religion*, Vol. X, No. 4, May, 1946. Tillich writes, for example, "Salvation is basically and essentially healing, the re-establishment of a whole that was broken, disrupted, disintegrated." On the point immediately under discussion, "All higher religions have fought against . . . calculating moralism with respect to disease and guilt. . . ." As to the unity of healing, "And this act of being made whole in relation to the ultimate ground and meaning of our existence influences all sides of our personality in the direction of wholeness, psyche, mind, and body."
5. Processes of the type described here in obesity and Parkinson's disease are becoming commonplace in the medical and psychiatric literature. Two good relatively popular books are Flanders Dunbar, *Mind and Body: Psychosomatic Medicine* (New York: Random House, 1947); and Franz Alexander, *Psychosomatic Medicine: Its Principles and Applications* (New York: W. W. Norton & Co., 1950). There is also C. A. Seguin, *Introduction to Psychosomatic Medicine* (New York: International Universities Press, 1950). For the special insight into Parkinson's disease I am chiefly indebted to Gotthard Booth in oral communication and in his "Variety in Personality and Its Relation to Health," *The Review of Religion*, Vol. X, No. 4, May, 1946.
6. The article by Paul Tillich cited in Note 4 above is relevant throughout the subsequent discussion. So also are Roberts, *op. cit.*; and Outler, *op. cit.*
7. *Op. cit.*, II, p. 363.
8. *Ibid.*, II, p. 362.
9. *Ibid.* Spencer had a pietistic view of "soul." Soul as such is of course not something uniquely the property of human beings.

10. *Ibid.*, II, pp. 249-69.
11. *Ibid.*, II, pp. 350-53.
12. *Ibid.*, II, p. 352.
13. *Ibid.*, II, pp. 186-206.
14. *Ibid.*, II, p. 187.
15. *Ibid.*, II, p. 190.
16. *Ibid.*, II, p. 191.
17. *Ibid.*, II, p. 192.
18. *Ibid.*, II, p. 193.
19. *Ibid.*, II, p. 196.
20. *Ibid.*, II, p. 197.
21. *Ibid.*, II, p. 204.
22. See the several discussions of acceptance, especially pp. 159-72, in Carl R. Rogers, et al., *Client-Centered Therapy* (Boston: Houghton Mifflin Co., 1951).
23. Paul Tillich, *The Courage to Be* (New Haven, Conn.: Yale University Press, 1952).
24. Matt. 5:24.
25. The literature on recent movements concerning religion and health has now become large. Carroll A. Wise, *Religion in Illness and Health* (New York: Harper & Bros., 1942), and I, *Religion and Health* (New York: The Macmillan Co., 1943), wrote general surveys. Especially more recent events have been dealt with by Charles F. Kemp, *Physicians of the Soul* (New York: The Macmillan Co., 1947), and by Carl J. Scherzer, *The Church and Healing* (Philadelphia: Westminster Press, 1950). More recent normative treatments may be found in the excellent symposium edited by Paul B. Maves, *The Church and Mental Health* (New York: Charles Scribner's Sons, 1953), and in A. Graham Ikin, *New Concepts of Healing* (New York: Association Press, 1956). A monthly magazine for the layman, *Religion and Health*, was until recently edited by Russell L. Dicks at Duke University. Dicks was coauthor with Richard C. Cabot of one of the great modern classics in this field, *The Art of Ministering to the Sick* (New York: The Macmillan Co., 1936).

Chapter 7. Sustaining

1. The initial and classic modern work on ministry to the sick is by Cabot and Dicks, *op. cit.* There has been much subsequent literature, including some by the present author. The impact on American ministers of this new attention to the sick has, however, been brought about far more by clinical (literal meaning, "bedside") experience and training than by the literature. Thousands of American ministers have now had such experience under supervision, in such a way that their own actual attempts to help sick persons have been recorded and analyzed to the benefit of their future parishioners. For a comment on the literature of bereavement see Note 6 below.
2. *Op. cit.*, II, pp. 61-71.
3. *Ibid.*, I, pp. 72-76.
4. *Ibid.*, II, pp. 408-19.
5. *Ibid.*, I, pp. 382-402.
6. Modern study of grief began with Sigmund Freud's article "Mourning and Melancholia," Collected Papers (London: Hogarth Press, 1925), Vol. IV, in 1917. Another great scientific article is by Erich Lindemann, "Symptomatology and Management of Acute Grief," *American Journal of Psychiatry*, Vol. CI, 1944. The work of Lindemann and his associates in Boston has been commented on and reported briefly in many subsequent publications, but a complete account is still not available. William F. Rogers' *Ye Shall Be Comforted* (Philadelphia: Westminster Press, 1950) makes use of the Lindemann findings in a book intended for bereaved persons. Paul E. Irion's *The Funeral and the Mourners* (New York: Abingdon Press, 1954) focuses on the funeral but also discusses pastoral care of the bereaved in general.

PREFACE TO PASTORAL THEOLOGY

Chapter 8. Guiding

1. For an elaboration of the argument in favor of the eductive principle in pastoral care and counseling see my *Pastoral Counseling* (New York: Abingdon Press, 1949).
2. *Conceptions of Modern Psychiatry* (now published in New York by W. W. Norton & Co., 1953; first published by the William Alanson White Psychiatric Foundation in Washington, 1940 and 1947), p. 45. The reference is to the original edition. Sullivan credits the original use of the term "parataxic" to T. V. Moore.
3. For the term "client-centered" see Rogers, et al., *op. cit.* In *Counseling and Psychotherapy* (Boston: Houghton Mifflin Co., 1942) Rogers used the term "nondirective."
4. *Spiritual Direction* (New York: Morehouse-Gorham Co., 1928).
5. *Op. cit.*, II, pp. 207-25.
6. *Ibid.*, I, pp. 247-49.
7. *Ibid.*, II, pp. 123-36.

Chapter 9. Communicating

1. For reference to a few modern studies of communicating, see Note 4, Chapter 4.
2. As one reader of this manuscript noted, I have a bias not only in the direction of shepherding but also in terms of work with individuals. While it is not the kind of bias for which apology is required, the reader is warned to consider carefully any possible unintentional distortions in material going beyond one-to-one relationships.
3. It would seem to us both possible and useful for someone to study the systematic treatises on homiletics in somewhat similar fashion to the way in which we examined the systematic works on pastoral theology in a previous chapter. Acquaintance with a few of them suggests that they were attempting to use all the communicative knowledge of their day (which was largely about rhetoric in the Aristotelian tradition) along with their theological understanding in order to create a systematic theory. No doubt the details of this would have to be subjected to critical scrutiny as has been done in a preliminary way with shepherding. But critically and systematically undertaken, as it seems not to have been done, we should expect such study to yield rich rewards in terms of comprehensive theory of communicating the gospel.
4. For this illuminating understanding of the meaning of the phrase "in principle," I am indebted to Paul Tillich in a lecture.
5. At this point the reader is warned against concluding incorrectly that I have paid insufficient attention to God in general and to the worship of God in particular, in my scheme. Worship as the act and liturgics as its study will always receive attention from the Christian community. But these are not of the same perspectival order as the categories of shepherding, communicating, and organizing. These categories, rightly understood, include the vertical (man and God) as well as the horizontal (man and man) dimension. They cannot take the place of the others, as I have indicated more than once; they are designed to get at different orders of truth or to get at the truth in different ways. If one of the perspectival categories were worship, then it would look as if the vertical dimension were found only here; so that we should quickly have to state that it is also found elsewhere. I believe the solution to this is not to avoid the use of categories like ours, but to remember steadily that each perspective (in all its aspects) has both vertical and horizontal dimensions.
6. *Op. cit.*, I, pp. 161-70.
7. His most readable book is *Resolving Social Conflicts: Selected Papers on Group Dynamics* (New York: Harper & Bros., 1948). The account in the text is drawn from several of the articles in that volume.
8. New York: Harper & Bros., 1935.
9. *Op. cit.*, II, p. vi.
10. *Ibid.*, II, p. vii.
11. *Ibid.*, I, pp. 65-71.
12. This is demonstrated in all the books on group dynamics, group work, group leader-

ship, and group therapy, for instance, in Thomas Gordon, *Group Centered Leadership* (Boston: Houghton Mifflin Co., 1955).

13. For instance, in Ruesch and Bateson, *op. cit.*
14. Especially interesting data bearing upon this point may be found in the voluminous collection of papers by O. Hobart Mowrer, *Learning Theory and Personality Dynamics* (New York: Ronald Press Co., 1950).
15. See, for instance, Hayakawa, *op. cit.*
16. It is my conviction that this is what the serious students of a systematic homiletics attempted to do in previous centuries, drawing on the best general knowledge at their command in addition to insights into the gospel itself.

Chapter 10. Organizing

1. Paul discusses the church or fellowship as a body briefly in Rom. 12 and at greater length in I Cor. 12. In both passages he indicates that we are not, and need not, all be alike in order to be in Christ; but the thrust of the discussions is that our very difference in function is positive for the whole body rather than negative. Rom. 12:4-5 reads, "For as in one body we have many members, and all the members do not have the same function, so we, though many, are one body in Christ, and individually members one of another." I Cor. 12 contains more details of the metaphor, such as, "If the whole body were an eye, where would be the hearing?" Even the weaker parts of the body, Paul asserts, are not only valuable but indispensable. The analogical discussion leads up to the conclusion of chapter 12, in which Paul states that "God has appointed in the church first apostles, second prophets, third teachers, then workers of miracles, then healers, helpers, administrators, speakers in various kinds of tongues." At times churchmen have treated this as a kind of diagram without solid recognition of the organic metaphor used as its context.
2. Although I am far from being an expert on biology, some of the volumes that have given me insight into trends in modern biology are: Kurt Goldstein, *The Organism: A Holistic Approach to Biology* (New York: American Book Co., 1939); Ludwig von Bertalanffy and J. H. Woodger, *Modern Theories of Development: An Introduction to Theoretical Biology* (New York: Oxford University Press, 1933); G. E. Coghill, *Anatomy and the Problem of Behaviour* (New York: The Macmillan Co. 1929); Paul Weiss, *Principles of Development: A Text in Experimental Embryology* (New York: Henry Holt & Co., 1939); Walter B. Cannon, *The Wisdom of the Body* (New York: W. W. Norton & Co., 1932), and *Bodily Changes in Pain, Hunger, Fear and Rage* (New York: Appleton-Century Co., 1920). Although I cannot agree with some of the philosophical assumptions in Edmund W. Sinnott's *The Biology of the Spirit* (New York: Viking Press, 1955), it is revealing and suggestive.
3. On biological integration and differentiation Weiss and Coghill, *op. cit.*, have been most striking and illuminating.
4. The classic works on both homeostasis and emotion are those by Cannon, *op. cit.* The concept of homeostasis has been somewhat generalized into areas like the psychological, and some now believe it gives promise of becoming a master linkage concept between the biological and social sciences. A forthcoming volume by Karl Menninger will present a discriminating account of homeostasis as a key notion in relation to all health and illness. My statement that homeostasis and emotion are the same process operating in reverse directions is a bold and probably oversimplified inference on my part, but it occurred to me while meditating on Cannon's contributions.
5. *The Social Teaching of the Christian Churches* (New York: The Macmillan Co., 1931), especially I, 331 ff.
6. *Op. cit.*, I, 202-15.
7. *Ibid.*, II, pp. 123-36.
8. *Op. cit.*

233

Index

Absolution, Luther's view of, 41
Accepance: ambiguous character of, 27-28; illustrated in psychotherapy, 27-28; relation of, to negative feelings, 111-12; relation of, to responsibility, 27; relation of, to threat, 27
Alexander, Franz, 230
American Association of Theological Schools, study of theological education by, 32-33
Angyal, Andras, 228
Anthropology, relevance of, to pastoral theology, 25
Apologetics, place of, in nineteenth-century conception of offices, 47
Aquinas, Thomas, 222
Attitude: in shepherding, 68-69; of shepherding, 16
Autonomy of branches of theology, 217-18

Baker, Oren H., 8
Balmforth, Henry, 227
Barth, Karl, 222
Bateson, Gregory, 228, 233
Baumgarten, S. J., 225
Baxter, Richard, 17, 30-31, 32, 47, 48, 61, 216
Bedell, Gregory T., 17, 48, 226-27
"Bent" of minister as asset, 35-36
Bereavement: communicating in, 195-96; relation of, to hope, 142; as requiring ministry of sustaining, 116
Berelson, Bernard, 228
Biblical stories: good Samaritan, 68, 146, 147-48, 179; man born blind, 94; prodigal son, 151
Biblical theology as logic-centered discipline, 20-21, 219
Bisseth, William, 5, 8
Blizzard, Samuel W., 228
Body of Christ: as focal in organizing, 199; Paul's analysis of, 233
Body of divinity: chart of, as understood by author, 28; explanation of chart on page 28, 218-19; integration within,

Body of Divinity—cont'd
218-19; as more than pigeon holes, 37; as organized in nineteenth century, 218-19
Boggs, Wade H., Jr., 230
Boisen, Anton T., 51, 228
Booth, Gotthard, 230-31
Boroth, J., 225
Braceland, Francis J., 230
Bryson, Lyman, 228
Bucer, Martin, 43, 225
Burnet, Gilbert, 45, 225

Cabot, Richard C., 231
Calvin, John, 43, 65-66
Cannon, James S., 226
Cannon, Walter B., 233
Case histories, methods of recording of, 71-72
Cases: of Mrs. Coe, 154-61; George, 119-23; Ichabod Spencer (see Spencer's cases)
Casuistry: method of, 150-51; Protestant attitude toward, 150-51; Protestant neglect of, 150-51
Catechetics: definition of, 15; as office of the church, 216; place of, in nineteenth-century conception of offices, 47, 216
Celebrating as aspect of communicating, 181
Chaplain in armed forces as pastoral theologian, 32
Chaplaincy, development of, 112-13
Child care and discipline, 66-67
Christian administration as office of church, 216
Christian eschatology, 141-42
Christian ethics: doctrine of freedom in, 148-49; relation of, to pastoral theology, 148 ff.
Christian faith: common currencies of, 21, 219; and culture, 22; as foundation of pastoral theology, 51; and personal problems, 24-25; place of doubt and despair in, 128 ff., 222; realization of,

234

Pastoral theologian: laymen as, 37 ff.; obligation of, to understanding other branches of theology, 35-36; sense in which every minister must be, 32 ff.; as specialist, 34 ff.

Pastoral theology: as autonomous, 20, 217; conception of, in American Association of Theological Schools' study, 32-33; content of, 64 ff.; decline of systematic works about, 49; definition of, 20, 24, 64; as different from pastoral psychology, 23; first American book about, 43; first use of term, 43; as function-centered discipline, 20-21; historical meaning of, 45; importance of being branch of theology, 220-21; method of, 21-22, 219 ff.; as more than application, 22-23; as more than practice, 22; not sole integrating theological discipline, 23; not theory of all functions, 23; organizing principle of, 219 ff.; as practical, 17; recent British conceptions of, 50; recent European conceptions of, 50; recent historical development of, 49 ff.; relation of, to moral theology, 148 ff.; structural norms in, 26-27; summary of content of, 68-69; summary of discussion of sin and healing, in, 113-14; as systematic, 21, 217, 219 ff.; as theoretical, 16-17

Pattison, T. H., 49, 227

Pauck, Wilhelm, 41, 42, 224

Paul: on discipline, 65; relation of love and grace discussed by, 29; relation of love and judgment discussed by, 29; sense in which insights are normative, 29

Peace of mind, relation of, to insecurity, 140

Pediatrician, 38

Pelikan, Jaroslav, 225

Penance, Protestant critique of, 41-42

Penology and discipline, 66-67

Personality sciences: development in, 221-22; as illuminating mixed motivation, 31-32; meaning of, for pastoral theology, 25, 51; that have led to new shepherding professions, 220-21; and theology, 22

Perspectives: cognate with shepherding, 55 ff.; as having aspects, 117; making shifts in, 152-53; meaning of, 18

Pietism, meaning of, 45-46

Plitt, J. J., 225

Plumer, William S., 48

Poimenics: definition of, 15; as office of church, 216; place of, in nineteenth-century conception of offices, 47

Pond, Enoch, 48, 225

Practical theology: critique of, 24; as nineteenth-century conception, 23-24, 218; Schleiermacher's view of, 46-47; Van Oosterzee's view of, 47

Preaching: meaning of, 19; method of studying, 177 ff.

Preliminary concern as metaphor in relation to theology, 57

Priesthood, Protestant conception of, 42

Prison chaplain as pastoral theologian, 32

Professions of healing, 25-26

Protecting as aspect of organizing, 201-2

Protestant principle, significance of, for pastoral theology, 222

Protestantism: attitude of, toward dependency, 139-40; and discipline, 65-66; essence of, 42; understanding of shepherding by, 15-16

Psychiatrist: as cautious about directing, 27; as shepherd, 25, 38

Psychiatry: contributions to understanding communication by, 192; as relevant to pastoral theology, 25

Psychoanalysis, contributions of, to understanding communication, 192

Psychologist as shepherd, 25, 38

Psychology: application of, to ministerial work, 36-37; as language of our century, 26; as relevant to pastoral theology, 25

Psychology of religion as logic-centered theological discipline, 36-37

Psychotherapy: place of acceptance in, 27-28; relation of freedom and responsibility in, 27

Purifying as aspect of organizing, 201

Pym, T. W., 162

Qualities required in shepherding, 30 ff.

Realizing as aspect of communicating, 181

Reformation view of discipline, 65-66

Reformed Pastor, The (Baxter), 44-45

Relating as aspect of organizing, 201

Religion and personality as logic-centered theological discipline, 36-37

Religious education: as aiding pastoral theology, 50-51; as of different order from shepherding, 55-56, 232-33

Reminding as aspect of communicating, 181

Roberts, David E., 224, 231

Rogers, Carl R., 154, 231, 232

Rogers, William F., 232

Role of unordained professional helpers, 38-39

Roman Catholicism and discipline, 66

Ruesch, Jurgen, 228, 233

Sacraments: function of, in care of souls, 41-42 Protestant view of, 41-42

Salvation, distinctiveness of, in Christian context, 100-101

Sanctification, 172

Sara, Edmond W., 227

Saving principles through shepherding, 31

Saving truth in communicating, 56-57